MW01169900

THE WORD: GOD WILL KEEP IT!

Titus 1:2 *In hope of eternal life, which* ***God, that cannot lie,*** *promised...*

Luke 21:33 *Heaven and earth shall pass away: but* ***my words shall not pass away.***

Psalms 12:6 *The* ***words of the LORD*** *are pure words...*
7 Thou shalt ***keep them,*** *O LORD, thou shalt* ***preserve them*** *from this generation for ever.*

THE WORD: GOD WILL KEEP IT!

THE WORD: GOD WILL KEEP IT!

THE 400 YEAR HISTORY OF THE KING JAMES BIBLE ONLY MOVEMENT

JOEY FAUST

2011

THE WORD: GOD WILL KEEP IT!

Note: The goal of the author has been to quote exactly from sources. Bold text within quotes and Bible verses generally indicate emphasis by the author of this book.

For information and resources contact:

Fundamental Books
700 Cordes Dr.
Venus, TX. 76084
http://www.FundamentalBooks.com
469-658-6046

Published in the United States of America

TABLE OF CONTENTS

CHAPTER 1

CONDITIONING FOR A ONE-WORLD CHURCH

Proverbs 24:21 My son, fear thou the LORD and the king: and meddle not with them that are **given to change**:

2 Timothy 3:1 This know also, that in the last days perilous times shall come.
13 But evil men and seducers shall wax worse and worse, deceiving, and being deceived.
14 But continue thou in the things which thou hast learned and hast been **assured** of, **knowing of whom thou hast learned them;**
15 And that from a child thou hast known **the holy scriptures**…

God will keep His Word! He preserves its purity from those who seek to destroy it (Psalms 12:6-7; Jeremiah 36:23, 32; Matthew 24:35, etc.). This book will reveal the degree that evil men and seducers have labored to change (i.e. corrupt) God's Word. And it also documents the multitudes of Christians throughout history that have defended this precious doctrine of Bible preservation. What use is an inspired Bible that is not preserved in purity and perfection?

The first thing the Bible teaches about the Devil is that he comes to cast doubt upon God's Word (Genesis 3:1). He uses men as tools to corrupt the Bible; and his ministers often disguise themselves as ministers of righteousness. Satan works to accomplish his plans within Christian churches and institutions, as well as outside of them.

For example, Philip Schaff (1819-1893) was the chairman of the American Standard Version translating committee:

"...he was convinced that such an ecumenical revision would foster the bond of interdenominational and international union..."
(George Shriver, *Philip Schaff, Christian Scholar and Ecumenical Prophet*)

Schaff's vision for an "international union" is seen in his final paper that was read at the Parliament of World Religions in Chicago (1893). Schaff associated with Theosophists (i.e. worshippers of Lucifer, that mixed Christianity with Eastern Mysticism), and called for an ecumenical council in Jerusalem led by the Pope (see chapter 17).

This plan to use new Bible versions to bring about a final, one-world religion (i.e. the false peace of Antichrist) is explained by Manly P. Hall. He has been called "the greatest cultist of all." He confessed to channeling the energies of Lucifer (see *The Lost Keys of Freemasonry*). Hall also admitted that he (and his "associates") had been laboring to change the world through a mass indoctrination program that includes promoting revised versions of the Bible! They worked to change and replace the King James Bible. He writes:

"The way of...**conditioning** would be the one used in Central Europe to condition Nazi minds...[It there] began in the public schools...[and] with the small child; which is where we will have to begin...To make things right we will have to **undo much** that is cherished error. The **problem of revising the Bible** shows how difficult it is to do this. **For the last hundred years, we**

have been trying to get out an edition of the Bible that is reasonably correct; but nobody wants it. **What's wanted [by the majority of people] is the good old King James version, every jot and tittle of it, because most people are convinced that God dictated the Bible to King James in English**...The solution to this whole problem...is...psychology...it should be an absolute requisite of education from the grammar school up...We must begin in the home with small children...[and] with the churches teaching the integrity of the religions of other peoples...We have to **be conditioned**..."
(Manly P. Hall, *Horizon*, "Asia in the Balance of the Scales," Volume 4, No. 1, 1944)

Hall praised the Greek manuscripts that modern versions are based upon as the greatest books in the world!

Multitudes have become occultists, etc., through believing the lie that there is no perfect Bible. Hall sounds eerily like Philip Schaff and other revised version leaders:

"The enthusiastic jot and tittle worshipper will insist that the words of the King James version are the words of God Himself...[But] every statement contained in the Bible should be checked with the Greek and Hebrew originals...The oldest existing codices of the New Testament reveal **considerable change** and amendment. The King James version omits a number of passages...the Bible student is not justified in accepting the King James version as an infallible production..."
(Manly P. Hall, *How to Understand Your Bible*, 1942)

It is probable that these men, with such diverse backgrounds, were connected and organized more than is often realized, through various secret societies, etc. However, it is certain that the prince of the power of the air (the god of this world) is organized, as he labors to unite men philosophically to accomplish his goals.

Things are "progressing" quickly according to such occult plans. Evil men and seducers are waxing worse and worse, deceiving, and being deceived (2 Timothy 3:13). Yet, in the early 1940's, Hall was complaining that KJV Onlyism was a major roadblock to the devilish goals of ushering in a one world religion, etc. (see Daniel 8:25, Revelation 13, 17, etc.). The great awakening of so many people to the King James Only viewpoint in recent decades continues to be a hindrance to their agenda.

The Roman Catholic Connection

While many believers are stirring, too many remain asleep! Over a century ago, Roman Catholics mocked the fact that multitudes of Protestant scholars were cutting up their own Bible with destructive criticism:

"One thing at least is certain; the Catholic Church will gain by the New Revision, both directly and indirectly. Directly, because old errors are removed from the translation; indirectly, because **the 'Bible-only'** principle is proved to be false...the New Version will be the death-knell of Protestantism...Their fundamental doctrine of verbal inspiration is undermined."
(*The Dublin Review,* Burns and Oates, 1881)

"...the Pope is calling on all Catholic lay-writers...fear not and shrink not...Catholic America is young...[The Reformation] was based upon Bible-and-Bible-Onlyism...[But now] **King Bible-and-Bible-Only is dead**, having turned destructive critic and sawn off the bough whereon he sat."
(John Hannon, *The Devil's Parables,* 1910)

This madness has continued today, causing many people to flock to the Roman Catholic Church, or liturgical forms of worship.

They are searching for the final authority that they no longer see in the Bible:

*"New converts flocking to an ancient church - Orthodox traditions dating back centuries attract members...*After 30 years as an Episcopalian priest, Petranek converted to the Antiochian Orthodox Church and leads a new but growing parish in west Houston, filled almost entirely with converts to the ancient faith. **'Most people come for the stability,'** he said...Members make the sign of the cross throughout the service, they kiss icons of Jesus and the saints and, sometimes, the Communion chalice and the priest's robes..."
(*Houston Chronicle*, January 9, 2011)

Rome grins at this state of affairs (see chapter 4):

"The Revisers have done an act of justice to Catholics...It is now at length too evident that Scripture is powerless without the [Catholic] Church...And it will now be clear to all men which is the true Church, the real Mother to whom the Bible of right belongs."
(*The Dublin Review,* Burns and Oates, 1881)

Many publishers of new versions want to keep Rome smiling:

"The future depends in part on the inclination of the largest religious family, the Roman Catholics, who are the 'sleeping giant' in the Bible market, said Robert Schwalb, Bible manager for Thomas Nelson Inc., the nation's largest Bible publisher. Another key to further growth would be the emergence of a translation that can gain broad, long-term acceptance."
(*Winnipeg Free Press*, "King James Version Holds On," February 8, 1986)

New version publishers, for decades, have hoped to gain the approval (and income) of the "sleeping giant" (Revelation 17), without overly offending Evangelical Christians. This is another reason why new versions increasingly affirm Roman Catholic doctrine.

This is a dire situation. But is "King Bible-and-Bible-Only" really dead? No, Bible-Onlyism is also growing. While many are falling away from the truth, a remnant is stirring. The pure Word of God is still with us today; and there are many Christians who are *certain* of it:

Isaiah 40:8 The grass withereth, the flower fadeth: but the word of our God shall stand for ever.

2 Timothy 2:9 ...the word of God is not bound.

Daniel 8:12 ...it cast down the truth to the ground; and **it practised, and prospered.**

The biggest bulwark to the expansions of Catholicism, liberalism, occultism, etc., is an ever-abounding, ever-growing King James Bible Only movement! This Bible is the Sword that is feared by infidels and false teachers (Ephesians 6:17). One 19th century convert to Catholicism (i.e. John Henry Newman) admitted that the Authorized Version is the great obstacle for Rome to overcome:

"Dr. Newman has been known to say that our Version of the Bible will make it difficult to bring the English people over to Rome..."
(Anson D.F. Randolph, *The Presbyterian and Reformed Review,* Volume 7, 1896)

Another Catholic leader also declared that the King James Bible is hindering the goals of Rome:

"Canon Barry's...declaration that it is impossible to supplant the Authorized version familiar to the English-speaking world, with any new translation, however excellent, has been met with considerable opposition...[Others argued that] converts would say that the [Catholic] Church was beginning to give way...[But Barry argued that] there is only one English Bible; there can never be another."
(*The Western World*, August 4, 1921)

He argued that Catholics should continue in their attempts to *change* the King James Bible more subtly, rather than attack its authority directly.

While these Roman Catholics were discussing the best way to remove the King James Bible from hindering their goals, many Christian leaders were attacking their own fortress with their textual criticism. Satan often seeks to destroy God's people from within. For example, in the Bible, Balaam greedily taught Balak, the king of the Moabites, to destroy Israel by provoking them to commit fornication, so that God would destroy the people in judgment (Numbers 25:1). He taught the Moabites to tempt God's people to forsake the words of the Lord, instead of trying to destroy them through direct warfare, or curses (Numbers 22-25, Jude 1:11, Revelation 2:14).

Today, God can ask the same questions of Christians that He asked of His people in the days of Jeremiah:

Jeremiah 2:5 Thus saith the LORD, What iniquity have your fathers found in me, that they are gone far from me, and have walked after **vanity**, and are become vain?
11 Hath a nation changed their gods, which are yet no gods? **but my people have changed their glory for that which doth not profit.**
13 For my people have committed two evils; they have forsaken

me the fountain of living waters, and **hewed them out cisterns, broken cisterns, that can hold no water.**
19 Thine own wickedness shall correct thee, and thy backslidings shall reprove thee: know therefore and see that it is an evil thing and bitter, that thou hast forsaken the LORD thy God, and **that my fear is not in thee**, saith the Lord GOD of hosts.
28 But where are thy gods that thou hast made thee? let them arise, if they can save thee in the time of thy trouble: for **according to the number of thy cities are thy gods**, O Judah.
31 O generation, **see ye the word of the LORD**...

False, so-called Bible versions have multiplied. Many Christians have turned to broken cisterns that cannot hold the water of life! God warns that His fear is no longer found in the land. Among other things, the so-called Revised Version of 1881 removed the "terror" of the Lord in 2 Corinthians 5:11; and "damnation" was downgraded to "judgment," etc. Modern versions have followed in this train. Discerning Christians, over a century ago, sounded the alarm against these changes in Bible words to no avail.

The tried, tested and true Word of God must be rediscovered in its fullness and perfection:

Psalms 119:105 Thy word is a lamp unto my feet, and a light unto my path.

Satan will continue to move the entire world toward the final world religion, and he intends to *change* everything that is associated with the *old paths* – especially the King James Bible:

Jeremiah 6:16 Thus saith the LORD, Stand ye in the ways, and see, and **ask for the old paths**, where is the good way, and walk therein, and ye shall find rest for your souls. But they said, We will not walk therein.
17 Also I set watchmen over you, saying, Hearken to the sound

of the trumpet. But they said, We will not hearken.
19 Hear, O earth: behold, I will bring evil upon this people, even the fruit of their thoughts, because they have not hearkened unto **my words**, nor to my law, **but rejected it**.

Many Christians have been infected with Satanic propaganda (disguised as knowledge, progress, etc.). In pride or carelessness, they are unaware of the errors already planted within their minds:

1 Corinthians 15:33 Be not deceived: evil communications corrupt good manners.

Colossians 2:8 Beware lest any man spoil you through philosophy and vain deceit, after the tradition of men, after the rudiments of the world, and not after Christ.

Satan, with his propaganda, pretends that dark delusion is enlightenment:

Isaiah 5:20 Woe unto them that call evil good, and good evil; that put darkness for light, and light for darkness; that put bitter for sweet, and sweet for bitter!
21 Woe unto them that are wise in their own eyes, and prudent in their own sight!

His government is vast and organized:

Ephesians 6:12 For we wrestle not against flesh and blood, but against principalities, against powers, against the rulers of the darkness of this world, against spiritual wickedness in high places.

His workers are often disguised as ministers of righteousness:

2 Corinthians 11:13 For such are false apostles, deceitful work-

ers, transforming themselves into the apostles of Christ.
14 And no marvel; for Satan himself is transformed into an angel of light.
15 Therefore it is no great thing if his ministers also be transformed as the ministers of righteousness; whose end shall be according to their works.

The battle is dreadfully real. This book documents how Satan and his ministers have infiltrated every area of modern culture (including churches, seminaries, etc.) with his, "Yea hath God said…?" philosophy. But it also reveals an encouraging number of Christians in history that stood in the way of his plans for "change." They boldly resisted his deceptions with simple faith in the "sword of the Spirit":

Ephesians 6:16 Above all, taking the **shield of faith**, wherewith ye shall be able to quench all the fiery darts of the wicked.
17 And take the helmet of salvation, and **the sword of the Spirit, which is the word of God**:

CHAPTER 2

SOME PLAIN PEOPLE IN THE WAY

2 Corinthians 11:3 But I fear, lest by any means, as the serpent beguiled Eve through his subtilty, so your minds should be corrupted from **the simplicity** that is in Christ.

John 7:47 Then answered them the Pharisees, Are ye also deceived?
48 Have any of the rulers or of the Pharisees believed on him?
49 But this people who knoweth not the law are cursed.

In reading the history of the KJV Only view, one will see that "the people" were often more discerning than many of the proud scholars. The same situation was found in the days of Jesus:

Mark 12:37 David therefore himself calleth him Lord; and whence is he then his son? And **the common people heard him gladly.**
38 And he said unto them in his doctrine, **Beware of the scribes**...

Both Jesus Christ and the Scriptures are called "the word of God" (Revelation 19:13, 20:4). Jesus is fully God; yet He is also a perfect man. The Scriptures are inspired and infallible; yet God used men to write them. If the "common people" readily heard the Lord (while the scribes often rejected Him), what should be expected in regard to the preserved, *written* Word of God?

Mark 11:18 And the **scribes** and chief priests heard it, and sought how they might destroy him: for they feared him, because **all the people was astonished at his doctrine**.

"...the **people are more conservative than the scholars**, and will not lightly suffer anything which savors of what they deem a tampering with the sacred text..."
(Thomas Harwood Pattison, *The History of the English Bible*, 1894)

There did arise a time when the religious leaders were able to move many of the people against the Lord, as they cried for Him to be crucified (Mark 15:13). But there is often a greater openness to truth among those who are considered "unlearned" by arrogant scholars:

Matthew 11:25 At that time Jesus answered and said, I thank thee, O Father, Lord of heaven and earth, because **thou hast hid these things from the wise and prudent, and hast revealed them unto babes.**

Matthew 21:15 And when the chief priests and scribes saw the wonderful things that he did, and **the children crying in the temple**, and saying, Hosanna to the Son of David; they were sore displeased,
16 And said unto him, Hearest thou what these say? And Jesus saith unto them, Yea; have ye never read, **Out of the mouth of babes** and sucklings thou hast perfected praise?

1 Corinthians 1:26 For ye see your calling, brethren, how that **not many wise men after the flesh**, not many mighty, not many noble, are called:
27 But God hath chosen the foolish things of the world to confound the wise; and God hath chosen the weak things of the world to confound the things which are mighty;

God certainly does not call His people to be simple-minded in a foolish manner. However, those who are humble and meek will see the Lord's truth long before those who are puffed up in their own knowledge or imagined accomplishments (1 Corinthians 8:1-2):

Psalms 25:9 The **meek** will he guide in judgment: and the meek will he teach his way.

Isaiah 5:21 Woe unto them that are wise in their own eyes, and prudent in their own sight!

Seeking knowledge without seeking humility, charity, etc., will soon blind us to the true knowledge of God (2 Peter 1:5-9). The pompous attitude that many have toward the King James Bible as the preserved, infallible Word of God is very similar to the attitude that many scholars had in regard to Jesus when He walked this earth as the Word made flesh:

"...the version [has been] used for nearly three centuries by English readers. **The people** cling to the English translation; they will quote it, and even when the translation can be shown **by scholars** to be in terms now obsolete or incorrect, **common readers** will be led by the version in their hands."
(Charles Augustus Jenkens, *Baptist Doctrines*, 1880)

"The Authorized Version is perfectly [understood by] **the people**...the 'less educated' are wedded to the splendid older version..."
(*The Literary Digest*, Volume 18, 1899)

"What has happened in the past has been this. Ignorant, illiterate people, in this country and in foreign countries, coming into salvation have been educated up to the book and have begun to understand it, **to glory in it, and to praise God for it**, and I say that we need to do the same at this present time. What we need is

therefore, not to replace the Authorized Version...We need rather to reach and train people up to the standard and language, the dignity and the glory of the old Authorized Version...men no longer read the Bible not because they cannot understand its language, but because they do not believe in it."
(D. Martin Lloyd-Jones, National Bible Rally, Royal Albert Hall, London, October 24, 1961)

"...scholarly critics have pointed to many inaccuracies in the King James Bible. They have insisted that it lacks clarity; is not true to original texts. But from the first, it was **immensely popular with the people**."
(*Indian Journal*, Oklahoma, December 19, 1957)

"The critical prefer it [the Revised Version], but **the people** still cling to the King James Version."
(*The Chautauquan*, Volume 11, 1890)

"In the long run, what may have been more important for the churches than the relative decline in attendance by 1901 was **the great gap that the second half of the century had opened between the theology of the people and the theology of its theologians**. The **theology of the people** by 1901 was very largely...what official theology had been in 1837. **It still depended upon a conscious or unconscious belief in the inerrancy of the King James Bible**...and of rewards and penalties in the hereafter."
(Lewis Charles Bernard Seaman, *Victorian England*, 1973)

Multitudes of the Lord's people (as will be fully documented in this book) have claimed that no other Book speaks like this King James Version. But the modern "Pharisees" and "scribes" answer the people with ridicule. They narrowly define "education" as indoctrination into their particular view of textual criticism; then they mock the "uneducated" for thinking that the AV is the preserved Word of God!

Interestingly, the same division occurred in regard to John the Baptist:

Matthew 21:25 The baptism of John, whence was it? **from heaven, or of men?** And they reasoned with themselves, saying, If we shall say, From heaven; he will say unto us, Why did ye not then believe him?
26 But if we shall say, Of men; **we fear the people; for all hold John as a prophet.**
46 But when they sought to lay hands on him, they **feared the multitude**, because **they took him for a prophet.**

The question is much the same today. Is the King James Version a gift of God's providence, or does it contain errors? Many scholars and pastors "fear the people" (see also 1 Samuel 15:24). They choose their words carefully, sometimes giving the impression that they believe that the AV is the inspired Word of God, inerrant, etc.:

Mark 12:13 And they send unto him **certain of the Pharisees** and of the Herodians, to **catch him in his words.**
14 And when they were come, they say unto him, **Master, we know that thou art true**, and carest for no man: for thou regardest not the person of men, **but teachest the way of God in truth**...

Washington Gladden (1836-1918) was an early modernist leader who denied the fundamentals of the faith. His words demonstrate how so-called "plain" people, with simple faith in the King James Bible, are a great obstacle to their liberal plans:

"Most of us who are now past middle life were brought up under influences in which the inerrancy of the Bible was always assumed. The Bible was God's Book...The time came when this sweeping chain of infallibility began to be widely challenged.

The doubts began to gather when the revision of the King James version was determined upon...The Bible never again could be to them the kind of Book which they had always supposed it to be...the theory of the Bible which is now held and taught by a large proportion of devout and intelligent Biblical scholars in all the Protestant churches is radically different from that which was taught at the beginning of my ministry...higher criticism has brought about this changed estimate of the Bible...few men graduate from these seminaries in these days who have not been convinced that the traditional theory...is erroneous...But it is also true that **there are many thousands of ministers and laymen who still adhere to the old theory...what are we going to do with the 'plain man'? He is the heart of the whole problem...unless his attitude toward the Bible can be changed**...[Indeed] the 'plain man' is the key to the situation..."
(Washington Gladden, *Biblical World*, Vol. 44, July, 1914)

This history of the King James Bible Only movement also documents centuries of ridicule and contempt heaped upon "plain people" for their firm faith in the King James Bible. It will become clear that the King James Bible, and the people who accept it as the infallible Word of God, are standing in the way of a vast, organized agenda (Revelation 17)! God will reward them for their fortitude as they despise the shame and seek His praise. Which side are you on?

CHAPTER 3

SOWING DEVILISH DOUBT

2 Corinthians 2:17 For we are not as **many**, which **corrupt the word** of God...

"What will be the effect on the minds of our people...Will not their minds be unsettled when they are told that some texts on which they had relied have been wrongly translated, when others disappear altogether...Will they not feel as if **all solid certainty** had been taken away?"
(George Salmon, *The Revision of the New Testament,* 1881)

The translators of the AV were incredibly gifted in languages. For example, John Bois (one of the translators) could read the Bible in Hebrew when he was only five years old:

"Not only had the English language...then ripened to its full perfection, but the study of Greek, and of the oriental tongues...had then been carried to a greater extent in England than ever before since...all the colleges of Great Britain and America, even in this proud day of boastings, could not bring together the same number...equally qualified by learning and piety...there has never been a time when a better qualified company could have been collected for the purpose..."
(Alexander McClure, *The Translators Revived*, 1858)

The *Preface* to the AV informs us:

"And in what sort did these assemble? In the trust of their own knowledge, or of their sharpness of wit, or deepness of judgment, as it were in an arm of flesh? At no hand. They trusted in him that hath the key of David, opening and no man shutting; they prayed to the Lord the Father of our Lord...'O let thy Scriptures be my pure delight, let me not be deceived in them, neither let me deceive by them...'"

The Lord was well able to answer this humble prayer of the AV translators. Yet, it is commonly argued by new version advocates that God has insured merely a "high degree" of "reliability" through modern textual criticism. Are we to believe that it is impossible for our miracle working God to providentially insure perfection? Unitarians, Universalists, liberals, and other infidels have always affirmed that this perfection is *impossible*:

"We do not make such remarks with a view to blame the translators, but to guard men against the **superstitious notion that our English version is perfect**. A perfect translation **needs not be expected** by imperfect men..."
(*The Expositor and Universalist Review*, Boston, 1834)

"Grant even that the Bible was originally infallible...and grant that all the books which have been excluded from the canon of Old Testament and New by us Protestants, are just the ones that ought to be excluded, and that all which have been included are just the ones that ought to be included, and that all which have been lost were spurious, so that the loss does not affect at all the perfectness of the canon - grant all that; yet even now how far have we got toward **certainty** that this Bible which we hold in our hand *today* is infallible - is infallible *as it comes to us?...* Have the translators of all the ages, who have translated Hebrew into Greek and Latin, and Greek and Latin into English, and Hebrew into English, in connection with the Old and New Testament books, been miraculously preserved from making errors? **If so, what mean the many thousands of errors which the great Commission of English scholars, who made for us a new Eng-**

lish translation of the Bible, found in the common translation or version of King James?...For example, the celebrated text (I. John v. 7, 8) of the three heavenly witnesses, which has been for a thousand years the strongest scripture bulwark of the doctrine of the Trinity, is admitted now on all hands to be an interpolation....So, then, what becomes of our infallible Bible? It has melted away into thin air..."
(Martin Kellogg Schermerhorn, *Renascent Christianity*, 1898)

God used "imperfect men" to give us the perfect Originals. Paul did not even write some of the Originals with his own hand (he used a "secretary"). God, who guided the hand of Tertius (one of Paul's scribes, Romans 16:22), did not fall asleep throughout the centuries. He is able to preserve through imperfect men the Scriptures that He originally inspired through imperfect men in the first place.

Many earlier Christians (though fallible) have recognized the exact books that belong in our Bible. Do we have merely a "reliable" canon of 66 books, or do we have the perfect set? The same God that can lead men to recognize the right books of the Bible, in perfection, can lead humble men to recognize the right words that make up those books:

Jeremiah 32:17 Ah Lord GOD! behold, thou hast made the heaven and the earth by thy great power and stretched out arm, and **there is nothing too hard for thee:**

The Devil's Foundational Lies

Satan, in the Garden of Eden, tempted Eve with two foundational lies, before deceiving her with the final lie that she and her husband "shall be as gods." His second lie removed her fear of the Lord:

Genesis 3:4 And the serpent said unto the woman, Ye shall not **surely** die:

This modern age has succumbed to these same lies. There is little fear of God in our culture, or even in many churches. But before Satan deceived Eve about the fear of the Lord, he first removed her *certainty* in the Word of God!:

Genesis 3:1 Now the serpent was more subtil than any beast of the field which the LORD God had made. And he said unto the woman, **Yea, hath God said**, Ye shall not eat of every tree of the garden?

Once Satan had shaken the faith of millions in the Word of God (so much so that many prominent, Christian leaders embraced the new claims), he then began to remove the fear of God from the land. Twentieth century Humanists soon began to mockingly proclaim that churches were losing the fear of God, and that a new age of Humanism was upon us. The nation, culture, and even many Christian churches, were then ready for the final lie of Satan. He then moved modern man (even many Christians) to become lovers of themselves (2 Timothy 3:1), and lovers of pleasures more than lovers of God (2 Timothy 3:4), and to practically seek their own godhood.

The New "Christian" Mysticism

Modern version advocates want Christians to believe that we have merely a "reliable" word of God today. They then desperately attempt to comfort modern, distressed Christians after destroying their faith in a perfect Bible that God has preserved for us:

"At that point an objection to the doctrine arises in the minds of many people. I am inclined to think it is a widespread objection, and I am inclined to think it troubles many thoughtful and intel-

ligent people. 'What is the use of the inspiration of the Bible,' people say, 'if no form of the Bible that we now have is inspired?'...I have deep sympathy with the people who raise it or who are troubled by it."
(John Gresham Machen, *The Christian Faith in the Modern World,* 1936)

Machen responds to this objection by saying that such troubled souls are guilty of *reasoning!*:

"...human though such reasoning is, it is very wrong."

After reading Machen's answer to this objection, it is not difficult to see why the Apostle Paul wanted to be delivered from *unreasonable* men!:

2 Thessalonians 3:2 And that we may be delivered from **unreasonable** and wicked men: for all men have not **faith.**
(*KJV*)

Yet, the new versions remove the word "unreasonable" from this verse:

"And pray that we may be delivered from wicked and evil people, for not everyone has faith."
(*NIV*, 2010)

God desires us to reason with Him, as we allow the Scriptures to enlighten our minds (Proverbs 20:27, Psalms 18:28, 119:105):

Isaiah 1:18 Come now, and let us **reason** together, saith the LORD...
(*KJV*)

But again, even this Old Testament command to be reasonable is subtly deleted in many new versions:

THE WORD: GOD WILL KEEP IT!

"'Come now, let us settle the matter,' says the LORD..."
(*NIV*, 2010)

It is obvious that neither new versions, nor their advocates, want believers reasoning (at least about this issue of the preservation of the Scriptures). The troubled souls, afflicted by "reason" in Machen's day, are still showing up in modern times. D. A Carson (a new version advocate) calls attention to it; and like Machen, he tries to console any alarmed Christians:

"All this sounds alarming. If not two manuscripts agree, how can we know what the Holy Spirit inspired the New Testament authors to write? The matter is, on the face of it, very difficult. All agree that one cannot simply take the oldest manuscripts and trust them...I should pause and set at rest the troubled concern of anyone who, on the basis of what I have written so far, concludes that the manuscript tradition is entirely **unreliable**, or that we cannot really be *certain* of **any** of it."
(D.A. Carson, *The King James Version Debate: A Plea for Realism*, 1979)

Notice Carson's carefully chosen words. *Certainty* has been replaced with a mere, general reliability. Christians can only be certain of *some* of the Bible. The fruit of these calculated insinuations has been seen in a countless number of people who have been "educated" (i.e. indoctrinated) out of their certainty by Bible seminaries. They have become unbelievers, or worse. Remember, the Devil never told Eve that God *did not say*. He simply created doubt (i.e. removing certainty). The Catholic Church hopes to capitalize on the spoil:

"...every critic of any textual pretensions makes a text for himself...To any one who knows what textual criticism is, how dubious in its methods, how revolutionary in its results, it is amazing that any Church calling itself Christian should hand over the Sacred Scriptures, the very title-deeds of its existence, to the chance

voting of critics."
(*The Dublin Review,* Burns and Oates, 1881)

Again, new version advocates are aware of this problem, but they attempt to minimize it with "good words and fair speeches" (Romans 16:18). For example, notice the following words from, *The King James Only Controversy,* by James R. White, a new version advocate:

"In this age of uncertainty, the last thing we need is the suspicion that the Word of God is somehow faulty and misleading... [p.1]...the 'argument for certainty' as I call it...is the 'glue' that holds the KJV Only position together...People do not want subjectivity, but desire **certainty** and clarity [p.93]...This argument is extremely powerful and should not be underestimated...many Roman Catholics find the idea of an infallible pope very 'comforting'...Protestants, however, should be *quick* to question any such notion of absolute religious certainty...As imperfect human beings we will make mistakes. [p. 94]...my desire is for the peace of Christ's church...[p. 250]."

Jeremiah 6:14 They have healed also the hurt of the daughter of my people slightly, saying, Peace, peace; when there is no peace.

White purposely confuses an infallible *pope* with an infallible *Bible.* This is an old trick. The infallible Bible teaches us to protest an infallible pope!:

"It is alarming to hear orthodox men say, **'Our fathers renounced an infallible pope - we must surrender an infallible book.'** Must we, indeed?...But what becomes of Christianity when the inspiration of the Bible is denied?"
(*The Methodist Review Quarterly*, 1882)

Is White certain that because people make mistakes that this means the *Bible* (in its *preserved* form) must have them as well? How can he be certain about his own view?:

"There are even some who go so far as to insist that the English translation of the King James is the infallible Word of God. I can understand and to some extent sympathize with people who think in this way. **We all prefer certainty to uncertainty**."
(Edward T. Babinski, *Leaving the Fold*, 1995)

The whole new version movement feeds on doubt; in fact, it was actually born in doubt. For example, Brooke Foss Westcott (1825-1901), one of the main leaders behind the Revised Version, wrote on May 5, 1860:

"My dear Hort...I reject the word *infallibility* - of Holy Scripture overwhelming."
(Arthur Westcott, *Life and Letters of Brooke Foss Westcott*, Vol. 1, 1896)

His partner, Fenton John Anthony Hort (1828-1892), likewise rejected infallibility:

"If you make a decided conviction of **the absolute infallibility of the NT** practically a sine qua non for co-operation, **I fear I could not join you**..."
(Arthur Fenton Hort, *Life and letters of Fenton John Anthony Hort*, 1896)

Modern Versions Diminish Certainty

It is therefore no wonder that that this uncertainty propaganda has been inserted into the modern versions themselves. We have already observed how these new versions delete verses dealing with reasoning. But there is much more that is changed or missing concerning certainty. Compare the King James Bible with some modern versions below:

SOWING DEVILISH DOUBT

Acts 1:3 To whom also he shewed himself alive after his passion by many **infallible proofs**...
(*KJV*)

"After his suffering, he presented himself to them and gave many **convincing proofs**..."
(*NIV*, 2010, etc.)

There is a considerable difference between *infallible* and *convincing*. Notice some other verses:

1 Timothy 6:7 For we brought nothing into this world, and it is **certain** we can carry nothing out.
(*KJV*)

"For we brought nothing into the world, and we can take nothing out of it."
(*NIV*, 2010, etc.)

Proverbs 22:21 That I might make thee know **the certainty of the words** of truth...
(*KJV*)

"teaching you to be honest and to speak the truth..."
(*NIV*, 2010, etc.)

2 Timothy 3:13 But evil men and seducers shall wax worse and worse, deceiving, and being deceived.
14 But continue thou in the things which thou hast learned and hast been **assured** of, knowing of whom thou hast learned them;
(*KJV*)

"...continue in the things you have learned and become **convinced** of..."
(*NASB*)

Examples could be multiplied of new versions changing verses that have to do with certainty, infallibility, reason, Bible study, etc. *Who* is *ultimately* behind such changes?:

2 Corinthians 4:4 In whom the god of this world hath blinded the minds of them which believe not…

Psalms 11:3 If the foundations be destroyed, what can the righteous do?

When Christians are taught that various verses are not found in the "most *reliable* early manuscripts," and such like, how can they truly prepare themselves for spiritual battle, and fight the good fight of faith?:

1 Corinthians 14:8 For if the trumpet give an **uncertain** sound, who shall prepare himself to the battle?
(*KJV*)

"Again, if the trumpet does not sound a clear call, who will get ready for battle?"
(*NIV*, 2010)

2 Peter 1:19 We have also a more **sure word of prophecy**; whereunto ye do well that ye take heed, as unto a light that shineth in a dark place...
(*KJV*)

"We also have the prophetic message as **something completely reliable**, and you will do well to pay attention to it..."
(*NIV*, 2010)

The "sure word" has become the merely reliable "something"!

Psalms 19:7 The law of the LORD is perfect, converting the soul: the testimony of the LORD **is sure**, making wise the simple.
(*KJV*)

"The law of the LORD is perfect, refreshing the soul. The statutes of the LORD are **trustworthy**, making wise the simple."
(*NIV*, 2010)

John 6:69 And we believe **and are sure** that thou art that Christ, the Son of the living God.
(*KJV*)

"We have come to believe and to know that you are the Holy One of God."
(*NIV*, 2010)

Psalms 93:5 Thy testimonies are **very sure**...
(*KJV*)

"Your statutes, LORD, stand firm..."
(*NIV*, 2010)

Roman Catholics, in preparation for the one-world-church of Revelation 17, have been rejoicing in changes like these for many years. In praising the Revised Version, Catholics stated:

"But perhaps the most surprising change of all is John v. 39. It is no longer 'Search the Scriptures,' but 'Ye search;' and thus Protestantism has lost the very cause of its being."
(*The Dublin Review,* Burns and Oates, 1881)

John 5:39 Search the scriptures; for in them ye think ye have eternal life: and they are they which testify of me.
(*KJV*)

"You study the Scriptures diligently..."
(*NIV*, 2010)

Many other verses are likewise changed in a manner that diminishes certainty and final authority in the Scriptures (e.g. see

Psalms 111:7; 2 Timothy 2:15; etc.). Satan works to replace true faith with *blind* faith; certainty, with some degree of doubt, etc. He desires strong, Bible-believing Christians to become subjective mystics with no sure anchor. The end result is an "emerging church" that is sure of nothing, with people lurking in the shadows of Dark Age liturgies and traditions, searching for stability and certainty. Along with this, worldliness is increased as others turn from the foundation of the Holy Scriptures to their own subjective hearts (Proverbs 18:2; 2 Timothy 4:3-4).

CHAPTER 4

THE ORIGINALS-ONLY SCHEME

"Revisions at moderate intervals of fifty years, will keep alive the idea of man's limited acquaintance with the original Scriptures in all the fullness of their meaning, and prevent superstitious attachment to the letter. Whatever checks bibliolatry is good and profitable."
(Samuel Davidson, *On a Fresh Revision of the English Old Testament*, 1873)

"...assuredly the *broad church* will widen their tents yet more, and rejoice in the liberty wherewith Textual Criticism has made them free."
(*The Dublin Review,* Burns and Oates, 1881)

Many unbelievers and liberals rejoiced in how the revised Bible versions were shaking the foundations of the faith:

"This translation [American Unitarian Association] is a decided help in the great battle against Bibliolatry and the doctrine of verbal and plenary inspiration. **Every new version**, even if it be not so good as this, **aids in overthrowing the power of the 'Paper-Pope' which has ruled Protestantism as with a rod of iron** [i.e. the King James Bible!]..."
(Sidney H. Morse, Joseph B. Marvin, *The Radical*, Vol. 5, 1869)

Sidney H. Morse (above) was an anarchist and free-thought infidel who was glad to see new versions ship-wrecking the faith of many Christians.

What many did not realize in their riot and revolution is that anarchy (political or spiritual) is used (and often planned) in order to bring about new chains and shackles out of the chaos:

2 Peter 2:19 While they promise them liberty, they themselves are the servants of corruption…

Power-mad leaders in history have set fires, etc., in order to justify assuming dictatorial powers. In a similar fashion, many have labored to destroy the faith of multitudes in the preserved Scriptures, so that they can capitalize on the vacuum. Laodiceanism (i.e. every man following his own heart in pride) is often followed by Nicolaitanism (Revelation 2:15), a totalitarian priesthood that robs Christians of their godly liberties, and even their lives (Revelation 17:4-6). The Bible is the anchor that keeps us from shipwrecking into these two extremes.

The devilish plan to use textual criticism (and thus, new versions) to destroy the faith of people in the Bible was formed centuries ago by the Jesuits.

The Roman Catholic Plot

"Wherever the so-called Counter-Reformation, started by the Jesuits, gained hold of the people, the vernacular was suppressed and the Bible kept from the laity. So eager were the Jesuits to destroy the authority of the Bible - the paper pope of the Protestants, as they contemptuously called it - that they even did not refrain from criticizing its genuineness and historical value."
(Ernst von Dobschutz, *The Influence of the Bible on Civilization*, 1914)

"If you answer, saying, that 'your judge and guide is not the translated copy as you have it now, but the original in Greek and Hebrew,' I ask you, what will your poor ignorant flock do, who neither hear what their rule of faith would have them to practice, nor see what it alleges?...you are deluded this day; because ye are

taught, on the one hand, by your ministers, to judge for yourselves; and on the other you are told, by your chiefest doctors and translators, that you have not in all Europe a true translation, whereby you can rule your judgments...**you stand in need of some infallible guide** to tell you which is the undoubted sense of those true copies, and which is not."
(Lawrence B. Sheil, Bishop of Adelaide, Australia, *The Bible Against Protestantism and for Catholicity,* 1846)

Richard Simon (1638-1712), a Catholic priest, is known as the father of textual criticism:

"Toward the close of the seventeenth century the scientific foundations of New Testament criticism were laid in four monumental publications of Richard Simon...a French Catholic scholar far ahead of his day..."
(Bruce Metzger, *The Text of the New Testament*, 1968)

"French Catholic priest and the real founder of Biblical criticism..."
(*The New Schaff-Herzog Encyclopedia of Religious Knowledge*, 1911)

Simon is a primary father of the "Originals only" viewpoint (i.e. that inspiration and infallibility apply to only the original autographs that are now lost):

"The distinction between 'inerrant autographs' and errant copies seems to have been first made by Richard Simon (1638-1712) ...to prove the necessity of textual criticism..."
(Philip Schaff, Samuel Macauley Jackson, *Theological Propaedeutic*, 1893)

The above testimony is from Philip Schaff (1819-1893), a historian, and chairman of the American Standard Version translation committee. The "Originals only" view is therefore Roman Catholic. Richard Simon (who studied with Jesuits) adopted this view in order to counter the "Bible only" doctrine of Protestants. If inspiration and infallibility pertain only to lost Originals (and never to copies or translations), Simon argued that the authority of Roman Catholic tradition was therefore necessary. He writes:

"...[Textual criticism] judges and determines the most authentic readings, which ought to be inserted into the text. By this means Origen acquired his reputation...Erasmus...is nevertheless guilty of very gross errors...In this piece, I have justified the Arians...I have no other intentions in composing this work, than the benefit of the [Catholic] Church...**As the Holy Books are not exempt from faults**, which either by the tract of time, or negligence of the transcribers [have slipped into them]...Is it possible (may some say) that God hath given to His Church, Books to serve her for a rule, and that He hath at the same time permitted that the first originals of these Books should be lost...?...**this rule [i.e. the Bible] is not altogether sufficient of itself...But it is much more reasonable only to admit this inspiration for the Originals** of the Holy Scriptures..."
(Richard Simon, *A Critical History of the Text of the New Testament*, 1689)

Simon even argued against the inclusion of 1 John 5:7 in the Bible (it is likewise deleted by new versions).

Notice again that Simon argued that only the Originals were inspired and infallible. He warned that the Scriptures in their present state are insufficient. He knew that the "Originals only" view of inspiration and infallibility would drive people away from "Bible Onlyism," in search of stability and final authority in the Roman Catholic Church:

"The great alterations...to the Copies of the Bible since the first Originals have been lost, utterly destroy the [Protestant's view]... it is almost impossible to translate the Holy Scripture...Instead of believing with the Protestants that the shortest and most certain

way of deciding the questions of faith is to consult the Holy Scriptures, we shall on the contrary find in this Work that if we join not [Catholic] Tradition with the Scripture, we can hardly affirm any thing for **certain** in Religion..."
(Richard Simon, *A Critical History of the Old Testament*, 1682)

Genesis 3:1 Now the serpent was **more subtil** than any beast of the field which the LORD God had made. And he said unto the woman, **Yea, hath God said...?**

Like Simon, the Knights of Columbus (i.e. Roman Catholic) argued in newspaper advertisements that there is no sure guarantee of Bible inspiration and infallibility without the Catholic Church:

"People differ radically in what they think about the Bible. Some seem to think that it was handed down from Heaven written in English and bound in morocco...the Bible is truly a Catholic book...it is the **infallible authority** of the Catholic Church that has always been the only **sure guarantee** of its inspiration."
(The Knights of Columbus, *The Salt Lake Tribune*, September 4, 1949)

With so many voices casting doubt on the Holy Scriptures, it is hoped that the history presented in this book will be refreshing to many who, like Elijah, may sometimes feel that they are alone in the battle (Romans 11:2-4). God has thousands who have not bowed the knee to Baal, or the constant "Bible Babel" of contradictory versions and texts. These saints believed that they possessed an infallible Bible - not one that only existed in ancient times - but a present Bible that they could read, believe and propagate. A countless number of Christians have believed that they possessed a Bible wherein *every* word is perfect (Matthew 4:4)!

THE WORD: GOD WILL KEEP IT!

CHAPTER 5

KJV ONLY: IS IT A NEW VIEW?

Acts 14:17 Nevertheless he left not himself without witness...

Hebrews 12:1 Wherefore seeing we also are compassed about with **so great a cloud of witnesses**, let us lay aside every weight...

"...**many** trust the English Bible as infallible...**millions** [believe]...our English Bible is the code and canon of all truth."
(Thomas Kingsmill Abbott, *The English Bible, and Our Duty with Regard to It*, 1857; 1871)

It has been 400 years since the publication of the King James Bible in 1611 (often called the Authorized Version or the AV). Multitudes of Christians (including this writer) believe that this translation is infallible; that it is the preserved Word of God in English for these last days. This view has been growing in acceptance for many decades, prompting a multitude of anti-KJV-Only books, websites, articles, etc.

One of the purposes of this book is to correct the oft-parroted claim that the KJV Only doctrine is a new or fringe viewpoint. The truth of the matter is, that it has been the most common view among Christians since the AV was printed!

It is hoped that this book will be an encouragement to many who have been ridiculed or intimidated by the false claims of anti-KJV-Only scholars. Notice this commonly repeated argument put forth by advocates of the new versions:

"There is not one...commentary or statement of faith or statement by a reliable authority that the King James Version is without an error in translation. Not one in the world!"
(John R. Rice, *The Sword of the Lord*, March 30, 1979)

"...no fundamentalist before mid-1950 ever claimed inerrancy for a translation..."
(Robert Leslie Sumner, *Bible Translations*, 1979)

"Before the 1950's there were no Christians, Bible Schools, church fathers, martyrs or scholars who restricted Christians to the use of only one version of the Bible...Only those poisoned by Ruckmanism [Peter Ruckman] are KJV Only...anyone who goes off after a new doctrine different from the accepted historic Christian position is bound to be wrong...It is a completely new man-made doctrine..."
(Dr. Robert A. Joyner, *King James Only?: A Guide to Bible Translations,* 2000)

"...this view that a translation is given by inspiration was unheard of throughout two millennia of church history until Ruckmanism reared its head after 1950...No Baptist or Protestant scholar believed that the KJV was given by inspiration before 1950!"
(Robert Hymers, *Ruckmanism Exposed,* 1998)

Robert Hymers offered to pay $1000 to anyone who could disprove the above claims. Another writer even places this objection in the very title of his book:

"The King James Only doctrine is a new idea...This new doctrine declares that the King James Bible is the providentially preserved Word of God...[The first advocate was] Seventh Day Adventist Benjamin G. Wilkinson [in 1930]."
(James D. Price, *King James Onlyism: A New Sect,* 2006)

KJV ONLY: IS IT A NEW VIEW?

"The arguments for the special role of the King James Version can be traced to Benjamin G. Wilkinson (d. 1968); a Seventh-day Adventist theologian..."
(J. Gordon Melton, *Encyclopedia of Protestantism,* 2005)

"The KJO movement originated with a 1930 book by Seventh-day Adventist theologian Benjamin Wilkinson."
(*The Daily Globe*, Michigan, July 21, 2001)

The above claims are refuted in the history section of this book that begins in the next chapter.

Introduction to the Historical Section

A few words should be noted about this history:

1. Quotations do not necessarily always imply full endorsement. Many sources are quoted. In the Bible, the enemies of Jesus sometimes attested to the fruitfulness of His ministry:

John 12:19 The Pharisees therefore said among themselves, **Perceive ye how ye prevail nothing? behold, the world is gone after him.**

In the same manner, the murmurings of unbelievers, modernists, etc., often unwittingly documented the views of Bible believers in their days. Many complained that the whole Christian world had gone after the Authorized Version as the infallible, written Word of God! In doing so, they became witnesses to the great prevalence of KJV Onlyism in history.

2. This history is mainly concerned with documenting the abundance of KJV Only believers throughout the past 400 years; their words should be an *encouragement* to Bible believers in this present time. However, many of the quotes in this history

also contain arguments that will serve as a *defense* of the King James Bible, and the KJV Only viewpoint.

3. Quotes could certainly be multiplied from KJV Only writers in recent decades. A bountiful supply of books, booklets and articles have recently been published proclaiming the infallibility of the Authorized Version. The goal of this book is not to document every KJV Onlyist in history, or modern times, but to provide many samples of the KJV Only view for the past 400 years. The various authors, pastors, etc., in modern times who have boldly promoted and defended the KJV Only view are numerous. Many of these modern writers are quoted or mentioned in this history in order to demonstrate that the KJV Only view is certainly alive and well today. However, the omission of any writer is not meant to imply that his contribution is insignificant.

4. Many of the men who defended the Textus Receptus (e.g. Burgon, Miller, and hundreds of others) have not been included in this history in any detail. Such men have diligently defended the inspiration and historicity of Bible passages such as Mark 16. However, this history mainly documents those who have advocated a clearer King James Bible Only view.

5. Some critics of this book will likely respond to the many quotes by stating that Christians should not base their doctrine on men's views or writings. But this will, generally, be a new way for them to argue. As already documented, most anti-KJV Onlyists have spent a considerable amount of time and energy alleging that the KJV Only view is of relatively recent origin, or that it began in cultic circles. The historical quotes will therefore refute this claim.

The Bible itself reproves the erroneous teaching that only the Originals are infallible, etc. We therefore are not dependent upon the views of men. However, when Christian history is "revised," and the testimonies of these many Christian witnesses are "deleted" (like so many Bible verses in the new versions, such as Matthew 17:21, 18:11, 23:14; Mark 7:16, 9:44, 9:46, 11:26, 15:28; Luke 23:17; Acts 8:37, etc.), it is important to set the record straight!

Some Early Fundamentalists Stopped Short

The fact that some of the early fundamentalists were (especially at first) blinded by the "new findings in textual criticism" propaganda in their days is not denied. Their statements are often contradictory. For example, notice the words of S. D. Gordon:

"The modern English and American Revisions have the advantage of the most recently found manuscripts, the latest scholarship, and the paragraphed printing. But one can rest content that the old common version is the most remarkable bit of translation ever done. In it we have the very Word of God, 'in' plain English, a sufficient guide for daily life."
(*Olean Evening Herald*, July 21, 1923)

A.W. Tozer (1897-1963) confessed that he was addicted and weary with the whole "new version" swindle:

"Since shortly after my conversion to Christ as a teen-ager I have been addicted to the habit of acquiring and being disappointed with new versions of the Scriptures, both revisions and new translations. It is a habit I cannot shake off. In spite of a long record of frustrated hopes and cruel disappointments, to this day I have but to hear a new version of the Scriptures has come out and I am off to the book-seller to pick up a copy...After poring over the new book for a few days or weeks and finding that it is just one more version, I put it aside and return to my first love,

the familiar King James Bible. I know its mistakes very well, its mistranslations and confused tenses; I should, for the Bible teachers are forever correcting it in public and the introductions to the new versions never tire of pointing out these flaws in the grand old English Bible...I believe that my error has been that I have nursed the hope, perhaps subconsciously, that my dullness of spirit and coldness of heart are the result of not hearing the truth expressed clearly enough in the common language of the street; that if I could hear a promise or a commandment couched in different words it would be easier to believe and obey. But this is a gross fallacy...Yet this is the latest religious word game in evangelical circles and we are all urged to play at it. For myself, I cannot keep serious while reading such a version...I have sometimes thought (and I trust not uncharitably) that the knowledge of a little Greek is a great convenience to such a man, for the Greek being a remarkably accommodating language enables him to preach anything he wants to without being challenged...I have not become a holier man nor a better preacher by my incurable addiction to new versions of the Scriptures..."
(*Confessions of a New Version Addict*)

Tozer requested to be buried with a King James Bible (with no notes) on his breast. Like many men with spiritual insight, Tozer was *close* to the KJV Only viewpoint. However, he still came short of understanding the full impact of the Lord's warning to "beware of the scribes" (Mark 12:38).

Evangelist D.L. Moody was also very close to discerning the danger and extent of the proud scribes:

"If every word between the covers of the Bible is not absolutely true, then we had better burn it..."
(D.L. Moody; quoted in H.M. Tabor, *Faith Or Fact?,* 1897)

The lost Originals were not between the covers of Moody's Bible! Again, Moody was close to putting his finger on the whole problem when he argued:

"...if you deny the story of Jonah and the whale you must deny the resurrection of Jesus Christ...And I believe the great and overwhelming majority of the common people with their English Bible in their hands will stand with me in that judgment...There's a false notion of authority associated with much that we hear in these days about the science of biblical criticism, as it is called...I believe there are a good many scholars in these days, as there were when Paul lived, 'who professing themselves to be wise, have become fools...'...I have said that ministers of the Gospel who are cutting up the Bible in this way, denying Moses today and Isaiah tomorrow, and Daniel the next day and Jonah the next, are doing the Devil's work...the cause of this state of things is in neglecting and apologizing to the natural man for the Word of God."
(Dwight L. Moody, *The Independent*, February 11, 1897)

Notice one more example. John R. Rice, in a sermon in 1936, defended the "Bible" from those who claimed it had mistakes. He argues:

"...**the Bible** does not claim that after it has been copied and re-copied and translated into the English language that then that English version or the King James Version are the very words of God...I do not say that. Intelligent Bible students do not say that. **The Bible** does say, however...**this Bible**, I say, claims to be the very words of God..."
(John R. Rice, *The Sword of the Lord*, June 26, 1936)

He was likely holding and preaching from the King James Bible! How confused or discouraged the people must have been. He finally attempts to comfort them by stating:

"...in the King James version, and even better in the Revised Version...not more than one word in every 10,000 is even in question."

There is no virtue in holding to the inconsistencies, weaknesses, or sins of our forefathers, regardless of how godly or blessed they may have generally been in their work. While some of the popular preachers came close to discerning the deceptions of the Devil concerning the Bible, others were foolishly gullible as they consumed the propaganda and marketing and allowed themselves to be intimidated.

In 1930, Charles F. Potter, the popular infidel, and founder of the first Humanist Society, laughed at how blind so many Christians had become to the fact that Humanists were controlling the public schools. He said that many Christians believed that evolution was the only issue of concern; to the contrary, Potter argued that children were receiving a five-day-a-week, *full* indoctrination into Humanism which Christians could never undo with their one-day-a-week Sunday Schools. This same blindness has occurred in regard to the Bible itself. Satan is far more wicked and crafty than many have realized; and the warnings of the Bible to beware of his devices, and beware of the scribes, have been little heeded. There is a dangerous tendency in many Christians to ignore the warnings of the Bible.

On the other hand, too often some popular, early Christian leaders are quoted as if their statements concerning the King James Bible represent the *only* viewpoint among believers in their day. The historical sections of this book document that these teachers were largely outnumbered by the many Christians who believed that the King James Bible is infallible! And these same teachers, when addressing the people, often implied that they too believed that the Bible in their hands is the infallible, inspired, inerrant Word of God. Religious leaders often feared the people during the Lord's ministry on earth; and sometimes the people feared their leaders. Even the Apostle Peter was once reproved by Paul for withdrawing from the Gentile believers when certain other teachers were in his company (Galatians 2:11-12). It is therefore no wonder that many otherwise good men throughout Christian history sometimes made contradictory statements on crucial issues.

As the controversy continues, let the proper history be proclaimed. Thousands of Christians (and even many Christian leaders) in the past 400 years have believed that the King James Bible is the inspired, infallible, inerrant, sacred, unalterable, preserved Word of God.

It is the author's prayer that this history will increase the reader's faith in the Holy Scriptures, and that he or she will be zealously encouraged to read the AV as the perfect, infallible, preserved Word of God for this age. This is the only way to truly prosper in the Scriptures:

Hebrews 4:2...the **word** preached **did not profit** them, **not being mixed with faith** in them that heard it.

1 Thessalonians 2:13 For this cause also thank we God without ceasing, because, when ye **received the word of God** which ye heard of us, **ye received it not as the word of men, but as it is in truth, the word of God**, which effectually worketh also in you that believe.

Matthew 9:29 Then touched he their eyes, saying, According to your faith be it unto you.

THE WORD: GOD WILL KEEP IT!

CHAPTER 6

1611-1699

The history of the KJV Only viewpoint should begin in the days of the KJV translators themselves. Their version was the **seventh one** in the line of the best English versions. This can be seen in one of the guidelines adopted by the translators of the KJV:

"These translations to be used when they agree better with the text than the **Bishop's Bible**: namely, **Tindale's**, **Matthews**, **Coverdale's**, **Whitchurch's** [i.e. Great Bible], **Geneva**."
(*Instruction to the Translators*)

Notice these versions placed in historical order:

1. Tyndale's (1526)
2. Coverdale's (1535)
3. Matthew's (1537)
4. Great (1539)
5. Bishop's (1568)
6. Geneva (1587)
7. **Authorized Version**

The Authorized Version (i.e. KJV) is the final purification. This is a fulfillment of God's promise to preserve His pure words:

Psalms 12:6 The **words of the LORD** are pure words: as silver tried in a furnace of earth, **purified seven times.**
7 **Thou shalt keep them**, O LORD, thou shalt preserve them

from this generation for ever.

What was begun by William Tyndale, was completed by the KJV translators:

"Three generations wrought upon [the English version]. It was begun...[by] William Tyndale...and it was **completed** when the able revisers of King James finished their labors in 1611. The 'King James," which we prize so much, was not, therefore, a new translation, but a sixth or seventh revision of a translation made in the first quarter of the preceding century...It has the seal of martyrdom upon it...our Tyndale was first exiled and afterwards strangled in a foreign land; Coverdale, who gave us our first complete Bible, by cruel exile barely escaped the stake; Rogers, author of the 'Matthews Bible,' was the first victim of the Marian persecution. Sir Thomas Cromwell, whose influence brought out the fourth revision, the 'Great Bible,' was beheaded; and Cranmer, life-long friend of the Word of God, whose picture stood with those of Henry and Cromwell on the frontispiece of the 'Great Bible,' perished with his friends, Latimer and Ridley, in the martyr fires at Oxford. A baptism of blood consecrated the English Bible to the Master's service...No other version of the Scriptures has been so widely or so reverently read..."
(*National Repository,* Volume 3, 1878)

"William Tyndale, a scholar of the highest rank, who took it, not, as others had done before him, from the Latin Vulgate, but from the original Greek...Wycliffe's translation had been very little known, and was entirely out of the reach of the poor. God then stirred up Tyndale's spirit to give his fellow-countrymen the Scriptures in their native tongue, that they might read for themselves the plain, simple word of God....When Tyndale's works first came abroad in England, Foxe says, 'It cannot be described what a door of light they opened to the eyes of the whole English nation'...**The translation made by Tyndale has formed the ba-**

sis of our principal subsequent versions, excepting only the late revision of 1881 [the RV]...Thus, the present Authorized Version is the work of these good men, combined with that of the Reformers before them. The Bible they produced still remains a monument of God's goodness...we fully believe that the hand of God was in the ordering and production of the Authorized Version, 1611..."
(*The Gospel Standard*, 1882)

"Is a revision of the authorized version of the Bible necessary?...emphatically No!...we prize our English Bible as one of our greatest blessings; as a book eminently distinguished above all others for its intrinsic worth; **a book that is ours at the cost of Tindal's blood**, the imprisonment and exile of Miles Coverdale, the manifold labours and sufferings of pious men...So far as its phraseology is concerned, we should remember that it is the language of inspiration...It is said that because a correction of the Geneva and the Bishops' Bible was found necessary, a revision of our present version is expedient. This we cannot admit...alter it now, in this present transitory state, and the charm of religion will have passed away, and infidelity will reign paramount in the land."
(*The British Controversialist*, 1857)

Tyndale began with a great, holy burden:

"I defy the pope and all his laws; and if God spare me I will one day make the boy who drives the plough in England to know more Scripture than the pope does."
(Tyndale, Virgil G. Townsend, *Translation and Spread of the English Bible*, 1922)

On another occasion, he wrote:

"I call God to record against the day we shall all appear before

our Lord Jesus, to give a reckoning of our doings, that I never altered one syllable of God's word against my conscience, nor would this day, if all that is in the earth, whether it be pleasure, honour, or riches, might be given me."
(Quoted in, *The Acts and Monuments of John Foxe*, 1838)

As Tyndale was dying, he prayed for the eyes of the king of England to be opened. The KJV Translators, diligently translating the original languages, used Tyndale's translation (and other good ones), as a basis of comparison to make their one, polished version:

"The final revision of the Tindale translations was published in 1534, and that becomes the notable year of his life. In two years he was put to death by strangling, and his body was burned...Tindale is the real father of our King James version. About eighty per cent, of his Old Testament and ninety per cent, of his New Testament have been transferred to our version."
(Cleland Boyd McAfee, *The Greatest English Classic*, 1912)

Tyndale (who was proficient in seven languages, including Hebrew, according to contemporaries) knew that his translation was only the *beginning* of something better to come!:

"Count it as a thing **not having his full shape**, but as it were born **before his time**, even as **a thing begun rather than finished**. In time to come (**if** God have appointed us thereunto) we will give it his full shape..."
(*Tyndale's Preface,* 1526)

God did not allow Tyndale to finish and polish his version. However, the KJV translators understood that their version was the perfected one, built upon the foundation of the previous good ones:

"Nothing is begun **and perfected** at the same time...we [are] building upon **their foundation**...that whatsoever is sound already...the same will **shine as gold** more brightly, **being rubbed and polished**...to make a good one better, or **out of many good ones, one principle good one**, **not justly to be excepted against**...we have at length, through the good hand of the Lord upon us, brought the work..."
(*Translator's Preface*)

What was planted and watered in these earlier versions became a fruitful harvest in the King James Bible. The translators worked, with the providential hand of the Lord upon them, to produce "one principle good one, not justly to be excepted against":

"The design of its authors [the KJV translators] was not to make an entirely new translation, but to gather up, **in one complete and final version**, all that England's wisest and holiest men had done to make the Bible the common inheritance of the English people. It was, therefore, at its birth a thousand years old, and stood forth in its gigantic and glorious youth as the grand result of all the revolutions in literature, in religion, in government which had made England what it was in the days of our fathers."
(John A. Albro, *The Congregational Quarterly*, Volume 12 , 1870)

It is true that the KJV translators, in their humility, left others to judge whether they had accomplished this goal of absolutely perfecting the work that others had begun:

"No cause therefore why the word translated should be denied to be the word...notwithstanding that some imperfections and blemishes **may** be noted in the setting forth of it."
(*The Translators to the Reader*)

But their humility is no proof that the Lord permitted them to make mistakes. God always used men who were little in their own eyes (Exodus 4:10, Judges 6:15). Did even all of the original writers of the Bible know that they were inspired and infallible in the writings they produced? Along this line, was Eliphaz the Temanite aware that his words would be quoted, not only in the Old Testament, but centuries later as inspired, New Testament Scripture (compare Job 5:13 with 1 Corinthians 3:19)? If such awareness was not necessary for the original writings, in every case, why would it be necessary for the mere *preservation* of these inspired writings?

God is able to insure perfect copies throughout the centuries. But it would have been presumptuous for each and every copyist to proclaim his own work as perfect. In the same manner, when imperfect men recognized the individual books that belong in the Bible, did they err in choosing 66? It is a fact that many did err, through the ages. Many of the various, so-called "church councils" added apocryphal works, or left out certain books of the Bible. But does this mean that no one in history ever made the right choices?

God preserved Daniel's three friends in the midst of the fiery furnace. They knew that He *could* preserve them; but they did not presume to say that they were absolutely certain that He *would* do so (Daniel 3:17-18). Millions of believers have recognized that God's guiding hand was with the translators as the English translation was being tried as silver in the fires, and polished to perfection. The translators were confident that He would indeed guide them to give the English translation a final polish; but they were careful not to use presumptuous or haughty language.

King James (1566-1625) also expressed his wish for "one uniform translation" during a meeting with various ministers in 1604 (according to an eye-witness):

"...my lord of London well added, that if every man's humour should be followed, there would be no end of translating. Whereupon his highnesse wished, that some special paines should be taken in that behalf for **one uniform translation**..."
(William Barlow, *The Summe and Substance of the Conference at Hampton Court*; quoted in, Edward Cardwell, *A History of Conferences*, 1841)

"...in the end its superior merits won it its due, and it became **the only Bible** of the English-speaking people..."
(*The Expository Times*, Volume 22, 1911)

The full awareness of what God had wrought in 1611 grew and increased among Christians in subsequent years.

The Early American Colonies

Many who desire to supplant the King James Bible in modern times, claim that it was not on the Mayflower, and that it was therefore rejected or scorned by the Pilgrims and the other early Christians who settled our country. A few years ago, this writer refuted this claim in a letter to *World Net Daily* ("Letter of the Week," Feb. 2, 2007). Notice some excerpts from this letter:

"Today, when the Pilgrims are mentioned, there is a great, misleading half-truth that many are promoting. Notice an example of this half-truth: 'In 1620, the Pilgrims arrived at Plymouth with their Bibles and a conviction derived from those Bibles of establishing a new nation. The Bible was not the King James Version.' (Gary DeMar, *The Geneva Bible: The Forgotten Translation*, www.reformed.org) I wonder how many 'Thanks-giving sermons' contained a sentence or two that stated that the early Pilgrims who came over on the Mayflower did NOT possess or use the Authorized Version (King James)? These preachers have simply repeated what they have heard from others. Notice the real truth about the Bibles the Pilgrims had when they arrived on the Mayflower as stated at the Pilgrim Hall Museum: 'Among the books in Pilgrim Hall are four Bibles of unusual interest. One belonged to Gov. William Bradford, the Pilgrim governor, and one to John Alden. These are among the very few objects existing today which we feel reasonably sure 'came over in the Mayflower'...**John Alden's Bible, rather surprisingly, is the 'King James' version...This is not a Geneva Bible, but the 'King James' or 'Authorized version...'** The early Pilgrims had both versions! Although the AV was new at the time, it would quickly outshine them all and become the cornerstone of civilization in the New World. Therefore, W.A. Criswell was correct when he stated: 'And when they [the Pilgrims] came to America, they brought with them this Bible, the King James Version of the Word of God. It had been placed in their hands, been translated just nine years earlier...So the little colony began with the Christian home, built around the Bible; with a Christian church, preaching the infallible Word of God; and a school whose textbook was the King James Version of the Bible'...Although the Plymouth Pilgrims used the AV and the Geneva (e.g. Gov. Bradford's 'Journal' quotes the Geneva version), the Massachusetts Bay Puritans, on the other hand, used the AV as their primary text (not the Geneva). The same thing is true of the separatists and the first Baptists in the New World who went out into the wilderness from them. For example, John Wheelwright's Fast Day Sermon in 1636 quoted from the AV, not the Geneva. Likewise, John Clarke (1609-1676), who is called the father of American Baptists, used the AV instead of the Geneva (see his *Ill-Newes From New England*). And the rest is well-known history. The AV would soon become 'Our Version,' and its fruit and authority in the lives of American Christians has been thoroughly documented elsewhere....It is God's Book. It soon outshined all other versions. They decreased and it increased; and so did our nation as long as it believed, honored and obeyed this Holy Bible."

Joseph H. Choate likewise proclaimed that colonial America was built upon the King James Bible. Speaking at the Centenary of the British and Foreign Bible Society, in 1904, he reminded his audience:

"When the Pilgrim Fathers embarked in the Mayflower in 1620, and when, eight years afterward, the great Puritan immigration from old England to New England set in, they carried with them, our fathers, and the brothers of your fathers, carried with them, as their best possession - in fact, the only one which was to have a lasting value - **King James's Bible**, upon which their infant state was built. It was their only book - their only readable book...That book was readable by every man, woman, and child. It was the ark of their covenant, and, really, they did find within those sacred covers their shelter from the stormy blast and their eternal home. Their faith was founded upon it...and they searched and found in it the golden rules of life."
(Joseph H. Choate; quoted in, Clayton Sedgwick Cooper, *The Bible and Modern Life*, 1911)

This proves that the KJV was more than merely *used* in the 17th century. However, even the view that the KJV is a true copy of the Originals was not lacking in those early days.

John Bunyan

John Bunyan (1628-1688) was a Baptist preacher who wrote, *The Pilgrim's Progress*. He believed the AV was an exact copy of the Originals, and he was not ashamed to proclaim it before the high-minded scholars of his day. Charles Doe was one of Bunyan's closest friends:

"The works left in manuscript at Bunyan's death were given to the world by his devoted friend and admirer, the good, simple-minded combmaker by London Bridge, Charles Doe, who soon after his decease set about a folio edition of his collected

works as 'the best work he could do for God.'"
(*Dictionary of National Biography*, Volume 7, edited by Sir Leslie Stephen, p.282, 1886)

Doe records one of Bunyan's confrontations with a proud scholar as follows:

"*Mr. Bunyan's dispute with a scholar to this effect:* As Mr. Bunyan was upon the road near Cambridge, there overtakes him a scholar that had observed him a preacher, and said to him, 'How dare you preach, seeing you have not the original, being not a scholar?' Then said Mr. Bunyan, 'Have you the original?' 'Yes,' said the scholar. 'Nay,' but, said Mr. Bunyan, 'have you the very self-same original copies that were written by the penmen of the scriptures, prophets and apostles?' 'No,' said the scholar, 'but we have the true copies of those originals.' 'How do you know that?' said Mr. Bunyan. 'How?' said the scholar. 'Why, we believe what we have is a true copy of the original.' 'Then,' said Mr. Bunyan, 'so do I believe **our English Bible** is a true copy of the original.' Then away rid the scholar."
(Charles Doe, *The Struggler,* 1691)

Doe's record of this dispute is found in several biographies of Bunyan:

"The design appears to have been undertaken principally by Charles Doe, a Baptist Minister, who entitles himself 'the Struggler for the preceding preservation of Mr. John Bunyan's labors in folio.' He furnishes a short narrative of the Author's life, with some particulars of the edition and index then printed; but by far the most valuable part of this very interesting literary document is the following...'**Bunyan could reprove even Biblical Critics.** Charles Doe says, 'A scholar overtook him near Cambridge, and asked him, how dare you preach, seeing you have not the *Original* (Scriptures), being no scholar? Then, said Mr. Bunyan, have

you the original? Yes, said the scholar. Nay but, said Mr. Bunyan, have you the very *self-same* copies that were written by the Penmen of the Scriptures? No, said the Scholar; but we have *true* copies of them. How do you *know* that? said Mr. Bunyan. How, said the scholar: why, we *believe* what we have is a true copy of the original. Then said Mr. Bunyan, - so do I believe our English Bible to be a *true* copy of the original. So, away rid the scholar!' *Doe's Circular*."
(Robert Philip, *The Life, Times, and Characteristics of John Bunyan*, 1858)

It is repeated in Stephen B. Wickens, *The Life of John Bunyan* (1853); George Offer, *The Whole Works of John Bunyan* (1862); and in the *Sunday School Teacher* (1871), etc.

Some modern researchers have supposed that the scholar (who was put in his place by Bunyan) was Thomas Smith of Cambridge, professor of Arabic.

Anti-KJV-Onlyites attempt to dilute the effect of this wonderful testimony by alleging that Bunyan sometimes quoted the *Geneva* version. However, in combing through Bunyan's *Works*, one can see that he constantly quotes the AV (not the *Geneva*). Notice one example among multitudes that could be cited:

"Oh that word! 'We have not preached unto you **cunningly devised fables**'...were blessed words unto me, in this my imprisoned condition."
(John Bunyan, *A Brief Account of the Author's Imprisonment*)

Bunyan is quoting the AV in this tract, not the *Geneva*:

2 Peter 1:16 For we have not followed **cunningly devised fables**...
(*AV*)

"For we followed not **deceiuable fables**...."
(*Geneva*)

Obviously, there are many *cunningly devised fables* alive and well today, such as the claim that the AV is imperfect. In the few places where Bunyan quotes the AV with minute differences, etc., it is obvious that he is quoting from memory, or he is freely quoting without exactness for literary purposes.

Even so, the *Geneva* was one of the six, *good* versions that the *King James Version* translators had asserted they were *perfecting* with their final, seventh version (i.e. the AV). We are not even out of the seventeenth century and we already have one of the most well-known, beloved Christian writers rebuking a pompous forefather of the modern Originals-Only movement!:

"...Bunyan presented his inability to read the Bible in its original languages as a virtue."
(*Reconsidering the Renaissance*: *papers from the Twenty-first Annual Conference,* State University of New York at Binghamton, 1992)

Bunyan was imprisoned for his Baptist faith. And while the establishment preachers were scorning him, Bunyan was drinking from the wellspring of the English Authorized Version; and he was used by God to write one of the greatest Christian classics ever penned! Bunyan's "Our English Bible" refers to the AV, which from the beginning was commonly called, "Our Version."

This is not the only place that Bunyan expressed his views against the "original languages only" doctrine. The following dialogue is titled, *A Relation of the Imprisonment of Mr. John Bunyan, Minister of the Gospel at Bedford, in November, 1660*:

"...I was desired by some friends in the country to come to teach...The justice, hearing thereof, (whose name is Mr. Francis Wingate), forthwith issued out his warrant to take me...and in the mean time to keep a very strong watch about the house where the meeting should be kept, as if we that were to meet together in that place did intend to do some fearful business…when, alas! the constable, when he came in, found us only with our **Bibles in our hands**...[When waiting,] in comes an old enemy to the truth, Dr. Lindale, who, when he was come in, fell to taunting at me with many reviling terms…when I came to the justice again, there was Mr. Foster [i.e. attorney William Foster, the brother-in-law to justice Wingate]...with such seeming affection [for me] as if he would have leaped on my neck and kissed me...it caused me to remember those sayings: 'Their tongues are smoother than oil, but their words are drawn swords.' And again, 'Beware of men,' etc:

Foster: '…We must not enter into...dispute now; but if you will say you will call the people no more together, you may have your liberty; if not, you must be sent away to prison.'

Bunyan: 'Sir, I shall not force or compel any man to hear me...'

Foster: 'That is none of your work; you must follow your calling, and leave off preaching...to have any such meetings is against the law...'

Bunyan: 'I do not make any such promise, for my conscience will not suffer me to do it...I look upon it as my duty to do as much good as I can...'

Foster: **'You are ignorant and do not understand the Scriptures; for how can you understand them when you know not the original Greek? etc.'**

Bunyan: **'It is your opinion that none can understand the Scriptures but those that had the original Greek, etc., then but very few of the poorest sort should be saved (this is harsh,) yet the Scripture saith, that God hides his things from the wise and prudent (that is, from the learned of the**

world,) and reveals them to babes and sucklings.'

Foster: 'There is none that hear you but a company of foolish people.'

Bunyan: 'There are the wise as well as the foolish that do hear me; and again, those that are most commonly counted foolish by the world are the wisest before God. Also, God has rejected the wise and mighty and noble, and chosen the foolish and base…'" (*The Complete Works of John Bunyan,* 1874)

It is reasonable to assume that many others in the 17th century had a similar faith in the AV as the preserved Word of God. As we enter the 18th century, King James Only advocates are certainly not hard to find.

CHAPTER 7

1700-1799

Michael Faraday (1791-1867) was an English chemist and physicist. He established the basis for the electromagnetic field concept in physics, as well as electromagnetic induction (the principle behind the electric transformer and generator), laws of electrolysis, etc. He is ranked #23 in Michael Hart's book, *The 100: A Ranking of the Most Influential Persons in History*. His inventions formed the foundation of electric motor technology. His work on electricity and magnetism revolutionized physics, and greatly influenced our lives today. He is called the best experimentalist in the history of scientific research.

Faraday's parents advocated the views of Robert Sandeman (1718-1771), the son-in-law of John Glas (1695-1773). Around 1730, Glas advocated the independence of local churches from the State. These men also taught that saving faith was simply intellectual belief in the finished work of Christ. They were also strong premillenialists. Michael Faraday, at the age of thirty, joined this church; he remained a member and lay preacher until his death. Faraday, and his church, believed in the absolute inspiration of the King James Bible:

"The founder of the sect had taught them that the Bible alone, with nothing added to it or taken away from it by man, was the only and sufficient guide for the soul. Apparently Faraday never admitted the possibility of human flaw in the printing, editing, translation, collation, or construction of the Bible...**Having once accepted the views of his sect as to the absolute inspiration of the English Bible as a whole**, he permitted no subsequent ques-

tion to be raised as to its literal authority."
(Silvanus Phillips Thompson, *Michael Faraday, His Life and Work*, 1898)

"Sandemanians were a small sect of Christians who believed in interpreting the King James version of the bible as literally true..."
(*Electrochemistry, Past and Present,* American Chemical Society, 1989)

Faraday was deeply devoted to the Holy Bible as the only sufficient guide for our lives:

"One day when he (Michael Faraday) was ill, his friend, Sir Henry Ackland, found him resting his head on a table on which lay an open book. 'I fear that you are worse today,' his friend said. 'No,' answered Faraday, 'it is not that; but why' - he asked, **with one hand on the Bible** – 'why will people go astray, when they have **this blessed book** to guide them?'"
(John Kenyon Kilbourn, *Faiths of Famous Men in Their Own Words*, 1900)

"Two well-worn Bibles that belonged to Michael Faraday (1791-1867) are now in the archives of the Royal Institution in London. Both are heavily marked in pencil. **Both are the King James version of 1611**."
(*Bulletin for the History of Chemistry*, Issues 9-14, 1991)

John Glas (mentioned above) argued with amazing foresight that the attack upon the King James Version by "scholars" would cause many people to seek authority in the Roman church (see chapters 1 and 4). He even exposed and rebuked these scholars for trying to keep the people dependent upon their own skill in the original languages!:

"...the first Christian school at Alexandria produced Arianism...You contend for the evidence that the testimony of God in the gospel carries in itself, and is beheld by them whose under-

standings he opens to understand the scriptures, and behold that evidence in them, and you do well. **But is that evidence to be seen only in the original Hebrew and Greek text?**...is this evidence that the word of God in the scriptures carries in itself, to be perceived only by the 'scribes and disputers of this world'...? Or also by the 'babes'...?...And are your consciences so far seared, as not to give you the least uneasiness, when you make your people believe, that others cannot be ministers for the want of that knowledge of the sacred languages which you yourselves least of all study?...And seeing you have taken up the **Jesuitical argument**, for the honour of the church and the clergy, against these illiterate men, and **their English Bible**, could you blame any of your people that should go off to the Roman church, because they know not if the translation be just...are you indeed for the people's believing in your church, instead of their English Bible? Or, perhaps you'll come next to a question, if a man can be saved without skill in the sacred languages, yea, without the original manuscripts? And clergymen have played the like of this, to **keep souls in dependence on their authority**..."
(*The Works of Mr. John Glas*, 1761)

Notice some other examples of KJV Onlyists in the 1700s:

1780: "Your zealous endeavours, my dear friend, to make me entertain the same idea of the great use of Hebrew learning which now so fully possesses your own mind, is owing to the real regard you bear for me. But, as this subject draws us into debate, and diverts us from better things, I now send you my reasons at large, which compel me totally to differ from you in this matter...when they bring satisfactory evidence for a reading different from the Authorised Translation, I adopt their corrections...upon the most exact inquiry, I cannot say that I have received from their labours one new spiritual idea, or any instruction in religious doctrines I possessed not before I adopted their emendations of the Text...I observe further, that even those excellent emendations, made by these celebrated critics, are still a *Translation* - not what you seem to lay such mighty stress upon, the Original Hebrew; so that, **when I adopt their corrections, in one place I receive Chandler's, in another Lowth's, version, instead of our established one. And the utmost the ablest Hebrew scholar can attain to, is no more than to prefer *his own interpretation* of the Original Text as better than that of a number of scholars more deeply learned in the same tongue than himself...what a high conceit of his own intellect must he possess**, who can think himself more able to *translate* the *Hebrew* than Forty-seven men skilled in that tongue, and therefore selected for the work out of all the divines then in the kingdom - men, who did not lean to their own understanding, but looked up to the Father of Lights for direction and teaching...men who studied more hours in a week than modern scholars in a month...Now, is there the least degree of probability that any individual Hebrew scholar should have acuteness, learning, and judgment so superior to these forty-seven truly venerable scholars, as to be justified in calling their version '*lies,*' but his own version the Word of God?...The experiment, in many instances, has been tried, and confirms my conclusion; for Lowth corrects Kennicott; Kennicott, Lowth; - a third great critic corrects them both! So much did I observe of this, early in life, to my great grief, **as to make me pay little deference, ever after, to critics, or their corrections in general...I must conclude we have the substance of the Word of God as truly in a Translation as in the Hebrew Bible; and that every real Christian, who now devoutly ponders on his English Bible, has before his eyes the Oracles of God; and no less hears His voice, than if he could read the Hebrew**...St. Paul, in his directions to Timothy and Titus, to choose pastors, never bids them be careful not to lay hands on any Christian who had sinfully neglected to read the Hebrew Bible...From this indisputable fact, I consider your position, 'that the Word of God is only to be known by reading the Hebrew,' as a sinful attempt to limit the Holy One of Israel to *one way* of revealing His salvation... by the English Bible their souls were converted; - by that, through the Divine Spirit's influence, they have been quickened, comforted, established, and made ready to every good word and work. Blessed are those servants whom the Lord, at His coming, shall find in this state! On the contrary, if the time and thoughts of those who are ministers of Christ are principally employed to become masters in Oriental learning (and such they certainly should be, who take upon them to vilify the Translation), their application to this business will leave but a fragment of time for secret prayer, devout meditation, or preparation to carry on family worship with any life or benefit or pleasure; and still less will it leave of that frame of mind which is essential to true worship...Smitten with the lust of correcting an established version, and, imperceptibly to themselves, filled with the flattering idea of their own great ingenuity, such scholars will be indefatigable in searching for evidence to support their own interpretation - be exceedingly partial, through self-love, to their own important discoveries - very violent and obstinate in defense of them...that no other effect is generally experienced, there are too many melancholy proofs...Our Saviour tells us, doctrines are to be tried by their fruits. We may safely apply this to our studies, and to scholars of greatest note...if we saw strenuous pleaders for the necessity and vast benefit of Hebrew learning go far beyond all others in compassion for perishing sinners...we should then, without hesitation, allow they did well, and could never too highly exalt the usefulness of that knowledge which brought forth such good fruits. But, where are these excellent effects found to proceed from an indefatigable application to Hebrew learning?...On the contrary, I know several Hebrew scholars, who no sooner came to the knowledge of themselves and of Christ, and were fired with an Apostolic desire to save sinners, than they relinquished their pursuit of Hebrew learning...The same was my own case...I believe not one of us has ever repented...I am grieved beyond measure to see the Children of God startled, and confounded, and distressed to the last

degree, from numberless and most peremptory accusations against the English Bible, as false...to have it asserted, with the most solemn airs of assurance, that the Translators are not to be trusted - what is this, but to fill them with endless doubts, and lead them to despise their English Bible, and think the Christian Religion itself an uncertainty? How often have you observed to me, what strange interpretations the Rector of a church in London would give of the Hebrew, and how unsupported! yet, to make way for even such interpretations as these, forty-seven men, who could 'render a reason,' are publicly branded as fools, compared with himself. Oh! it will neither please God, nor be of any use to men!...ask yourself what real good you have received to your immortal soul from so much study, and such violent pursuit of Hebrew learning? How different was your judgment, when we were first acquainted..."
(Henry Venn, Jan. 3, 1780; quoted in, *The Life...of the Late Rev. Henry Venn*, 1836)

If Henry Venn was so discerning in 1780, what would he say today, after seeing the rotten fruits that he predicted come to full manifestation? He was very, very close to King James Onlyism!

1783: "I cannot help thinking a new translation of the Bible an attempt extremely dangerous, and quite unnecessary. Instead of serving the cause of religion, which is the ostensible motive for the wish, I am convinced that nothing would more immediately tend to shake the basis of the establishment...**It is true, indeed, that some very devout and wellmeaning people** carry the prejudice too far, **when they profess to believe, that our translation was written with the finger of the Almighty, and that to alter a tittle of it is to be guilty of blasphemy**. But still, as the faith of such persons is strong, and their intentions pious, it would be imprudent to shock their minds by an innovation, which they could not help considering as an insult on heaven."
(Vicesimus Knox, *Essays, Moral and Literary,* Volume 1, 1783)

"Our translation" refers to the King James Bible, that some very devout people in 1783 believed was written with the finger of God, and is inerrant and sacred!

1788: "...were the alteration [of the AV] now proposed to take place, we should not be surprised to see numbers of the worthiest and best meaning men in the kingdom united with the whole tribe of fanatics under a formidable standard of rebellion against what they would deem - and loudly in our ears pronounce - an impious, an **abominable**, yea verily a heathenish innovation...it would hardly be possible to carry it into execution without creating very serious dangers both to church and state."
(*The European Magazine, and London Review*, Volume 14, 1788)

These testimonies reveal that the early KJV Only advocates believed that altering the KJV is *abominable.* And they were so numerous that prudent observers warned that a revision would cause such a storm of protest and confusion that the foundations of church and state would crumble! As we look around us today in these perilous times and observe the moral decay, it is past time to realize that we have been experiencing the dire consequences that these writers predicted:

Psalms 11:3 If the foundations be destroyed, what can the righteous do?

2 Timothy 3:16 All **scripture** is given by inspiration of God, and is profitable for doctrine, for reproof, for correction, for instruction in righteousness:
17 That the man of God may be perfect, throughly furnished unto all good works.
4:2 Preach **the word**...
3 For the time will come when **they will not endure sound doctrine**; but after their own lusts shall they heap to themselves

teachers, having itching ears;
4 And they shall turn away their ears **from the truth**, and shall be turned unto fables.

Dan Gilbert, in *Evolution: The Root of All ISMS* (1935), documents that the sexual revolution (and many other evils) was the offspring of the scientific revolution (i.e. the lie of evolution, etc.). But what was the root of the widespread *acceptance* of evolutionary thought? One of the main contributing factors was the revision of the King James Bible, with the accompanying proclamation by scholars that only the Originals were inspired. Since these original manuscripts are now lost, many people lost faith in their present Bible, and embraced the sinking sand of scientific philosophy (Colossians 2:8), and science falsely so-called (1 Timothy 6:20).

The truth of this claim is easily seen in the fact that the principle fathers of the "new version movement" praised Darwin and his theory of evolution. Brooke Foss Westcott (1825-1901) and Fenton John Anthony Hort (1828-1892) were Anglican scholars at Cambridge University. They developed a system of textual criticism, with a new Greek New Testament in 1881. The Wescott and Hort Greek text was used as the basis for the Revised Version (which is the mother of modern versions such as the NIV, NAS, etc.). On April 3, 1860, in a letter to John Ellerton, Hort praised Darwin:

"But the book which has most engaged me is Darwin. Whatever may be thought of it, it is a book that one is proud to be contemporary with. I must work out and examine the argument in more detail, but at present my feeling is strong that the theory is unanswerable."
(Arthur Fenton Hort, *The Life and Letters of Fenton John Anthony Hort,* Vol. 1, 1896)

On March 4, 1890, Westcott wrote a letter to the Archbishop of Canterbury denying the literalness of the Creation story in Genesis:

"No one now, I suppose, holds that the first three chapters of Genesis, for example, give a literal history - I could never understand how anyone reading them with open eyes could think they did."
(Arthur Westcott, *The Life and Letters of Brooke Foss Westcott,* Vol. 2, 1903)

Quotes linking Westcott and Hort with spiritism (occultism), Catholicism, and higher criticism could be multiplied (see chapter 16). Clearly (as will also be seen from other quotes in this history), the so-called revision of the King James Version was used, and even designed, to destroy the foundations of Biblical Christianity. (See also the history under "1831").

CHAPTER 8

1800-1849

In the 19th century, Satan zealously labored to dilute the power of the King James Bible by inspiring new translations, and heretical cults and movements; yet the KJV Only viewpoint continued to abound:

1822: "...**most Protestants**...take their **English Bible in hand with the same confidence as if they had immediately received it, as Moses received the Tables of the Commandments, from God himself**, on Mount Sinai..."
(John Milner, *A Vindication of The End of Religious Controversy*, 1822)

John Milner (1752-1826) was a Roman Catholic writer.

1822: "...the belief of wellmeaning, but illiterate, minds would be liable to be shaken by a change in what they have been accustomed to **revere as the standard of their faith** [i.e. the AV]. The style and phraseology of the authorized version have become venerable; it has acquired a sacredness of character by being handed down, for two centuries, from father to son, **as the Word of God**...At present all sects and parties have one common standard, to which they appeal in their interminable controversies..."
(George Holden, *An Attempt to Illustrate the Book of Ecclesiastes*, 1822)

1 Corinthians 1:20 Where is the wise? where is the scribe? where is the disputer of this world? hath not God made foolish the wisdom of this world?

1828: "So ill taught are **many Christians** that they **cannot think that any translation of the scriptures deserves the title of the *Word of God* except that of King James**...If King James' version is the only Word of God on earth, then all nations who speak any other language than the English, have no Revelation...Much of the reasoning of both priests and people, on this subject, is as silly as that of an old lady...Her husband was reading in the *new version*...'That is a good *explanation,*' said she, but *it is not the scriptures,* not the Word of God.' So our good logicians reason...I would thank some of those ignorant declaimers to tell us *where the Word of God was before the reign of King James!"*
(Alexander Campbell, *The Christian Baptist*, 1828-29)

Alexander Campbell was the founder of the so-called "Church of Christ" denomination, which believes in baptismal regeneration. He had published his own translation of the Bible in 1826; so it is no wonder that he resented the King James Version:

"The people had only one Bible. This was the 'old family Bible that lay on the stand.' This they implicitly believed to be the word of God from lid to lid. And *here in their midst was the daring critic, Alexander Campbell,* telling them that this only cherished Bible of theirs was not what they thought it to be...Those who walked in the wake of his new-shed light were termed *Campbellites*...Yet, after more than half a century of such pleading [against the King James Version], a dear sister...greeted the minister as he stepped from the pulpit one beautiful Lord's day morning, with the warm, heart-felt demand that he read no more the new version of the Bible because those higher critics who had gotten it up so shocked her nerves! But said she, 'Read that pulpit Bible; that's what it is there for; **read that good old King James authorized version which we know to be the word of**

God!'...One thing is certain, *Alexander Campbell,* in his never-flinching agitation for a better Bible during the 19th Century, helped, in no small degree, to beat down the prejudice in the way, and give to the world the revised Bible which we now enjoy."
(James Egbert, *Alexander Campbell and Christian Liberty*, 1909)

As Campbell scornfully objected to the many KJV Onlyists in his day, he unwittingly testified to their historic existence for future generations.

New version publishers and promoters in modern times often use the same objections that Campbell used. And it is no wonder; they are also trying to sell or promote a new version!

It is interesting that in an address before the Bible Union convention, at Memphis, Tenn. (1852), Campbell was far more correct than he realized as he attempted to argue for a new translation:

"The living critics and translators of the present day, in Europe and America, **are like Saul** amongst the people - head and shoulders above those of the early part of the seventeenth century."

Campbell did not intend to rebuke the modern textual scholars. Nevertheless, he hit the nail on the head! Saul was esteemed for his appearance. But God sees more than just the outward appearance of things (1 Samuel 16:7, John 7:24). Saul was rebuked for rejecting the Word of the Lord in his self-will:

1 Samuel 15:22 And Samuel said, Hath the LORD as great delight in burnt offerings and sacrifices, as in obeying the voice of the LORD? Behold, to obey is better than sacrifice, and to hearken than the fat of rams.
23 For rebellion is as the sin of witchcraft, and stubbornness is as

iniquity and idolatry. **Because thou hast rejected the word of the LORD**, he hath also rejected thee from being king.

1829: "So badly taught are **many Christians** that they cannot think that any translation of the scriptures deserves the title of the Word of God except that of king James."
(Alexander Campbell, *The Christian Baptist,* Volume 6, Number 9, April 6, 1829)

Luke 10:21 In that hour Jesus rejoiced in spirit, and said, I thank thee, O Father, Lord of heaven and earth, that thou hast hid these things from the wise and prudent, and hast **revealed them unto babes**...

1829: "Patiently and learnedly had they [the KJV translators] explored the Divine Originals; and neither few nor feeble were the grounds upon which, after mature deliberation, upon the deepest conviction, and assuredly in the spirit of dependence upon the guiding counsel of the Most High, they retained 1 John V. 7 as an integral and essential text of Holy Scripture. Therefore, when that Volume, the Authorised Version of the Bible, was placed in my hands at my ordination...I should have deemed myself guilty of an unworthy dissimulation, had I virtually assented with my lips, and by my written subscription, to the integrity of that Authorised Version as the Revealed Will and Word of God, while I tacitly obliterated so important a verse as 1 John V. 7. I could not conscientiously profess myself a Minister of the Established Church, while I deliberately stamped Falsehood and Forgery upon an entire text in her Authorised Version, promulgated by the Supreme Ecclesiastical Authority in the realm, as the very Word of God...Now, let me ask you, My Brethren...opponents of this important text, Are you aware of, or indifferent to, the inevitable results...? Will your flocks, who readily follow in their shepherd's track, as readily stop when he cries out *'Halt?'* You are sedulously endeavouring to convince

them, that an entire text in the Authorised Version of the Bible is spurious and interpolated. You have perhaps succeeded: they receive your *conclusion* as it were an axiom; but think you, *Will they stop at that conclusion?* Indeed No! **Blind must be the man who does not already discern the effects of your - shall I call it, rash and unwarrantable - impeachments of the integrity of our Authorized Version**; who does not already take alarm at the wide-spreading Scepticism, and the popular and palatable delusion, that the Established Church of England circulates a spurious Bible, and imposes the fictions of man as the Oracles of God...**The transition, from *your* conclusion to that of the Unitarians, is natural and easy. *You* reject one verse of John's First Epistle: *they* reject the first fourteen verses of his Gospel (John I. 1-15.)** It is but a step, and we reject the Sacred Canon altogether. This is no imaginary or visionary alarm: late circumstances indicate, if not its actual arrival, its very near approximation...During the discussions which lately agitated the Bible Society on the subject of the Apocryphal Books, a great laxity of opinion was developed, as to the inspiration of the Sacred Canon."
(William Alleyn Evanson, Translator's Preface, Franz Anton Knittel, *New Criticisms On the Celebrated Text: 1 John V. 7*, 1829)

1830: "...does not the most uninstructed person **who thinks the very words of King James's translation the original diction of the Holy Spirit**, familiarly speak of the respective style of St. Paul or St. John...?"
(*The Christian Observer*, 1830)

1831: "...It has been urged on your Committee, by an enlightened member of your [Unitarian] Society, that the theological information which they seek to diffuse [i.e. Unitarian doctrines] **must meet with serious obstructions so long as the Authorized Version of the Scriptures**, notwithstanding all its merits of general accuracy, and its greater merits of taste, **continues to be**

the final appeal of the English reader in matters of controversy...the mere circulation of another translation of the Scriptures would tend to shake the undiscriminating veneration for the Common Version (as if the translators were infallible or inspired) which prevails...Three plans presented themselves; either to attempt a new translation; or to adopt and circulate some existing version of the New Testament..."
(*The Monthly Repository of Theology and General Literature*, Volume 12, 1831)

The above journal embraces Unitarian viewpoints (i.e. denying the Trinity, etc.). Unitarians of the nineteenth century became the Humanists of the twentieth century. These Unitarians believed that the Authorized Version (and its advocates) stood in the way of their movement. Their goals were partially realized in the publication of the Revised Version (1881-1885). [See the notes under the year 1838] The above quote not only reveals the goals and methods of these unbelievers (with their form of godliness), it shows that people in their age held to the KJV Only viewpoint.

1832: "If alterations of the received version once commence, where will they end?...The reception of the 'authorized version of the Bible,' by the whole Christian community wherever the English language is spoken, is a blessing the value of which cannot be estimated, and the loss of which would be one of the heaviest curses which could befall the Church of Christ...If one substitution may be made, another may be; and the Bible, by this impious transmutation, become, after a few successive changes, the book of man, and not the Book of God...If to the curse pronounced on him who should remove his neighbor's landmarks, all the people were required to say Amen, what shall be said of them who would remove the landmarks of the faith, and turn aside the wanderer from the path that leads to heaven!"
(*Banner of the Church*, Stimpson & Clapp, 1832)

1833: "In my estimation there is nothing more deserving of respect and protection, than the honest confidence with which an unlettered peasant looks upon his English Bible as expressing to him the genuine word of God."
(*The British Magazine*, J. Petheram, 1833)

Matthew 11:25 At that time Jesus answered and said, I thank thee, O Father, Lord of heaven and earth, because thou hast hid these things from the wise and prudent, and hast **revealed them unto babes.**

1833: "It has a tendency, they think, to unsettle the minds of the vulgar; who had better be left to receive the Bible, *i. e.* our authorized version of it, as the Word of God, without any suspicion of the possibility of error in any passage they read; since if once (it is urged) they doubt the infallibility of our translators, they may go on to doubt whether this, and that, or any passage of Scripture may not be mistranslated; till at length the Bible will be, to them, no revelation at all."
(Richard Whately, *Essays on Some of the Difficulties in the Writings of St. Paul*, 1833)

1833: "The people of this country are as much interested in whatever relates to King James's Bible, as the people of England. It is the authorized, or at least the generally received and accredited version of the Scriptures, wherever the English language is spoken. In England and most of its dependencies, and in this country, it is looked upon, not so much as a translation of the Bible, **as the Bible itself**."
(*The Christian Examiner*, Volume 14, 1833)

1834: "...the practice of explaining, or, to speak more properly, getting rid of difficulties, by suggesting new and ingenious interpretations for the passage in the original...**we always look with suspicion on any, even the slightest departure from the**

authorized version - a version which should by no means be brought, however remotely, into disrepute, upon light or trivial grounds, as it is the only version in the hands of the unlearned: it is wrong to diminish, by groundless alterations, **their confidence in its correctness**. The authorized version is, besides, the most faultless translation that has ever been performed; and though many ingenious commentators have exercised their skill in endeavouring to amend it, we have **never** been fortunate enough to meet with a proposed alteration, which would have been an improvement."

(William Curry, *The Dublin University Magazine*, Volume 4, 1834)

1835: "Dear Sir, one of our teachers in this county has refused to have the new translation read in a public meeting because it is not the word of God, alleging that **the common version is received as the word of God,** but that the new translation is not considered such...Answer this, if you please, for some of us are in doubt upon this subject."

(*The Christian Baptist*, edited by Alexander Campbell, Volumes 1-7, 1835)

1835: "...this is the version universally received by Protestants, wherever the English language is spoken, and there exists no probability that any other will ever supersede it...It is the Bible which our godly fathers have read, and over which they have wept and prayed. It is the Good Old English Bible, with which are associated all our earliest recollections of religion. As such let it go down unchanged to the latest posterity. We give it in charge to coming generations, and bid them welcome to all the blessings it has conveyed to us. It is our fervent prayer, that the light of the resurrection morning may shine on the very book which we now read...what has the Bible already wrought for the world through its English translation! and what mightier results are yet to follow! This may not be the time or the place to discuss the interesting question, but there are not wanting many prob-

abilities that the English tongue is destined to become as nearly universal as it is practicable for any one language."
(William Adams, Preached Oct. 4, 1835, in commemoration of the first printing of an English Bible)

What amazing foresight this preacher possessed!

1836: "Yet **there are some sectarians who almost worship their English Bible, as the Jews do their own**...It was reserved to modern learning in Germany and France chiefly to begin to lift the Mosaic veil...The modern geologists and the blind, vulgar Biblicists have often been at variance..."
(Constantine Samuel Rafinesque, *The World*, 1836)

1837: "Again, **many of the unlearned (even in...what are called the educated classes)** have grown up in the habitual belief of the **unerring correctness in every part, of our version** of the Bible."
(Richard Whately, *Essays on the Errors of Romanism*, 1837)

1838: "...I believe almost every thing that has been written on this subject [the sphere of the woman], has been the result of a misconception of the simple truths revealed in the Scriptures, in consequence of the false translation of many passages of Holy Writ. My mind is entirely delivered from **the superstitious reverence which is attached to the English version of the Bible**. King James's translators certainly were not inspired. I therefore claim the original as my standard, believing that to have been inspired..."
(Sarah Moore Grimke, *Letters on the Equality of the Sexes*, 1838)

This is another clear testimony that the KJV Only view was alive and well in 1838. Sarah Moore Grimke was an early feminist that disliked the Authorized Version when it came to certain commandments concerning women. Years later, Elizabeth Cady

Stanton would publish, *The Women's Bible* (1895), with feminist notes, wherein she mocked Biblical inspiration, and called for women (and society) to abandon the Bible, altogether! Her publication prompted the *Chicago Post* to write:

"The **attack of the new woman on the King James Bible** will be observed with interest where it does not alarm."

We can behold in all of this a constant pattern. Those who cannot endure the plain, sound doctrine of the AV (2 Timothy 4:3, Proverbs 8:8-9), usually end up attempting to revise it to fit their own lusts. One keen observer had already called attention to this fact in 1830:

"We may consent to go with them as far as the Old Version will authorise; but when we shall have arrived at a limit, they... substitute a New Version...The Unitarians, finding the Old Version rather a dead weight upon them, constructed a new dress for the Testament...And now Mr. Campbell has a Version...**Why is it that all innovators become tired of the Old Version and seek new ones?**...none of the leaders of [heretical] innovation so far as we know, have remained contented with the old fashioned Book in its present dress."
(W.T. Brantly, *The Columbian Star and Christian Index*, 1830)

"The design, however, of publishing an Improved Version of the New Testament was never totally abandoned: and it was resumed with great unanimity and spirit at the annual meeting of the [Unitarian] London Society, in April 1806..."
(William Newcome, *The New Testament, in an Improved Version,* Unitarian Society, 1817)

These Unitarians denied the Trinity and were the forefathers of the Modernists and Humanists of the twentieth century. In their so-called "Improved Version," they removed or altered foundational verses that prove the Trinity, such as 1 Timothy 3:16 and 1 John 5:7. The Revised Version would later follow in this same Unitarian pattern, removing or altering these same verses (just like the NAS and NIV, etc.). In fact, the RV was so similar to the earlier Unitarian version, that an observer in 1881 argued to the editor of *The New York Times* that the revisers must have used the earlier, Unitarian version as their very basis!:

"*The Revision of the New Testament criticized. Certain striking coincidences discovered - A comparison with the Unitarian Version published in London in 1808.* To the Editor of the *New York Times*...On comparing the examples referred to in the article I have been forcibly struck with their curious resemblance to the alterations made in the Unitarian version of the New Testament...published in London in 1808...The new revision omits altogether the Doxology of the Lord's Prayer: 'For thine is the kingdom, and the power, and the glory, for ever. Amen.' [Matthew 6:13]. The Unitarian version of 1808 omits it also. [Other similarities are found in Matthew 6:1, 19:17, Mark 8:36-37, Luke 16:8, John 5:2-9, Acts 8:26-40, etc.]...These striking coincidences of sense, and even of phraseology, as well as the omissions and changes made in the text, would seem to indicate that the revisers must have had constantly in view the Unitarian version of 1808, if they did not, indeed, make it the basis of their revision. It would hardly seem as if such coincidences could have been accidental...the work [the RV] will be a remarkable tribute to the learning and skill of Mr. Belsham..."
(*The New York Times*, February 14, 1881)

Thomas Belsham was one of the main Unitarian editors of the Unitarian version. He denied the Trinity and repudiated the Virgin Birth as a fable. The similarity between the RV and the Unitarian versions was certainly not accidental. A noted Unitarian, Dr. Vance Smith, was actually a member of the RV committee! He argued that the changes made in the RV were certainly doc trinally significant. Among other heresies, Smith believed that Hell and the Lake of Fire are mythological. His association with the RV caused a storm of protest from many who were aware of it:

"*An Unitarian Revisionist intolerable - The Westminster Abbey Scandal*...That while engaged in the work of interpreting the everlasting Gospel, you should have knowingly and by choice associated with yourselves one [Dr. G. Vance Smith] who, not only openly denies the eternal Godhead of our Lord, but in a recent publication is the avowed assailant of that fundamental doctrine of the Christian Religion, as well as of the Inspiration of Holy Scripture itself, - filled me (and many besides myself) with astonishment and sorrow...In the meantime, this same person was invited to communicate with his fellow-Revisers in Westminster-Abbey, and did accordingly, on the 22nd of June, 1870, receive the Holy Communion, in Henry VII.'s Chapel, at the hands of Dean Stanley...So conspicuous a sacrilege led to a public Protest signed by some thousands of the Clergy..."
(John William Burgon, *The Revision Revised*, 1883)

The Unitarians of 1881 were indeed very pleased. They believed the RV was ushering in a new, liberal age that no longer trembled before the Holy Scriptures:

"*The Revised Version of the New Testament*...Rational Christians of all churches appear to view with pleasure the departure of the old words 'damnation' and 'damned'...**a more temperate tone will be the result. The effect of the publication of the new version will, however, be far more felt in the breaking of the spell**...Already it is plain here that the Bible will be read and quoted in a far more open, free, and reasonable way...**a great work has been done**..."
(*The Unitarian Review and Religious Magazine,* Volume 16, 1881)

Yet, seven years later, while still rejoicing in the RV, the Unitarians were disappointed that the common people had largely rejected it. They thought it was due to the unpolished English of the RV:

"We have seen of late several **expressions of regret**, surprise, or blame, coming from persons highly to be respected, that the Revised Version of the New Testament has failed to take the place, in private or public reading of the Scriptures...The revisers had not sufficiently felt the fact that the English Testament is an English classic; that, apart from all others, it is *the one* popular English classic...To the liberal theologian, especially, this version is strictly invaluable, as showing how much that he has all along contended for, almost hopelessly, in the face of **vulgar prejudice**...This one debt to them we frankly acknowledge...But, for all that appears, that text [the AV] will continue, for the **common mind**, to be the same it has been..."
(*The Unitarian Review*, Volume 29, 1888)

But the AV is more than beautiful English. It is the sword of God's Spirit (Ephesians 6:17).

Universalists (i.e. those who believe every person will one day be saved) also applauded the Revised Version in 1881:

"In the Third Universalist Church...the Pastor, the Rev. S. A. Gardner, read his scripture lesson from the revised edition of the New Testament...In the new version, he said, we have a more liberal view...the word 'hell' is practically rejected...never before have [Universalist, liberal interpretations]...been so authoritatively acknowledged by orthodox Christians..."
(*The New York Times*, May 23, 1881)

Annihilationists (i.e. those who deny the doctrine of the endless punishment of unbelievers) likewise praised the "revised" version:

"Indeed, it must be admitted on all hands that all the recent amendments that have been made in our Old Version have been directly in the line of the doctrine we hold, and are contributing greatly to strengthen our position."
(John Hancock Pettingell, *The Life Everlasting*, 1883)

1838: "There are many passages in the Douay which we could not say were *inspired Scripture*...we could not pronounce over its text, this is the word of the Most High which he has graciously given; this is our infallible rule of faith and practice. **But we can with truth speak thus of our authorised version**. Taking it altogether, we have no hesitation in saying, *here is the Book of God.*"
(W. M'Comb, *The Orthodox Presbyterian Theological Review and Missionary Recorder*, Volume 1, 1838)

1838: "A distinguished and influential supporter of the Union has repeatedly said that it would be necessary to spend ten thousand dollars in order to destroy the 'bigoted' attachment of **our people** to the **commonly received version**..."
(*Annual Report*, American and Foreign Bible Society, Bible Convention, 1838)

Luke 5:1 ...**the people** pressed upon him to hear **the word of God,** he stood by the lake of Gennesaret,

1839: "Of this there are perpetual illustrations in the sermons of some admirable preachers, and even in their manner of reading the scriptures, a manner often of itself demonstrative, **that the English Bible, and the English Bible only, is to them the word of God**."
(Charles Hodge, *The Princeton Review*, 1839)

Charles Hodge (1797-1878), and some earlier men before him (e.g. Richard Simon, etc.), helped lay the foundation for the erroneous "Originals only" viewpoint (i.e. that only the Originals were inspired and infallible, and that this inspiration and infallibility is not preserved in any copy or translation we possess today). This view was later articulated and promoted by A. A. Hodge (the son of Charles Hodge) and B. B. Warfield.

1839: "...it [the KJV] is now held forth by the American Bible Society as **a standard** for the whole pagan world, **so sacred** as to justify the extinction of existing translations in languages spoken by more than half the heathen on the globe...In other words, King James' version is to become **the standard** of translation. Here then, is, virtually, a decree that the English translation is **The Bible**...a decree that is perfectly analogous to that of the council of Trent, in the sixteenth century, which declared the Latin Vulgate the *authentic* version; and commanded that that alone should be read publicly, and in all sermons, expositions and disputations; one effect of which was, that soon, multitudes considered it as dictated by the Holy Spirit; at least was providentially guarded against all error; was consequently of divine authority, and more to be regarded than even the original Hebrew and Greek text."
(*Quarterly Papers*, American and Foreign Bible Society, July, 1839)

The official teaching of the Catholic Church does not hold that the Latin Vulgate was inspired or infallible. It believes it is trustworthy or reliable:

"The traditional and official attitude of the Roman Catholic Church toward Sacred Scripture and its use was formulated in the fourth session of the Council of Trent (Apr. 8, 1546)...[It] enacted that [the Latin Vulgate] which was declared **a substantially correct** translation of the original Scriptures, should henceforth be considered as the official text...Underlying these and similar enactments is the fundamental Roman Catholic doctrine that the authority of the living Church - **not the letter of**

Scripture - is the proximate rule of belief..."
(*The New Schaff-Herzog Encyclopedia of Religious Knowledge*, Vol. 10, 1911)

"It may be thought that, having in the Vulgate an **approved** version of the works of the evangelists, I have uselessly expended time in **frequent references to the Greek text**. To this it must be answered that in any exposition of the gospels which is worthy of the name, a frequent reference to the original text is not only useful, but necessary...the thoughts of sacred writers expressed in that language **cannot be fully rendered** in the most faithful version. But it will be urged that the authenticity of the Vulgate has been declared in the most solemn manner by the Church in the Council of Trent...The Vulgate has, indeed, been **declared authentic**...but **this rule has many exceptions** which are not affected by the declaration of the Council. Thus it appears safe to say that in the decree...**the Fathers of Trent did not declare even by implication that the Vulgate is free from all errors** in matters not affecting faith and morals...If we keep in mind, then, the **limited scope of the declaration** regarding the authentic character of our Latin version **we must admit that an appeal to the original text** is in many cases necessary and in every case useful for those who wish to know fully the meaning intended by the evangelists."
(Cornelius J. Ryan, D. D., late Professor of Sacred Scripture and Hebrew, Holy Cross College, Dublin, quoted in, *The American Catholic Quarterly Review*, Volume 31, 1906)

"This first installment of a 'Complete Course on Scripture' [by Auctore R. Comely] has been followed by the Introduction to the New Testament by the same...The most interesting chapter of the book is the History of the Vulgate, and the discussion on the authority of it, which may be summed up thus: - (1) **By the Decree of the Council of Trent, the Vulgate has not been preferred either to any other authorized translation, or to the original text**. (2) **The Vulgate has not been declared free from every**

fault in points not concerning faith and morals; (3) but has been declared to be a genuine source of revelation...It is well known how Sixtus V. published an edition of the Vulgate, and how this edition had to be withdrawn on account of faults that had crept in."
(*The Irish Ecclesiastical Record*, 1886)

Therefore, the promoters of modern versions have more in common with Roman Catholicism than King James Bible Only advocates! They continually use words such as "reliable," "trustworthy," etc., for their new versions, while never advocating perfection or infallibility. Roman Catholics teach that tradition is another source of revelation. They do not teach that the Bible alone is their final authority. This is a major reason why they reject the infallibility of any Bible version.

Nevertheless, there is a big difference between multitudes of Catholics allegedly viewing the Latin Vulgate as infallible, and multitudes of born again Christians viewing the Authorized Version as infallible. The Catholics are filled with superstition; the Christians are filled with the Spirit of God, faith and discernment:

James 2:5 Hearken, my beloved brethren, Hath not God chosen the poor of this world rich in faith...?

Luke 10:21 In that hour Jesus rejoiced in spirit, and said, I thank thee, O Father, Lord of heaven and earth, that thou hast hid these things from the wise and prudent, and hast **revealed them unto babes**...

1840: "It does not therefore seem strange to me now, though it once did, **the attachment the Christian world** has to this venerable Book [AV], nor the tenacity with which they, who speak the English tongue, hold on to our common version, in spite of the

defects which **criticism** justly points out."
(*The Boston Quarterly Review*, Volume 3, 1840)

The above quote is from Orestes Augustus Brownson (1803-1876). He was a Unitarian preacher who converted to Transcendentalism in 1832. With no final authority (i.e. no infallible, inspired Bible), he converted to Roman Catholicism in 1844, and spent the rest of his life trying to make America a Roman Catholic nation.

1841: "Look, for example, at the exclusive confidence - we might say the superstitious reverence - with which **the people of this country** have been led to regard what is known as **the authorized version**, a confidence which it is reckoned by some persons so dangerous to shake; to what a multitude of mistakes, and artifices not a few, are **the millions of Great Britain** attaching thc authority of everlasting truth!"
(*The Eclectic Review,* Vol. 1, 1841)

John 12:19 The Pharisees therefore said among themselves, Perceive ye how ye prevail nothing? behold, the world is gone after him.

1841: "...the version of King James's translators...The popular translation is **sacred to the millions**..."
(*The Monthly Miscellany*, Volume 5, 1841)

1842: "The English Scriptures issued by the American and Foreign Bible Society, although a literal transcript of King James' version of 1611, **have been frequently stigmatized from the press and the pulpit as 'the Baptist Bible.'** Such has been the popular cry, and numbers of Peedobaptists have believed it."
(William Henry Wyckoff, *The American Bible Society and the Baptists*, 1842)

1844: "The notion that the English translation of the Scriptures

is the word of God, is a very mischievous notion..."
(Joseph Barker, *The Christian,* Volume 1, 1844)

Jude 1:10 But these speak evil of those things which they know not...

1845: "...**many good folks** believe the 'authorized version,' to be *the Bible,* and the only Bible that has ever existed."
(Allan Freer, *The North British Review,* Volume 2, 1845)

1846: "...it has been, also, discovered that by the Bible, and the **Bible only**, is meant, not what the words would seem to imply, **but the authorized version**, and **the authorized version only**... On what grounds do ultra-protestants insist on the exclusive use of the authorized version?"
(Walter Farquhar Hook, *The Church of England Vindicated Against Romanism and Ultra-Protestantism*, 1846)

1847: "*The Authorised Version as a Test of Truth...*'The Bible and the Bible only is the Religion of Protestants.' Such is the fundamental principle...That the Bible is the whole and sole rule of the Protestant religion is more than a popular prejudice ...plainly is the Bible and the Bible only the Religion of the Protestant Church...since the Bible in the original languages is the sole religion of Protestants, it follows that so long as there exists doubt respecting the true text of the original, and so far as there are uncertainties respecting its meaning, so long and so far the real religion of Protestants is not only uncertain but is actually unknown. Upon Protestant principles, until the original Bible is definitely settled and properly understood, the Protestant religion can have no existence...these same Protestant Englishmen affect to **set up the 'authorized version' as the standard of truth**..."
(*Dolman's Magazine*, 1847)

This Roman Catholic magazine reveals how Catholicism preys upon doubts in Christians concerning the preservation of the Scriptures. They see the infallible, preserved Bible as a threat to their (so-called) infallible church.

1847: "Is it not strange, that a superstitious veneration should so generally prevail among **the people** for King James' version…"
(*The Primitive Expounder*, Volume 4, 1847)

1848: "[The clerical mind of the day possessed]...a fond belief in the absolute perfection of the 'authorized version'..."
(William Scott, Francis Garden, James Bowling Mozley, *The Christian Remembrancer*, 1848)

1849: "According to Mr. Morris [i.e. William Morris, of Plymouth], our Authorized Version is infallible..."
(John Howard Hinton, *Anathasia*, 1849)

1849: "Some persons seem to have thus been led practically to forget that there is no *inspired book* in the *English* language… Some members, however, of our Church, are accustomed to speak of the 'authorized version,' as if they understood that version to be the 'SCRIPTURE' which is referred to in the Articles as the standard and rule of faith..."
(Richard Whately, *Sermons on Various Subjects*, 1849)

CHAPTER 9

1850-1899

"Not a few seem to believe, or at least act as if King James' version was inspired, and consequently infallible, that to touch it with the rod of criticism, is like laying sacriligious or unpriestly hands upon the ark of God."
(James Challen, *The Necessity of a New Version and the Means of Procuring It*)

In 1850, many Baptists united against the proposal suggested by some to issue a new Bible translation with the word *baptism* changed to *immersion*, etc. Some Baptists met at Oliver St. Baptist Church, N.Y, on April 4, 1850 to defend the King James Bible and the traditional words (arguing, for example, that *baptism* was an English word, and they had no desire to be called *Immersionists* instead of *Baptists*). The proceedings of the meeting were recorded in a booklet titled, *The Common English Version: An Argument Sustaining the Common English Bible, Addressed to the Members of the American and Foreign Bible Society, and to the Baptist Denomination in the United States*, 1850. Although some of the speakers wrongly believed that the AV had slight defects (which they referred to as "faint spots on the sun's fiery disk"), some of their arguments for retaining the KJV are worthy of notice:

"...a dedication to James the First of England has been prefixed to many copies, though not to many other...The Bible - which is embalmed in so many hearts - interwoven with so many solemn recollections, - indissolubly blended with our most sacred hopes

- sending its influence through the whole sphere of our duties, - our best support in life, and our cherished consolation against the hour of death - we have yet to be convinced that its dear and venerable phraseology, so familiar to our ear, and which falls with such a thrill of emotion upon our hearts, should be exposed to desecration and danger by any change... The Baptists have always planted themselves on the solid ground of Scripture...With the old translation in their hands, they have gained distinguished triumphs...loving the brethren much, we love the Bible more..."
(Dr. Welch)

"The Lord by his prophet asks, 'Hath a nation changed their gods, which are yet no gods? but my people have changed their glory for that which doth not profit.' Shall the Baptists substitute some other version of the Scriptures, which is yet no version, for that which has hitherto been their **sufficient light and their unceasing glory**?...beside my conviction that our English Bible is a good and truthful version of the Scriptures, I have a sort of veneration for its simple and sublime phraseology...I should make a sad work of learning a new phraseology for my pulpit, - indeed I should feel as Mary felt when she said, 'They have taken away my Lord, and I know not where they have laid him.' No, the English Bible as it is, is stamped on my memory and fixed in my heart for ever. I protest against this change..."
(J. L. Hodge)

"For my part, Mr. Chairman, I regard our present Bible as a Baptist Bible. It has made one million Baptists since Roger Williams went into the waters of Narragansett Bay. We have stood on this platform, and have always stood firm...Cling then, brethren, to the old-fashioned Bible; frown down every attempt to set it aside; give no countenance to such a measure, from whatever quarter it may be recommended."
(John Dowling)

1850: At the inaugural meeting of the American Bible Union in 1850, William Stone also pleaded against revising the King James Bible:

"...think you that the associations of two hundred and forty years can thus be erased? Think you that Christians who have learned to lisp the Saviour's name from this book, can thrust it aside and take up a new version? Dear old English Bible! We will not forsake thee. Thou may'st be slandered with 'blasphemy,' but we will not part with thee; and when we lay our heads on our last bed of sickness, this slandered, blessed book, shall be our pillow, and in its glorious words we will breathe out our last prayer..."
(Quoted in *Millennial Harbinger*, August, 1850)

1851: "Often, too, I find families without any other than the Common Version of the Bible...The Family Testament (New Version) is not, except in a few cases, read or consulted..."
(William Kimbrough Pendleton, *The Millennial Harbinger*, Volume 1, 1851)

A common argument among revisionists (i.e. promoters of new versions) is that it takes some time before the people will accept a new version. After many new versions arose, and then faded away, many Christians who were against any revision began to argue that, "the chief value of translations subsequent to King James' has been to better satisfy the great mass of Bible-readers with the received version." In other words, nothing exposes a counterfeit like comparing it to the real thing. With the rise of mass marketing and propaganda, the initial excitement and novelty of new versions can be somewhat extended; but always, each new version fades away, while the King James Bible continues to be, "the old-fashioned Bible, the dear blessed Bible, the family Bible that lay on the stand." It stands alone against all contenders; and before long, it always vanquishes its rivals.

1852: "**...many very sincere and pious Christians** have

hitherto strenuously resisted either a new translation of Scripture, or **any amendment** of the present English text...Such persons to a great extent entertain the unreasoning prejudice that our English translation is not only a faithful exposition of the word of God, but **they actually regard it as if it was also an inspired translation**."
(J. H. McCulloh, *Analytical Investigations*, 1852)

1853: "...And the manner in which that version has met the wants of the most free and intelligent nations in the old world and the new, may well confirm us in the persuasion, that the same illuminating Spirit which [brought forth the] original Scriptures, was imparted in rich grace to aid and guard the preparation of the English version...Whosoever attempts to shake **the confidence of the common people in the common version**, puts their faith in imminent peril of shipwreck...Against all such attempts let them be fully warned...The best fruits of Christianity have sprung from the seeds our translation has scattered..."
(Alexander Wilson M'Clure, *The Translators Revived,* 1853)

1853: "I can appreciate, therefore, and go along with those who would shrink from doing anything which may tend to lessen either the influence or the use of **the Authorized Version**...I can appreciate, and partly go along with, remonstrances such as this: - Is it wise, is it safe, to undermine the reliance which **thousands place in it as the very Word of God?**...It is their Scripture, - their **only Scripture**."
(Samuel Hinds, *Scripture and the Authorized Version of Scripture,* 1853)

1854: "The words of our English version are invested with Divine authority, only so far as they express just what the original expresses. I present this thought because **there is, in the minds of many, a superstitious reverence for the words and phrases of our English version**."
(John Quincy Adams, *Baptists: the Only Thorough Religious Reformers*, 1854)

1854: "Though the general trustworthiness of our noble English version of the Scriptures, and its venerableness as the purest fount of our language, will be admitted with gratitude, and with an almost religious feeling of attachment, by every cultivated person, it has been long felt that a revision of the translation is not unnecessary. And so, a great deal of popular error has been preserved, and not a little bad theology has been sanctioned, by the something like **superstitious respect with which our common version has been adhered to**..."
(*Nonconformist*, October 14, 1854)

1855: "Alexandrian legends claimed for the Septuagint Version that infallible inspiration...and **many** betray a feeling as if they would prefer the same claim in behalf of our own Authorized Version."
(William Webster, William Francis Wilkinson, *The Greek Testament*, 1855)

1855: "*Resolved*...That we have unshaken confidence in our **common version**...that we deprecate the incalculable evils that would inevitably result from such an attempt, by any denomination or denominations, to introduce a new version, destroying, as it would, confidence in our common version...sadly wounding and marring our beautiful Protestantism...That all our ministers be careful, in expounding the word publicly, so to expound, as to inspire and sustain confidence in our excellent version, **as truly the Word of God**..."
(*Minutes*, Presbyterian Church in the U.S.A., Presbyterian Publication Committee., 1855)

1855: "...the superstitious reverence paid by others to the authorized version..."
(*Unitarian Principles*, John Wilson, American Unitarian Association, 1855)

1856: "**Many of the pious members of Christian congregations imagine, that the authorised version of the scriptures is in every iota absolutely correct and infallible**... [They regard] as impious, any insinuation tending to impeach the absolute correctness of the authorised text..."
(Nathan Rouse, *A Dissertation on Sacred Chronology*, 1856)

1856: "He had heard his brethren here utter the most singular remarks in relation to the forty-nine translators appointed by King James; and **some had gone so far as to pronounce the Bible as translated by the distinguished forty-nine, *a perfect work!*** Had we ever heard of a work so lauded to the skies?... In considering the question of 'revision,' [of the AV] as connected with Mr. Cone, nothing strikes us with such entire surprise as the storm of abuse [from Baptists] which assailed him on account of it...Why was Spencer Houghton Cone accused of being a destroyer of all that was stable in language, or reverend in faith, for proposing a revision on this side of the Atlantic?...But there is another, a more general and plausible objection to the alteration of our common version: - it ought not to be touched, because it has, for centuries, been **held in reverence by the people**. We admit the fact...."
(Edward Winfield Cone, Spencer Wallace, *Some account of the Life of Spencer Houghton Cone,* Livermore & Rudd, 1856)

Matthew 11:25 At that time Jesus answered and said, I thank thee, O Father, Lord of heaven and earth, because **thou hast hid these things from the wise and prudent, and hast revealed them unto babes.**

Matthew 21:46 But when they sought to **lay hands on him**, they feared **the multitude, because they took him for a prophet.**

Luke 19:47 ...But the chief priests and the scribes and the chief of the people sought to destroy him,

48 And could not find what they might do: **for all the people** were very attentive to hear him.

1856: "Since the year 1611, we of the English tongue have been taught to look for the **infallible Word of God in King James' translation**...Rev. John L. Dagg, D.D., President of Mercer University, wrote in 1837: 'I much dislike the superstitious regard which some seem inclined to render to King James' version.'"
(*Tiffany's Monthly,*, Volume 2, 1856)

This magazine advocated spiritism (necromancy). The authors despised the KJV as uninspired. Yet, in 1856, they were calling for a new version that would be produced by modern scholarship that would be inspired by these same spirits that they believed were giving revelations through automatic writing, psychic mediums, etc.!

1856: "The facts brought out in this interesting volume serve to diminish the *superstitious reverence* which has been cherished for the *Common Version...*"
(*Friends' Intelligencer*, Volume 13, 1856)

Acts 26:25 But he said, **I am not mad**, most noble Festus; but speak forth **the words of truth and soberness**.
26 For the king knoweth of these things, before whom also I speak freely: for I am persuaded that none of these things are hidden from him; for this thing was not done in a corner.

1857: "...the time, to all appearance, is forever past, when any alteration can be made in [the KJV] without a shock to a thousand holy things..."
(A. Cleveland Coxe, *An Apology for the Common English Bible,* 1857)

1857: "[A revised version] would unsettle the minds of thousands, as to which was the Word of God - the old translation or the new. What a door it would open for the workings of Satan

...what a confusion this would create in almost every place! At present, all sects and denominations agree in **acknowledging our present version to be the standard** of appeal...If the new translation were at once to begin, where would it end?...The present English Bible (Authorized Version) has been blessed to thousands of the saints of God...It is, we believe, the grand bulwark of Protestantism; the safeguard of the Gospel."
(Joseph Charles Philpot, *The Gospel Standard*, April, 1857)

1857: "The general excellence of the English Version being admitted, **its perfection is assumed**, and therefore all preceding and subsequent versions must be unworthy of notice; nay, even the original text need not be consulted...It is not strange, then, that any proposal for its improvement should be looked upon with as much alarm as if the British Constitution were to be revised, or the Scriptures themselves brought up to the present state of science...**many trust the English Bible as infallible**...Hence some make it a positive objection to a revision that it might be followed in time by another...**millions** [believe]...our English Bible is the code and canon of all truth."
(Thomas Kingsmill Abbott, *The English Bible, and Our Duty with Regard to It*, 1857; 1871)

1857: "It is on this account, we believe, that so many deprecate a new translation, or even revision, of the Bible. **They consider the authorized as sacred as the original text. Indeed, some have such a superstitious reverence for their own version, that we are told that any change in it is such an alteration of the 'Word of God' as that against which there is so fearful a warning in Rev. xxii. 18, 19**...Again, we are told that this *innovation* would destroy all biblical stability; that there would then be no end to revisions and emendations, but an end to all permanence and respect for it..."
(*The British Controversialist and Literary Magazine*, Volumes 3-4, 1857)

1857: "...he nevertheless observes [that our Authorized Version] is 'faulty,'- in which latter respect we disagree with him...**What is the number of the learned men of the present day who find fault with the authorized version of the Bible? We cannot tell; but surely we know this much, that they are few, very few, in comparison with the whole of the learned men; therefore we may be well assured that the small response which has been made to the desire of the discontented for revision is pretty fair proof that the general feeling is *against* it**...If once a revision be permitted, how often *might* a similar demand be made?...Once begin to revise, and there would, beyond doubt, be a tumult and uproar which could not be easily appeased. The Bible is, and has been, the foundation whereon we ground, and have grounded, all good things, because that holy book has, for so long a period, remained unaltered ...Suspicion would thereby be entertained of the Scriptures; the regard now paid to them would become lessened; confidence therein would be shaken...It would thus eventually be classed with writings of a worldly description, and its inspired character be forgotten...The *large majority* of thoughtful and wise men are entirely *against* the movement of those who are fond of change ...Readers, believe not that the authorized version of your Bible needs revision, rather, much rather, treasure it as it is. You would be none the better off with any other than that you have. It is an old, a tried, and a true friend. Respect and reverence it accordingly...Whenever, therefore, there be talk of revision and of 'improvement,' it is right and proper to protest against it...*Let well alone!* God grant that this concluding remark may be engraven on the hearts of all, and that the Bible, in its present form, may always so continue."
(*The British Controversialist and Literary Magazine*, 1857)

1857: "**The second objection to any alteration in the Authorized Version is founded** on the **veneration felt towards it by the people**...let them think, if they will, that the English Version

is the very Word of God; but we object in every case to a reverence for words..."
(Hilkiah Bedford Hall, *A Companion to the Authorized Version*, 1857)

Psalms 138:2...for thou hast magnified thy word above all thy name.

1858: "We must never leave out of sight that **for a great multitude** of readers the English Version is not the translation of an inspired Book, **but is itself the inspired Book**."
(Richard C. Trench, *On the Authorized Version of the New Testament*, 1858)

1858: "...it would throw the Christian world into inextricable confusion, it would destroy the universality of much of our existing literature...it would annihilate the common dialect of the English and American Christian world, to substitute a new for our beloved old version of the Scriptures. We may confidently hope that the Providence of God will never permit such a measure to be carried out. We may expect that the English Bible, which has comforted so many Christian, and converted so many unchristian, hearts, which has enlightened and guided so many erring intellects, which has been the rhetorical no less than the spiritual teacher of such authors as Bunyan and Baxter and Addison and Wordsworth, will still teach and gladden and guide their successors to the end of time."
(*The Bibliotheca Sacra*, 1858)

1859: "...**those** who wish to compel its use in the Public Schools mean the Protestant Bible of King James...I confess my astonishment at this whole train of argument, which is the stereotyped one **all over the country**, for the compulsory use of the Bible in our National Schools. It runs in this style: '**Our translation is the inspired Word of God**...'...But my friends urge with great zeal, that our Bible must be placed in the schools, because it has been blest to so many millions, and because it has been so

blest, **it must be the Word of God, and is the best and only proper translation**, and must therefore be used in the schools."
(William Anderson Scott, *The Bible and Politics*, 1859)

1859: "The Princeton *Review,* in repelling a charge 'that our English translation was not taken directly from the original,' says: 'That is to say, the translators have published a deliberate falsehood in the very title page of their great work; and either falsehood or less information concerning them than we now possess, must be charged upon those of their contemporaries who have represented them as the most learned, pious, and venerable company that was ever united in one great literary undertaking. There is no fact in history better ascertained than that the men called upon in 1607 to translate the Holy Scriptures were men eminently qualified for their task...'...Foes and friends alike have subjected it [the AV] to the most searching tests of criticism. Romanism led the way...The efforts of Romanists for the last twenty years, to exclude it from American schools is but a part of this plan...Deism, indeed infidelity in all its forms, assailed the translation next, but assailed it in vain. Semi-infidelity next followed...Never, since the world began, has any book been so thoroughly tested by friends and foes, and from the crucibles of infidelity, and true scholarly criticism alike, it comes forth pure as gold tried in the furnace...How sad their influence [revisers] on the minds of the **millions of Christians**, who are unacquainted with the original languages of the Holy Scriptures; **all they have is the English Bible; they believe every line of it; they have hitherto known it as the simple, unadulterated word of God**, and built all their hopes of eternity on the system of redemption which it reveals. How sad to have this child-like faith and confidence shaken by such assertions and reasonings...In view of these facts, let them possess their souls in quiet, and continue as heretofore, to love and cherish, and, confide in the good old book as being, in very truth, the unadulterated word of God. When the new theory is urged against their faith, let

them point its advocates to the undivided testimony of all truly learned men for the last two hundred and fifty years; to the unanimous voice of the Evangelical Church during those years; and above all, let them point to the endorsement of the book by the Holy Ghost, as his instrument in converting sinners and sanctifying saints...let me here say that I do not doubt the sincerity of [those who praise the AV while attacking it] and, indeed [these praises] are necessary to save the whole theory from the just charge of utter, absolute infidelity. But while they are doubtless sincerely made, and while, as a sort of Christian baptism, they may serve to lighten the shock which every Christian mind must experience in reading his theory, they will not be considered and weighed by the Romanist and Deist, or by any other enemy of the English Bible. All this class will rest their arguments on *his admission, that it is sectarian and not the unadulterated word of God...*"
(W.C. Anderson, *Dr. Scott's Bible and Politics*, 1859)

1859: "This is the doctrine of *plenary* inspiration, as it is usually styled. The advocates of this theory take the ground, that there is not **a single erroneous statement** in the Sacred Volume, from the first verse of Genesis to the last of the Apocalypse. They contend that the whole, **as it reads in our English version**, is perfect, unmixed, **infallible** truth - as true in point of fact as the elements of Euclid, or the Multiplication Table."
(Theodore Clapp, *Theological Views*, 1859)

1859: "The manner in which the New Version movement has been advocated, has had, as I conceive, a tendency to lessen the confidence of the public mind in the Divine origin and the uncorrupted preservation of the Sacred Scriptures...It should therefore be exposed and resisted...A brainless fanatic may destroy in an hour a temple which required ages, and incalculable treasure...to complete. Let the confidence of the masses of the people in the truth of the Bible be once destroyed, and what may we not ex-

pect?...**should they succeed in destroying confidence in King James's version, how will they manage to secure confidence in their own?** They will not be able to do so...they must demonstrate that they are *infallible*: that is, under the influence of *Divine inspiration*...'If the foundations be destroyed, what can the righteous do?'...they have made some of the very same objections to our translation which Paine and others of the lower class of infidels have made...though these *'nibbling critics'* have generally little talent...yet they have misled many of the unwary...'Hath a nation changed their gods, which are yet no gods? But my people have changed their glory for that which doth not profit...'...No person deeply imbued with piety, not to say sound learning or good judgment, can ever finally give up 'The Old-fashioned Bible' for any such a mutilated and spiritless thing..."
(N.H. Lee, *The Babel Builders Confounded*, 1859)

1859: "...there is an ignorant word-worshiping which still requires to be laboriously taught that neither Moses nor Christ spoke in English, and **that King James's translators were not miraculously inspired for their work**."
(*The Christian Reformer; or, Unitarian Magazine and Review*, September, 1859)

These Unitarians (i.e. heretics) mocked the King James Bible Only believers in their age. Yet, in so doing, they attested to their existence in history:

1 Corinthians 1:20 Where is the wise? where is the scribe? where is the disputer of this world? hath not God made foolish the wisdom of this world?

1860: "...the model Scotch Presbyterian is jealous of *everything* that might by possibility bring in question **the inspired character of King James's translators**, - his blind and dogged faith wherein (- **not usually knowing the originals, and still more**

rarely caring for them, -) is the solitary thread by which he thinks that he can safely hold on to the Rock of Ages...there is little to choose between the bigotry of the self-styled Catholic with his Papal infallibility, and the model Scotch Presbyterian with his bibliolatry - **his worship of the Authorized English Version**..."
(James R. Ballantyne, James Madden, *The First Three Chapters of Genesis*, 1860)

1860: "The faith **of millions** reposes on their English Bible. Wherever our tongue is heard, this version is read, and learnt, and loved, as **the very word of God**."
(William Davy Watson, *Netley Hall*, 1860)

1861: "Now, **to all ordinary readers, the authorized version is the Bible.** An uneducated man or woman attaches precisely the same authority to the punctuation as to the other parts of the book…The Koran prides itself on the perfection of its composition. Its pure Arabic style is regarded as a proof of its divinity…The book is believed to be in every word and point the transcript of the Divine original…compare that with the authorized version of the Bible and you have a very distinct picture of the difference of view between those who suppose that the Bible contains, and those who suppose that the Bible constitutes, the revelation which God made to man."
(Sir James Fitzjames Stephen, *Defence of the Rev. Rowland Williams, D.D.*, Delivered in the Court of Arches, Dec. 21st, 1861)

1862: "We are not of those who believe in a literal inspiration of the New Testament...But the Protestant, having only the Scripture for his rule of faith, or thinking that he has nothing else, has been led to insist more on what he calls 'literal inspiration'...It is for this reason that many object to any new translation of the Bible...They are afraid to unsettle **the respect with which men regard even the English words chosen by doctors of divinity in the time of King James.** For the same reason, they continue to

quote texts like that in the First Epistle of John, of the three witnesses, in proof of the Trinity...this worship of the letter does not stop with what is really the letter, **but applies itself to every thing within the lids of the Bible**, - even to the headings of the chapters, and the divisions into chapter and verse."
(*The Monthly Journal of the American Unitarian Association*, Volume 3, 1862)

1863: "...**this has been fostered by, and in turn tends to foster, that over-zealous and almost idolatrous veneration for our present Version,** which forbids the gradual introduction from time to time even of the smallest and most obvious improvements..."
(Richard Whately, *Condition of a Church Militant*, 1863)

1864: "But the question now is merely to what book do intelligent Englishmen refer when they speak of the **infallible word of God?** And to that question the answer clearly is, - **the English Authorised Version.**"
(Evan Powell Meredith, *The Prophet of Nazareth*, London, 1864)

1865: "**We have one party lauding our Authorized Version as if it were inspired**, and condemning every attempt at revision ..."
(*Journal of Sacred literature*, Volume 11, 1865)

1865: "...we might remark at length upon the representation which Mr. Beecher has given of the spirit and details of his father's [Lyman Beecher] ministry in Boston, to which he was summoned as the most hopeful assailant and the virtual extinguisher of Unitarianism...His **fundamental views about the Bible**, and about the philosophy of things human and divine, were utterly discordant with those held by Unitarians...**His daughter tells us, as his writings show, that he drew his arguments of doctrine and appeal from the literal statements made on any page and in any part of the Bible, 'without the shadow of a**

doubt, that we do have in our English translation the authoritative, inspired declarations of God.' His daughter's admission is a candid one; and it is none too frank a statement of the Doctor's bibliolatry. But what a stupendous assumption it involves! Unitarians *know* that it is false..."
(*Christian Examiner*, Volume 79, 1865)

Lyman Beecher (1775-1863), was a Presbyterian minister (the father of Henry Ward Beecher) who was known for his strong anti-Catholic and anti-Unitarian views. In the above words, Unitarians are mocking Lyman Beecher's strong views concerning the Authorized Version, based mainly on his daughter's testimony. His daughter (Harriet Beecher Stowe) wrote of her father:

"After this followed the scriptural argument, on which **he always and unhesitatingly relied**, without the shadow of a doubt that we do have, in our English translation, the authoritative, inspired declarations of God."
(*Autobiography, Correspondence, Etc., of Lyman Beecher*, Volume 2, 1865)

Lyman Beecher's son, Henry Ward Beecher, later advocated most of the views of his father concerning the AV:

"In the study of the word of God he [Henry Ward Beecher, the son of Lyman] discards, somewhat unceremoniously, the help of critics and commentators...He complains, as we think somewhat unjustly, that commentators have 'betrashed' the Bible..."
(Lyman Abbott, Samuel Byram Halliday, *Henry Ward Beecher: A Sketch of His Career*, 1887)

1866: "To alter the words of the Authorized Version would be to the poor man, if I may use such an expression, to *dislocate his faith*...To him the Authorized Version is the *Word of God* as he *now reads it*...I cannot imagine any greater shock given to the religious feelings of a nation, than by the publication of a Revised Version of the New Testament. Such a crop of infidelity

would spring up as would satisfy the most ardent wishes of the whole of rationalists."
(*The Journal of Sacred Literature and Biblical Record*, 1866)

James 2:5 Hearken, my beloved brethren, Hath not God chosen **the poor of this world** rich in faith, and heirs of the kingdom which he hath promised to them that love him?

1866: "And yet this is the version [1611] which some would have us regard as infallible, and receive as the written word of God!..."
(Henry Alford, *The New Testament for English Readers*, Hebrews 10, 1866)

1866: "To him [the uneducated] the **Authorized Version is the Word of God** as he now reads it..."
(John Kitto, *The Journal of Sacred Literature*, 1866)

John 7:15 And the Jews marvelled, saying, How knoweth this man letters, having never learned?

1867: "Do the Psalms lose their claim to Divine inspiration by being translated from one language to another? If so, all other books of the Bible are subjected to the same loss, and the English reader has not the inspired word of God at all. If this be so, **the great mass, of the people of God** must be labouring under a sad delusion..."
(*The Evangelical Repository and United Presbyterian Review,* Volume 45, 1867)

1867: "In New England, then, we see reflected in a glass the English Protestantism of the future; a society of thoughtful, serious, hardworking men, by nature more prone to labour than amusement, and penetrated by a strong traditional religious teaching, the substance of which is a superstitious reverence for the letter of King James's Bible, a belief that each man ought at

least to profess to have learned from it, for himself, all social, moral, and religious truth; and a conviction that the doctrine of the so-called orthodox Protestant sects is true, and must be maintained by all who value their salvation, while the Catholic Church is clearly wrong."
(*Dublin Review*, 1867)

1868: "There is danger, we are told, in unsettling the minds of those who **simply rely on their English Bibles as the word of God.** I am amazed at hearing this plea from lips which **frequently** utter it."
(Henry Alford, quoted in, *Good Words*, Volume 9, 1868)

Luke 24:25 Then he said unto them, O fools, and slow of heart to believe all that the prophets have spoken:

1868: "It is a common trick of those who deprecate **all** correction of our **authorized version**, to charge those who publish abroad the necessity for such correction, with want of regard for **the sacred text**."
(Henry Alford, *How to Study the New Testament*, 1868)

Proverbs 8:8 All the words of my mouth are in righteousness; there is **nothing** froward or perverse in them.
9 **They are all plain** to him that understandeth, and right to them that find knowledge.

1869: "With this supreme reverence for the Bible, **there lurks in the minds of many something very like a belief in the inspiration of our translation of the Bible**; **an idea that the authorized English version is infallible; and that matters of faith are to be settled by an appeal to the words of the English translation**. Thus, it is not uncommon for Anabaptists to quote certain texts, as they appear in English, as supporting their peculiarities, where the words of the original Greek do not con

vey the meaning which the English words are supposed to bear."
(Edwin Clennell Leaton Blenkinsopp, *The Doctrine of Development in the Bible and in the Church*, 1869)

1869: "And yet there is a tendency in certain classes - **even an increasing tendency, to regard the Anglican Bible as a resultant of inspiration**...the admitted errors of confessedly incompetent translators are regularly read to English congregations, and **habitually taught to English readers as the uncorrupt and genuine Word of God**."
(Anon., *What Saith the Scripture? Bible Difficulties,* 1869)

1869: "This translation [*The New Testament, Translated from the Greek Text of Tischendorf*, by George R. Noyes, American Unitarian Association] is a decided help in the great battle against Bibliolatry and the doctrine of verbal and plenary inspiration. Every new version, even if it be not so good as this, aids in overthrowing the power of **the 'Paper-Pope' which has ruled Protestantism as with a rod of iron...it is asserted on good grounds that nine-tenths of the members of Protestant churches in this country believe as implicitly in the infallibility and absolute freedom from error of King James's version** as the Catholics of Spain do in the infallibility of Pope Pius IX..."
(Sidney H. Morse, Joseph B. Marvin, *The Radical*, Vol. 5, 1869)

Sidney H. Morse was a Transcendental anarchist, dedicated to so-called "free thought" and a "new church" of infidelity. Transcendentalists believed spirituality was acquired through individual intuition rather than traditional, Biblical Christianity. When Satanists, Transcendentalists, Theosophists, Humanists, Unitarians, Roman Catholics, etc., all unite against one Book, it should cause Christians to take note!

1870: "To disturb is sometimes a duty. When men are mistak

ing the imperfect for **the perfect**, accepting **as absolute** what is conditional merely, **declaring** the fallible **to be infallible [i.e. the KJV]**...then it is both wise and kind to disturb their false security."
(*The British Controversialist and Literary Magazine,* 1870)

Genesis 3:1...And he said unto the woman, Yea, hath God said...?...

1870: "Have we, then, the *Word of God* as it is revealed in the original Scriptures? And in the use of this book which we now call the *Bible,* can we be sure that we are reading, not man's thoughts, but that Word of God of which one apostle says, that it 'liveth and abideth forever,' and another, 'that it is able to make us wise unto salvation'? It is a *translation.* But is the translation *identical* with the original? Is it *inspired?* Is it of *Divine* authority?...We cannot doubt that it was the Divine intention that the Word of God should be read or heard by all people. It was given in the language of those to whom the revelation was first made. God spoke to the Hebrews in *Hebrew,* to the Greeks in *Greek.* The apostles preached to a great multitude on the day of Pentecost, in many languages, so that every man heard in his own tongue wherein he was born...The only question of interest to us now is, whether *our English Bible* is a translation which, in all the doctrines it inculcates, in all the commands it addresses to the conscience, in all the promises and threatenings by which it strives to arouse the heart, in all the influence it exerts upon the mind of the people, truly reflects the light which first shone upon the minds of Prophets and Apostles, and utters with Divine authority those truths that were recorded in the original Scriptures by holy men, who wrote as they were moved by the Holy Ghost...In answer to this question, which is an eminently proper and necessary one, I will endeavor to show what ground of confidence we have in the Divine authority of this book...It must suffice here to say that this translation is the work of men who, as all scholars know, were the most eminent Greek, Latin, and Oriental scholars of the learned age of one of the most learned nations of the world...the consummate fruit of the greatest and exactest philological scholarship of the sixteenth and seventeenth centuries...And all parts of the country were searched to find the most learned men...[Furthermore, when] we look upon its glorious features, and listen to its heavenly voice, and walk in its Divine light, who will not be grateful to the Puritans for demanding it; to the King for the judicious exercise of his authority in requiring the work to be done; and to each and all of those learned and venerable men whose intellectual and spiritual life was so freely poured into this living and abiding Word?...The design of its authors was not to make an entirely new translation, but to gather up, in one complete and final version, all that England's wisest and holiest men had done to make the Bible the common inheritance of the English people. It was, therefore, at its birth a thousand years old, and stood forth in its gigantic and glorious youth as the grand result of all the revolutions in literature, in religion, in government which had made England what it was in the days of our fathers...We should never have had such a Constitution, such laws, such freedom, such a Union, but for this Book. They all have their roots and their nourishment in this soil...We are told that a new translation of the Scriptures is needed. But if that were true, - which it certainly is not, - who is to make it? We cannot translate or transfer to another version the associations which make our English Bible the peculiar inheritance and treasure of all who speak the English language. We cannot translate the martyr spirit with which *every* word of this translation has been baptized. We cannot translate the influence which this book has exerted upon the character, the speech, the affections, the literature, and the customs of New England. A new translation would be, for us, a new Bible, and even though it should represent the original *as* faithfully, - no version could be more faithful, - we should sigh for the old Bible of our fathers, of our own childhood, of our country, and say, for once, wisely,

'The former times were better than these.' No, the only translation which our English Bible really needs is a transfer of its precious doctrines to the heart and life of the people...The sooner we have such a translation, the better for us and for our children... May we hold fast by this safeguard of our freedom, our religion, and hopes! And may the God of the Bible be with us as He was with our fathers, and by His Spirit inspire us with a deeper reverence and a holier love for that Word which is our salvation and eternal life! Let us bind this precious Book, not to our churches alone, but to our hearts, with bands purer and stronger than gold, that we and our children may have it as our guardian and our joy forever."
(John A. Albro, *The Congregational Quarterly*, Volume 12 , 1870)

1870: "He is not bound to hold, **as some people** appear to hold, that **every word** of the authorised version is strictly true."
(*Fraser's Magazine*, Volume 81, 1870)

1870: "...no one has succeeded in constructing English that commends itself to English speaking people, as the **Authorised Version** does: and there is such a general conviction as to the impossibility of making another of equal merit, that **some persons have imagined there was some special gift of quasi-inspiration bestowed upon the translators of past days**."
(John Henry Blunt, *A Plain Account of the English Bible*, 1870)

1870: "...we believe that no English Protestant denomination now habitually reads the Bible in any other text than in that of the Version of 1611...The Bible of 1611 is the common property, and **substantially the religious oracle, of sixty or seventy millions** of English speaking Protestants..."
(*The Nation,* Volume 11, 1870)

1871: "Nobody can doubt the sincerity or ability of the writer or writers of these two curious tracts; but they would be just now as

utterly thrown away as **the old theories about the evils of popular education and the immaculate perfection of the 'authorized' version of the Bible.**"
(*The Contemporary Review*, Volume 16, 1871)

1871: "A superstitious reverence for King James' version of the Scriptures - so that its very errors and absurdities were regarded as inspired, and all attempts to remove them by faithful and learned criticism as sacrilege."
(David King, *The Ecclesiastical Observer*, 1871)

1871: "Among **many pious people**, accustomed to use only the authorised version, and to attach to it a feeling of reverential regard, the proposal to revise and alter it has excited a feeling almost of horror and indignation. It seems to them as if we were about to play a part as profane as that of Uzzah of old, when he laid his hands rashly on the ark of the Lord; and they seem almost to expect (I hope they don't wish) that some such terrible judgment as befell him will surely befall those who have ventured on so audacious an attempt. But such persons surely forget that the authorised version is, as a version, the work of men..."
(*Scottish Congregational Magazine*, 1871)

The preserved, Written Word is maligned as a work of men. They forget that God used men to write the originals. Will He not use men to preserve them? People likewise pointed to the humanity of Jesus as a justification for their unbelief:

Matthew 13:54 And when he was come into his own country, he taught them in their synagogue, insomuch that they were astonished, and said, Whence hath this man this wisdom, and these mighty works?
55 Is not this the carpenter's son? is not his mother called Mary? and his brethren, James, and Joses, and Simon, and Judas?
56 And his sisters, are they not all with us? Whence then hath

this man all these things?
57 And they were offended in him. But Jesus said unto them, A
prophet is not without honour, save in his own country, and in
his own house.
58 And he did not many mighty works there because of their unbelief.

1871: "...it is obvious that **the popular notion that every word of the authorised translation of the Bible is inspired** opens the door to endless errors..."
(John Moore Capes, *Reasons for Returning to the Church of England*, 1871)

1872: "With **many good people, the practical impression, doubtless, is that the English Bible, which they are in the habit of reading from day to day, is itself an infallible book**, and any intimation as to the incorrectness of any portion of it is apt to bc rcgardcd as a spccies of impiety."
(J.F. Winks, *The Christian Pioneer*, 1872)

1872: "With that **popular bibliolatry which sees in King James' Bible the matchless model**, the almost inspired ideal, of a perfect Bible version, he had the smallest sympathy."
(*The Semi-Centennial Anniversary of the Divinity School of Yale College,* 1872)

1873: "Numbers have grown up with the highest love and veneration for their old English Bible. They admire its superb diction, its elevated style, its pure and simple English, which has become 'household words' in Great Britain and America. **Some, indeed, regard it as 'the Word of God'**...Many look upon it almost as a fetish..."
(*Appletons' Journal*, Volume 9, D. Appleton and Co., 1873)

1874: "**Most of those** who believe the Holy Scriptures to be infallibly dictated attach their reverence to the words of their

English Bible..."
(Frederick Willliam Farrar; quoted in, E.H. Plumptre, *The Bible Educator*, 1874)

1875: "It is, therefore, no matter of wonder that a treasure so priceless should be guarded with the most scrupulous and jealous care, or that a proposal to revise it, however urgently such revision may be demanded in the interests of truth, should at the outset meet with opposition. 'Why,' it may naturally be asked, 'attempt to improve that which is universally admitted to be so excellent? Why meddle with a version which presents the word of God in all its substantial integrity, - which has gone home to the hearts of the people, **and is by them regarded as containing the very words of inspiration?**' And we need not be surprised to find some going even further, and charging would-be revisers with **profanely touching the ark of God, and tampering with the very fountain of revealed truth.** These and other objections, some of which will be noticed presently, were urged when proposals were first made for a revision of our English Bible..."
(Henry Charles Fox, *On the Revision of the Authorised Version of the Scripture*, 1875)

1875: "Perhaps in Scotland more thoroughly than in any other part of the British empire, **the 'Authorised Version' has been exclusively reverenced as the only true version - as the Bible itself.**"
(John Hill Burton, *The History of Scotland from Agricola's Invasion to the Extinction of the Last Jacobite Insurrection*, Volume 6, 1875)

1876: "...popular readers who regarded **every letter** of the English version as directly dictated by the Holy Ghost..."
(Sir Leslie Stephen, *History of English Thought in the Eighteenth Century*, Vol.1, 1876)

1876: "Dr. Davidson [his new translation] does more than run counter to a phraseology which has become stereotyped in our

sacred literature, and is cherished as something inviolable by the pious instincts of every devout reader of the Authorized Version, for he is inflicting a positive injury on his mother tongue…"
(*The Church Quarterly Review*, Volume 2, 1876)

1877: "...[There are] those who are so far given to Bibliolatry as to think the AV absolutely infallible..."
(*Clerical Guide & Churchman's Directory,* 1877)

The accusation of Bibliolatry was commonly used by Roman Catholics against Christians who believed in the final authority of the Bible, in contrast to the Catholic popes!:

"...excessive reverence for any book of authority on any subject: **specifically applied by Roman Catholic divines** to the exaltation of the authority of Scripture over that of the pope or the church."
(John Ogilvie, *The Imperial Dictionary of the English Language,* 1882)

The same type of propaganda is used to mock those who believe the Authorized Version is the infallible Word of God. When the authority of the Bible is usurped by any group of people, the cry of "Bibliolatry!" is set up as a scarecrow in an attempt to gain or keep power. F.W. Faber, a Catholic priest, once complained that the AV was a powerful stronghold of Protestantism (which he considered heresy):

"...Who will say that the uncommon beauty and marvelous English of the Protestant Bible is not one of the great strongholds of heresy in this country? It lives on the ear, like music that can never be forgotten...Nay, **it is worshiped with a positive idolatry**...It is a sacred thing which doubt has never dimmed..."
(Dr. F. W. Faber, quoted in, Isaac Hollister Hall, *The Revised New Testament,* 1881)

Indeed, the Roman Catholics were as numerous and vocal as the

Unitarians in heaping praise upon the RV, and applauding the fact that it confirmed their own doctrines and versions.

In regard to Bibliolatry, many of the more conservative scholars who accuse KJV Onlyists of this bugbear are themselves accused of the same thing by liberals for believing that the Originals were inspired. Some have learned to meet the objection by accepting it as a compliment. For example, Girdlestone writes the following about Dr. Sewell:

"The late Dr. Sewell, in his *Last Words,* makes a touching and striking confession...'I had no doubt whatever of its inspiration, but I fear I did not cling to it, revere it, adore it, as the voice of the Holy Spirit, as I now do, when twelve years of uninterrupted leisure have enabled me to examine a portion of it with a most minute and impartial and fearless criticism as a Greek scholar. I cannot describe *the awe, the wonder, the loving thankfulness, the entire unshaken*...which that examination has impressed on my mind. **There was a time when the word 'Bibliolatry' sounded to my ears as it has sounded to others; as if in worshipping the Bible we ran too great risk of idolatry. I now confess for myself that I do worship the Bible as the voice of the Holy Spirit, I do bow down and adore it as the perfect oracle of God.**"
(Robert Baker Girdlestone, *How to study the English Bible*, 1894)

Likewise, KJV Onlyists, "cling to [the AV], revere it, adore it, as the voice of the Holy Spirit"!

Years later, the liberal leaders of the National Council of Churches also accused Bible believing Christians of *Bibliolatry*:

"It is a well-known fact that many of the leaders of the NCC openly accuse evangelicals of 'Bibliolatry' and are on record as denying the infallibility of the Word. These men no longer be

lieve the Word...They are talking psychiatry, substituting Freud for Jesus Christ. They are substituting socialism for the Kingdom of God."
(James De Forest Murch, *The Growing Super-Church*, 1952)

"'Bibliolatry' is a word the modernists coined to describe those who believe in the infallibility of the Bible."
(Carl McIntire, *The New Bible: Why Christians Should Not Accept It,* 1953)

"*Bibliolatry*: One who idolizes the Bible (used of believers in its verbal inspiration)."
(*The New American Encyclopedic Dictionary*, 1907)

Talmage, the well-known preacher, laid the blame upon some scholars and ministers who were trying to impress the world:

"Many of them are engaged in picking holes in the Bible and apologizing for this and apologizing for that. In an age when the whole tendency is to pay too little reverence to the Bible, they are fighting against Bibliolatry, or too much reverence for the Bible. They are building a fence on the wrong side of the road... ministers pretending to be friends of the Bible...doing the Book more damage than all the blatant infidels on all the earth."
(Thomas DeWitt Talmage, quoted in, *Logansport Pharos,* Indiana, December 15, 1892)

1878: "Departures from ancestral faiths **are rapidly increasing**...Such dogmas as the six days' creation of the world; the fall of man through Adam and Eve; the total innate depravity of the human race; the salvation of the soul through the literal blood of the Lord Jesus...[the] personality of the devil; **the plenary inspiration of King James' Bible**...hell...and kindred theological dogmas, are fast dying out of all cultured minds. Freethought, scientific research, and a potent Spiritualism...have, with united persistence, undermined the theologies of the ages."
(J. M. Peebles, *New York Freethinker's Association*, 1878)

2 Timothy 4:3 For the time will come when they will not endure sound doctrine; but after their own lusts shall they heap to themselves teachers, having itching ears;
4 And they shall turn away their ears **from the truth**, and shall be turned unto fables.

Notice that the so-called "free-thinkers" linked the belief in the inspiration of the King James Bible with the other fundamentals of the faith. They were glad to see these fundamentals being discarded by many.

1878: "If it were proposed to take away this version of centuries and to put a new one in its place, then, indeed, would there be a loud and persistent protest. **To many the proposition would savor of sacrilege.**"
(*National Repository,* Volume 3, 1878)

1878: "A certain class...will be certain to regard it [the RV], from the start, with disfavor. It is made up of worshippers of the letter, **to whom the traditional version has all the sacredness of the inspired original**...the most conservative sticklers for the old version unaltered are found among those who entertain extreme theories relative to the inspiration of the Biblical writers. It is they who are most afraid of unsettling, if not their own faith, the faith of other people on the writers of Scripture, by the suggestion that errors are found in the popular translation of the sacred books."
(*The New York Times*, September 23, 1878)

1878: "...these very words [of the King James Version] have for a long time, and by millions of our race, been held to be the very words of God...Is it wise to lift the anchor...?"
(*The New York Times*, September 27, 1878)

1878: "...the common English Bible made the Baptist system

possible, and was, and is the chief 'stock in trade' of the 'immersers' or 'dippers'...Of so much value have the renderings 'much water,' 'in Jordan,' 'down into and up out of the water'...[etc.] been to the 'dipping' theory that Baptists have been known to claim the 'King's version' as the 'Baptist Bible.'"
(Thomas Gallaher, *A Short Method With the Dipping Anti-Pedobaptists*, Presbyterian Publishing Company Print, 1878)

1879: "*A Translated Bible is the Word of God - If the foundations be destroyed, what can the righteous do?* - Ps. xi:3...**It is urged that infallible inspiration cannot attach to translations.** This objection should be calmly met...If Christ were to preach to us today, He would employ King James' version, with which the people are familiar, just as of old He did the Septuagint. Doubtless, if He found any important errors, He would correct them, but this would be the Bible He would use, and use it with all its inherent Divine authority...The conclusion of the whole matter is this: We have a literary, historic, moral and spiritual demonstration that our Bible is the Word of God, and the Word of God is our Bible."
(Thomas H. Skinner, in *The Preacher and Homiletic Monthly,* Volume 3, 1879)

1879: "There is no better argument for revision, than the existence of such errors [in the KJV]. If they could not be corrected, it would be unwise and unkind to make them known to **those to whom the English Bible, and the English Bible only, is the Word of God**..."
(Joseph Packard, *Anglo-American Bible Revision*, American Sunday-School Union, 1879)

Pro-revision writers often saw themselves as heroes, riding in to save the ignorant masses from the alleged errors in the KJV. Yet, they left behind many testimonies such as this, proving how popular the KJV Only view was with the people in their days.

1879: "...Timothy Dwight opens his essay on the true conservativism in respect to changes in the English text by saying, 'The **authorized English Version** of the New Testament and the Greek text on which it was founded have attained a sort of independent existence of their own. **They have been accepted for so many generations as the true original** and the accurate translation of the sacred books, **that to multitudes of persons, both in England and America, there seems to be no doubt that they, and they only, are the Word of God'**...It is a very grave matter to touch words which through centuries have borne the joys and sorrows, the deepest despairs and highest aspirations, of millions of men."
(*New York Times*, May 18, 1879)

Timothy Dwight served on the translating committee of the *American Standard Version* (see chapter 17). He counseled his associates to make their new version sound as much like the King James Bible as they could, while introducing changes. He did not want the whole project resisted before it even got off the ground, due to the fact that there were so many conservative "KJV only" believers.

1880: "Many ardent lovers of the Bible are taunted with believing practically in the infallibility of the English version. In popular Bible readings and other uses of Scripture, it is quite common to take a particular word, turn up all the passages where it occurs, and deal with them as if in the original the word were always the same."
(William Garden Blaikie, *The Catholic Presbyterian*, Vol. 3, 1880)

1880: "The English public is rather more conservative than our own...The American recommendations are in the interest of a more complete and modern scholarship...In summing up, then, what we suppose to be the results of this work: I believe one result will be that **this revision will help to destroy the New Tes**

tament as a fetish in the public mind. People have come, in this modern age, almost to worship the letter of the Book."
(*Unity Pulpit*, Vol. 2, 1880)

1880: "The revised version of the New Testament receives in some quarters more favorable notice, but it makes no way with the public. The *Athenaeun* says it is impossible to assign it a high standard even of accuracy, but it considers that the revision will do good by exorcising **the notion that the old version was infallibly inspired**."
(*Literary News*, Volumes 1-3, 1880)

1880: "Now, for two centuries and a half the Authorised Version has been the sole text-book of the English-reading student of the Bible. Launched without legislative or ecclesiastical enactment, it has, by its own intrinsic merits, absolutely superseded and supplanted every predecessor, not only in the Church of England, but in every English-speaking Protestant community in the world...**Familiarity for generations with the *ipsissima verba* [i.e. very words] of the Authorised Version has led to an unconscious acceptance of the English words as being themselves literally inspired**."
(Walker Purton, *Churchman*, Issue 1, 1880)

1881: "It is further affirmed that the evil is done by disturbing popular associations with biblical language. The Bible of the people, again, it is affirmed, is King James's translation. Their faith in the whole may be impaired by the loss of their faith in a fraction."
(Austin Phelps, *The Theory of Preaching,* 1881)

1881: "One dignitary thought that to revise the English Bible would be 'like touching the Ark'...And Lord Panmure had solemnly declared at a public meeting at Edinburgh 'that the prospect of a new version is fraught with the utmost danger to the

Protestant liberties of this country, if not to the Protestant religion itself'...**What will the good people in England and Scotland think who believe in the verbal inspiration of the English Bible, looking upon it as the pure, authentic, and unadulterated Word of God?**"
(*The Dublin Review,* Part 2, Burns and Oates, 1881)

1881: "Many thought that there *was* such risk of greater mischief; they have said – 'What will be the effect on the minds of **our people who have been in the habit of using our English Bible, not as if it were the translation of the inspired book, but the inspired book itself?** Will not their minds be unsettled when they are told that some texts on which they had relied have been wrongly translated, when others disappear altogether, and they hear that they never had had a right to be regarded as part of God's Word? Will they not feel as if all solid certainty had been taken away?'..."
(George Salmon, *The Revision of the New Testament; A Paper Read Before the Irish Church Conference*, April, 1881)

1881: "Another class will oppose the new revision from motives very much less respectable. They are necessarily ignorant people. **To them, the King James version of the Bible is the inspired Word of God, in all its language. They regard a revision as a tampering with the sacred text, and as essential profanation.**"
(J. G. Holland, *Scribner's Monthly*, 1881)

John 7:47 Then answered them the Pharisees, Are ye also deceived?
48 Have any of the rulers or of the Pharisees believed on him?
49 But this people who knoweth not the law are cursed.

1881: "[In the RV] there will be enough...change to disturb the minds of those who have not only believed in verbal inspiration,

but practically in the **verbal inspiration of the authorized Eng lish version.**"
(*The Bystander,* Volume 2, 1881)

1881: "But it is certain, nevertheless, that they will try the faith, or at any rate hurt the feelings, of **numbers** who have been accustomed to believe that **they had in the Authorised Version the authentic and unadulterated Word of God**..."
(*The Academy,* Volume 19, 1881)

1881: "For nearly three centuries the King James version has been read and studied by all English speaking peoples...**It is not commonly felt to be a translation**...The man of letters as well as the pious zealot, the lover of good ripe old English as well as the Christian, can not fail to deplore useless tampering with a text so long read with devotion and delight by millions of people."
(*Appletons' Journal,* Volume 11, 1881)

1881: "The most important event in the world of letters this year is the publication of the revised edition of the New Testament Scriptures...because of the progress of the Christian world out of superstitious reverence for mere words, and the growth of the sentiment that Christianity does not depend at all for its power or truth upon any words or sets of words...**Some denominations have even declared that to alter a word was to mutilate the Scriptures.** It is within the recollection of one who has not passed his allotted days, that **the great 'body of believers' would fling the stones of malice at the man who would for a moment doubt that King James's version was the most perfect, truthful, sublime, in fact the only version that would be sanctioned by God, and that to alter it in the slightest particular would bring upon the daring vandal the anathema, which was written, 'God shall take away his part out of the book of life, and out of the holy city**, and from the things which

are written in this book'...People who once looked upon the very letter as sacred have come to believe that the letter and the word are but symbols...and that the word may change, but no decay of truth will follow."
(*Potter's American Monthly*, Volumes 16-17, 1881)

1881: "And we think one of the certain effects of this acceptance of the revised version will be the increase of more rational views about the Bible...**thousands of readers of the King James version have read it in the firm belief that they were reading an infallible book.** They will **now** begin to see that that belief, at least, was a mistake...From this point of view, therefore, **the revised New Testament has a special interest for Liberals.** That the revision, on points where any doctrinal change is involved, favors liberal Christian rather than orthodox interpretation is also apparent. But this is a matter of much less moment than setting the Bible-reader's wits to work on the question whether the Bible he is reading is an infallible book. Let that question once fairly get started among the plain-thinking people of Christendom in the nineteenth century, and the twentieth century will answer it by placing the Bible on the library shelves alongside of other historical religious books, classified as one of the **human** literatures of the world's religions."
(William James Potter, Benjamin Franklin Underwood, *Free Religious Index*, Free Religious Association, Boston, Mass., 1881)

Again, we see that Liberals and Infidels loved the whole idea of shaking the confidence of the people in the Authorized Version.

1881: "...**thousands of earnest Christians**...have been brought up to look upon the Book as the inspired word of God, and have not considered the fact that the English Bible is a translation...to those who have been taught to look upon the English Bible as the one source of religious authority changes of this nature [in the RV] will appear harsh and repulsive...The devil, the prince of

darkness, still holds his place...under the translation of revised edition, but he holds a somewhat subordinate one. **He does not enter so largely into the complications of human affairs as in the old version.**"
(*The New York Times*, May 20, 1881)

Satan certainly desires people to think that he is presently occupied in exploring Hell, rather than walking to and fro, throughout the earth, tempting men to corrupt and pervert the Scriptures with subtle changes:

1 Peter 5:8 Be sober, be vigilant; because your adversary the devil, as a roaring lion, walketh about, seeking whom he may devour:

2 Corinthians 2:17 For we are not as many, which corrupt the word of God...

1881: "The Brooklyn Tabernacle held an overflowing congregation yesterday morning. Mr. Talmage recited the Lord's Prayer to the doxology and then solemnly said: 'There we are compelled to stop.' Taking up the Bible he turned to the fifth chapter of John, but passed it with the remark, 'I will not read that, for it has been abolished or made doubtful by the new revision.' He next started on the eighth chapter of John, but soon stopped reading, saying 'that also has been abolished, so I will pass it.' The fifth chapter of the First Epistle of John was next announced, but was quickly abandoned also, Mr. Talmage saying, 'I will progress no further in that reading, for that too has been abolished.' (Laughter)...When the time for the sermon was reached, Mr. Talmage took for his text: 'And when they came to Nachon's threshingfloor, Uzzah put forth his hand to the ark of God, and took hold of it; for the oxen shook it. And the anger of the LORD was kindled against Uzzah; and God smote him there for his error; and there he died by the ark of God.' Second Samuel, vi: 6

and 7. We have, he said, an ark of the covenant, which is the Bible, and like the old one, it is precious. Let not the hands of worldly criticism, pedantry, or useless disturbance touch that ark! Remember the fate of Uzzah! We are in the midst of an agitation caused by the revision of the New Testament. We had a translation 270 years old...satisfactory to all Christendom except a few doctors of Divinity...After great and universal advertising of the book [the RV]...it comes forth...All the Christian world wanted to know what had been done...That accounts for the 1,000,000 or 2,000,000 [sold]...monopoly would, if it could, rule religion as it rules the money market or the Legislature...**the voice of the great masses of people [has been hurt], 999 of whom out of every thousand regret from their very soul that any revision was attempted, and look upon it as a desecration, profanation, and religious outrage (Applause)**...put it upon my study table, into my family room, or into my pulpit, as a substitute for the King James translation, I never will. (Great applause.) I put my hand upon the old book and take an oath of allegiance to it, so help me God!...why this shock to sacred associations?...It is too late to revise the Bible or to make a new translation...Who are the men who undertook this impertinence?...D.D. and Ph. D. and L.L. D. are often only the heavy baggage of a slow moving train...I agree with several friends of mine in pronouncing the revision a literary botch, which will never be adopted if the people of this country speak out their true sentiments...If you have more control over your sense of the ridiculous than I have, you can read without smiling some of the changes made...I have sometimes wondered how much good could have been accomplished if the...revisers...had spent the last 10 years preaching the old version instead of finding fault with it, and if, instead of spending the vast sums of money subscribed, they had been given toward sending abroad the old translation from whose loins sprang civilization and Christianity...[The revision] comes at a time when the battle has opened with sin and unrighteousness, and we are asked to stop and see if our swords are hammered out

correctly, or if we can't replace the tassel on the hilt with a handsomer one. In this Armageddon of the nations we are asked to stop and discuss the definite and the indefinite article...I reject it because it shakes the faith of a great multitude in the Bible...**Religion has not so much to fear from infidels as from mistaken friends of the Bible**...I believe this revision will sow infidelity...**What I say may be derided in high places, but I am putting into words the sentiments of more people...These are only the mutterings before the storm. Hands off from the word of God!**...An advocate of the revision told me the other day, 'Of course we are to have another revision, and another and another'...Christianity will finally go into a paroxysm of revisions, and nothing intelligent, satisfactory, or appropriate will be left in the Bible...**I have some practical advice for private Christians. Hold on to your Bible. The old Bible is for me; it is good enough for you...The Bible in your houses is the Bible that will be quoted for all time to come. I call upon all private Christians, all teachers and Superintendents of Sunday-schools, all ministers of religion whose utterance is unterrified, to be quick in protesting against this scholarly profanation. Speak out now, or forever hold your peace**."
(*The New York Times*, June 6, 1881)

1881: "...clergymen in their pulpits discussed and criticised the revision. To those who with fond and devout affection cling to the English form of the Greek version as in itself an **inspiration**, and who thus **ascribe to the work of King James's translators the sanctity with which they invest the very word of God**, any disturbance of that work, **any change** of word or phrase, or even of traditional form of chapter and verse, must seem to be sheer sacrilege. This, indeed, has been the tone of a few clergymen...The great mass of persons in Christendom to whom the Christian gospels are the word of God do not know in what way that word has taken its present form...**they assume that it was inspired as it is presented to them**...if they go so far as to know

that in their own language it is a translation, **they assume that the infallible wisdom** which dictated the original record, in whatever tongue, **also guided** the reproduction in other forms of speech. To this feeling **a change of any kind is blasphemous tampering** with the Word of God."
(*Harper's Magazine*, Volume 63, 1881)

Mark 12:37...And the common people heard him gladly. 38 And he said unto them in his doctrine, Beware of the scribes...

1881: "It is to be regretted, that upon the part of some a species of idolatry has arisen, in which the Bible, possibly the English Bible of King James, has been regarded as a thing to which no error could attach, and which is faultless in all its forms."
(George E. Merrill, *The Story of the Manuscripts*, 1881)

1881: "The journalist asked [Uncle Rufus] whether he had read the revised edition of the New Testament. 'I have not,' he replied. 'I have read extracts published in some of the wicked newspapers. The old version was good enough for my ancestors, and it's good enough for me. I never knew anyone who governed his conduct in life by the rules laid down in the old version to go astray. I take no stock in new-fangled theological combinations based on a change of the Bible. They all carry grist to Bob Ingersoll's mill...'"
(*The Sayings of Uncle Rufus,* Jesse Haney & Co., 1881)

1881: "No heathen ever gave the objects of his worship more superstitious reverence than these ignorant Christians do the Bible. Of course they would oppose any change in it...It would be a real benefit to Christendom to break up **the idea** that there is anything sacred and not to be touched in the language of the old English Bible..."
(*The Century*, Volume 22, 1881)

1882: "...one point of **popular opinion**, which has almost been elevated into an article of faith by **the great mass of uninstructed Christians**, namely, the quasi-infallibility of the English Bible in its ancient and accustomed dress."
(Alexander Gordon, *Christian Doctrine in the Light of New Testament Revision*, 1882)

1882: "...instead of being a help [i.e. the RV of 1881] it acts as a club in the hands of the infidels to destroy, if possible, the influence of the Holy Scriptures...King James' translation is the Protestant Bible, **and always will be...agreeing perfectly with the Divine revealment, whether in the Bible or in nature**; and as a matter **well understood by enlightened ministers and people**, to have come out with **the Divine sanction** in the days of peril when the glory of God was the consideration, not money...**The OLD VERSION [AV] has for its source Jesus of Nazareth**, the Apostles and the Holy Ghost. The NEW VERSION has for its source...the spirit of the age...The OLD VERSION is a Trinitarian Testament...The NEW VERSION with its sister - the *American Bible Union Version,* are **Unitarian Testaments**...[bringing] the whole Bible into disrepute...strife and divisions...[driving] millions into skepticism...**I unhesitatingly say, that the same Holy Ghost who gave inspiration to the Apostles to write out the New Testament, presided over and inspired those men in the translation and bringing out of the entire Bible in the English language**. And I also say, that ***no version*** **since, brought out in the English language, has the Divine sanction**...Now, why would God cause at this age and in these trying times, versions in the same language to be brought out, to conflict...?...He would not...**I furthermore say, that *King James' Translation* of the Bible is the <u>only</u> Divinely Inspired translation *directly*** [in modern ages]..."
(William Washington Simkins, *The English Version of the New Testament, Compared with King James' Translation*, 1882)

1882: "It is computed that at this time the Authorized Version is the Word of God to as many as ninety millions of souls. No words can exaggerate the amount of interest with which any alterations in a possession of such vast importance, and in which so many human beings have a share, must be viewed by those whose religious belief or cherished religious sentiments may be affected by such alterations. No wonder, therefore, that the work of the Revisers has been acutely examined and severely criticized..."
(Charles Frederick Bryan Wood, *Notes Designed to Illustrate Some Words and Expressions in the Greek,* 1882)

1882: "It is written: 'Knowing this first, that there shall come in the last days scoffers, walking after their own lusts...This is evidently the spirit of the present age - the age of infidelity; and everything is swiftly turning toward these evil ways of mocking God and his Word...Infidelity now rides forth with a high hand and unblushing face, and everything seems to be tending to lift it up on high...The new revision is in no way equal to the good Book sought to be removed...Yes, this old Book has stood the test of all the power of Satan, the criticism of infidels and papists, and every grade of error. All who believe in inspiration have admitted it to be *the* authority; but now-a-days men are aiding the infidel, by undermining the certainty of God's Word with questions as to its genuineness. We consider the omissions of words, clauses, and whole verses, and the marginal notes in the Revised Version, can accomplish no other purpose...we fully believe that the hand of God was in the ordering and production of the Authorized Version, 1611; and it is a noble national treasure to the English nation."
(*The Gospel Standard*, Pastor D. Allen, 1882)

1882: "In the margin of our Testaments - I mean those of the authorized version **which will never be parted with** for the so-

called revised version..."
(C.H. Spurgeon, "Acceptable Service," Sermon No. 1639, *Metropolitan Tabernacle Pulpit;* sermon delivered on January 15, 1882)

Spurgeon's words are included here since his prediction is certainly correct! Many others reasoned in the same manner as Spurgeon:

"...its authority has been owned by all. No other version will ever become the Bible of the nation...In the old Bible we have unity; in the new version, a division throughout the whole nation."
(*The Gospel Standard*, 1882)

"The twentieth century, we have no doubt, will still read the Bible in those pure rhythms of the Authorized Version..."
(*The Literary Digest*, Volume 18, 1899)

Spurgeon did not appear to ever absolutely understand or embrace the infallibility of the AV. He nevertheless did, from time to time, get a whiff of some of the dead flies in the ointment of the RV and the textual criticism behind it (Ecclesiastes 10:1):

"...they miss no chance of saying, 'The Greek is so-and-so.' It makes a man an inch and a half taller by a foolometer, if he everlastingly lets fall bits of Greek and Hebrew...making every old lady distrust the only Bible she can get at, or what is more likely, mistrust you for falling out with her cherished treasure."
(Spurgeon, *Commenting and Commentaries,* 1876)

Like many preachers, he appears to have grown closer to the KJV Only view as he aged. He was aware of this change in his views:

"...we are less and less disposed to countenance any tampering with the text. The older we grow the more conservative we become."
(*Sword and Trowel*, January, 1884)

In 1881, Spurgeon doubted that the RV would replace the AV; yet sometimes he included pro-RV articles and reviews in his magazine. By 1884, he was including anti-RV reviews. In a review of a book by Tilney Bassett, which documented how the RV attacked the Deity of Christ, Spurgeon wrote:

"Our author in this instance acts as one of the watch-dogs of the flock, and his deep baying must be very unpleasant music for the wolves."
(*Sword and Trowel,* March, 1884)

Notice some other quotes from Spurgeon concerning the AV:

"I would quote John Bunyan as an instance of what I mean. Read anything of his, and you will see that it is almost like reading the Bible itself. **He had studied our Authorized Version, which will never be bettered, as I judge, till Christ shall come...**"
(*The Last Words of Christ on the Cross, MTP,* Vol. 45; sermon delivered on June 25, 1882)

"They never rest, for they will have nothing to do with an infallible revelation...As for us, we cast anchor in the haven of the Word of God...The Word of God is quite sufficient to interest and bless the souls of men throughout all time...If this book be not infallible, where shall we find infallibility? We have given up the Pope, for he has blundered often and terribly; **but we shall not set up instead of him a horde of little popelings fresh from college. Are these correctors of Scripture infallible?** Is it certain that **our Bibles** are not right, but that the critics must be so?...**Striplings fresh from reading the last new novel correct the notions of their fathers, who were men of weight and character.** Doctrines which produced the godliest generation that ever lived on the face of the earth are scouted as sheer folly...But where shall infallibility be found?...Are we now to believe that infallibility is with learned men? **Now, Farmer Smith, when you have read your Bible, and have enjoyed its pre-**

cious promises, you will have, to-morrow morning, to go down the street to ask the scholarly man at the parsonage whether this portion of the Scripture belongs to the inspired part of the Word, or whether it is of dubious authority...**All possibility of certainty is transferred from the spiritual man to a class of persons whose scholarship is pretentious**, but who do not even pretend to spirituality. We shall gradually be so bedoubted and becriticized, that only a few of the most profound will know what is Bible, and what is not, and they will dictate to all the rest of us. **I have no more faith in their mercy than in their accuracy**: they will rob us of all that we hold most dear, and glory in the cruel deed. This same reign of terror we shall not endure, for **we still believe that God revealeth himself rather to babes than to the wise and prudent, and we are fully assured that our own old English version of the Scriptures is sufficient for plain men for all purposes of life, salvation, and godliness**. We do not despise learning, but we will never say of culture or criticism. 'These be thy gods, O Israel!'"

(Spurgeon, "The Greatest Fight in the World," delivered at the Pastor's College Conference, April, 1891)

In these forceful, Spirit-filled words, Spurgeon was acutely discerning the times (perhaps even more than he realized), and arriving at the very doorstep of the KJV Only view. The infidels and liberals answered Spurgeon's *Manifesto* with observations like the following:

"Mr. Spurgeon, in this 'Final Manifesto,' makes everything turn upon the Bible...Mr. Spurgeon appears to forget that it was not originally written in English, and he assumes that we have it just as God communicated it...He asks; 'If this book be not infallible, where shall we find infallibility?' We frankly answer; Nowhere. But why wish for infallibility?...One thing must be said, and greatly to Mr. Spurgeon's credit: - he takes the Bible just as it is..."

(*The Coming Day*, Aug., 1892)

In 1887, until his death in 1892, Spurgeon reproved what he called the "Down Grade" (i.e. Broad School) in the churches and Christian institutions. Had he lived longer, it is probable that Spurgeon would have been able to discern (even more than he already did) that these liberals were the prime movers behind the RV and the ASV. (See chapter 17, *Heretics Behind the ASV*).

1883: "Probably **with many of them in this country the hitherto authorised English version is the inspired one**, and the original Greek, Hebrew and Chaldean Scriptures are somewhat less sacred. Perhaps their reverence, which has been said to extend to the punctuation..."
(*The Literary World*, Volume 28, 1883)

1883: "The popular mind is passing through a curious transition of opinion...a transition from the superstitious view to that of common sense...The root of the superstitious view is a gross literalism founded on the mistaken doctrine of **Verbal Inspiration and applied to the Authorized Version**."
(*Dickinson's Theological Quarterly*, Jan., 1883)

1883: "This [i.e. thousands of differences] sounds formidable, and may seem sufficient, in the judgment of timid conservatives, **who look upon the English version as the inspired Word of God**, to condemn the Revision..."
(*The Homiletic Review*, Volume 7, 1883)

1883: "The strongest condemnation and the most formidable assaults have come from conservative admirers of the received Greek text and the Authorized Version. Most of them had previously resisted all attempts at revision as a sort of sacrilege, and found their worst fears realized...How many sacred associations, they said, are ruthlessly disturbed! How many edifying sermons spoiled! Even the Lord's Prayer has been tampered with, and a discord thrown into the daily devotions. The inspired text is

changed and unsettled, the faith of the people in God's holy Word is undermined, and aid and comfort given to the enemy of all religion. **We need not be surprised at such talk, for to the great mass of English readers King James's Version is virtually the inspired Word of God**...It may take a whole generation to emancipate the mass of the people from the tyranny of ignorance and prejudice."
(Philip Schaff, *Companion to the Greek Testament, and the English* Version, 1883)

Philip Schaff's arrogant sarcasm is not surprising in light of his heretical views and dark connections (see Chapter 17).

1883: "I have heard of apparently intelligent Christians who oppose Bible revision because they want the very words of Christ and the apostles and the prophets, and seem to think they have them in the King James version."
(Edwin W. Rice, quoted in, *The Sunday-School World*, Volumes 23-24, 1883)

1883: "...even if it were true that every word, as originally spoken or written, was inspired, we have none of the original documents, and the Scriptures are now read in copies containing many various readings, interpolations, omissions, and errors of various kinds...**multitudes of pious** but ignorant people in our own country and in England, until very recently, **regarded King James' version with a reverence due only to inspiration**, the day is past when such a view can be seriously entertained."
(Isaac Errett, *Leading Theories of Inspiration, A Lecture delivered before the Summer School of Christian Philosophy, at Richfield Springs, 29th of August, 1883*)

1 Corinthians 1:27 But God hath chosen the foolish things of the world to confound the wise...

1884: "In fact, any new version [revision of the AV] is **contested by that ultra conservative spirit that will not brook**

any interference with 'God's word.' But no English version is God's word. The Greek original comes nearest to that. It is an irreverent reverence that invests any version with such sanctity as to repel any attempt at communion with the divine original for the purpose of bringing a more accurate report to men. It is to make a fetish of a book, and perpetuate mistakes."
(*The Universalist Quarterly and General Review*, Volume 21, 1884)

Notice that these Universalists (who deny a literal Hell, and/or eternal Lake of Fire) use the same arguments and mocking attitude as modern day critics of the King James Bible Only viewpoint.

1884: "These godly, liberty-loving but self-controlled, Protestant, Americanized Englishmen of the fourth generation, **had not let go their English Bible as the Inspired Word**, nor sold their God-given birthright for any mess of pottage..."
(F.H. Palmer, Edward Payson Crowell, *Two Centuries of Church History*, First Congregational Church, Essex, Mass., 1884)

1885: "As early as 1832, Joseph Livesey contended for a revised version of the Scriptures...To advocate such a reform fifty-three years ago **amongst the common people, whose religion was tinctured more or less with a species of bibliolatry, was taking the surest course to be dubbed 'infidel' or 'atheist,'** both by the clericals and their followers..."
(Joseph Livesey, *The Life and Teachings of Joseph Livesey*, 1885)

1885: "This conclusion is just in view of the manner, in which the new version of the New Testament was received in 1881, and the insignificant influence its changes have had on the mass of Christian believers. The old-version of the New Testament is as much the vital, **infallible** factor in popular orthodox opinion today as it was before the new version was given to the Protestant public. We predict the same fate for the new version of the Old Testament. The experience of 1881 showed that **the people who**

care anything about the bible at all look upon the King James version as unalterably *the* bible...It is to them as authorative as the original text could be to a thorough biblical scholar. Aside from the fact that many of its phrases have become a part of our literature is the fact that these phrases, for centuries, have been the method by which phrases of spiritual life and religious emotion have been commonly expressed."
(*Semi-Weekly Jackson Sentinel*, June 6, 1885)

1885: "**I once heard a tutor of a college defend** the use of the word *wages,* in reference to the salaries of ministers of the Gospel, **on the ground that it was the word which Divine Inspiration had stamped with its authority**, inasmuch as Paul had said to the Corinthians, that he had 'robbed other churches, taking *wages* of them to do them service.' If to one who knew Greek, the English had become **the inspired representation** of inspired Greek, it is likely to become so to a still larger extent to those who are indebted solely to it for their knowledge of the word of God...old fashioned beliefs are becoming curiosities...The inspiration that is now believed in is the inspiration not of words but of men. As long as the old theory was held the value of textual criticism was underrated. In a general sense the *words* [of the Bible] were believed to be inspired...With the progress of the change...[an] impetus was given to textual criticism...the authorized version has been revised...the *Textus Receptus* failed...The Liberalism of today will be the Conservatism of tomorrow, and as for the Conservatism of today, it will be utterly forgotten and ignored in the future, which is near..."
(Frederic Edwards, *The Revised Old Testament*, 1885)

1885: "It is very painful to hear scholars who should know better, affirming the *absolute perfection, the infallible accuracy, of our Bible*."
(Rufus Phineas Stebbins, Carlton Albert Staples, *A Common-Sense View of the Books of the Old Testament*, Unitarian Sunday-School Society, 1885)

1885: "Some persons regarded our English Bible with such superstitious reverence that they were opposed to any modifications of its phraseology."
(*The Unitarian Review*, Volume 24, 1885)

1886: "...**multitudes** of pious but ignorant people in our own country and in England, **until very recently**, regarded King James' version with a reverence due only to inspiration..."
(Charles Force Deems, *Christian Thought*, Volume 1, 1886)

John 7:48 Have any of the rulers or of the Pharisees believed on him?
49 But this people who knoweth not the law are cursed.

1886: "There is doubtless **a considerable body** of opinion... opposed to **any change in that Authorised Version** of Holy Scripture which men have been accustomed from their childhood **to receive as the Word of God**."
(Annie Wood Besant, *Our Corner*, Volumes 7-8, 1886)

Annie Besant was the successor to Blavatsky in the Theosophist Society (i.e. New Age, Lucifer worshipping in doctrine). The Theosophists, such as Besant, often objected to the AV, and promoted the readings of the RV.

1886: "One objection made by plaintiffs, to the use of the Bible in the schools under defendants' control, is that they use **the Protestant or King James version**...the plaintiffs are members of the Roman Catholic church...On the other hand, the defendants deny that the translation of the Holy Bible known as the King James version is incorrect, unauthorized or sectarian, or that any inspired portion of the Word of God has been omitted or excluded from the said Bible; they maintain and aver that the 'King James' version, is nearer the original writings through which the Deity has revealed Himself to man than any other

translation."
(*The Chester County Reports*, Volume 2; Pennsylvania, Supreme Court, 1886)

1887: "And the remarkable dictum of Chillingworth, that the Bible, and the Bible only, is the religion of Protestants, coupled with the grotesque idea of **the verbal inspiration of the English version**..."
(John William Horsley, *Jottings from Jail*, 1887)

1887: "...the light cast on a subject which is more likely to be rightly understood by calm scholars than by the **adherents of sects, who worship the letter of King James's Version**."
(*The Critic*, Volume 8, 1887)

Psalms 119:11 Thy **word** have I hid in mine heart, that I might not sin against thee.
105 Thy **word** is a lamp unto my feet, and a light unto my path.

1887: "This unfaithfulness to truth is certainly not so great a sin against the light as **the habit which seems to be still prevalent** of **treating the old authorized version alone as the *ipsissima verba* [i.e. very words] of inspiration**...Let us hope that the **increasing use of the new revision**...may win over its readers to the true stand-point and to right practice."
(James Frederick McCurdy; quoted in, William Rainey Harper, *The Old Testament Student*, Volume 6, 1887)

McCurdy (1847-1935) was a modernist (i.e. one who denies the fundamentals of the faith):

"James Frederick McCurdy...entered Princeton Seminary in 1868 to study biblical languages. He taught there 1871-82, but **resigned when his 'modernist' views on the Bible were attacked**. After studying in Germany he was hired by the University of Toronto in 1885..."
(John S. Moir, *Called to Witness: Profiles of Canadian Presbyterians*, Vol. 3, 1991)

1888: "There are so-called evangelists, and some ministers, who have forgotten their Hebrew and Greek, who scorn the Biblical training of theological seminaries, and who think that **the English Bible is good enough for them. They think that they have the key to unlock its treasures that Greek and Hebrew professors have not found**."
(*The Presbyterian Review*, Volume 10, edited by Charles Augustus Briggs, 1888)

1888: "The theory is put by a distinguished dignitary of the Church of England in very strong form. According to him, 'Every chapter, every verse, every sentence, every word is absolutely inspired by God.' This is the idea of verbal inspiration followed out to its ultimate issue...**They talk of their English Bible as though it were the original of the Divine message. The story of the good divine who, being confronted by an objection from some of his hearers that the interpretation which he had given to his text was not in accordance with the original Greek, naively answered that 'the gospel was always foolishness to the Greeks,'** is only an extreme illustration of the spirit in which some men indulge, and which not unfrequently found more or less distinct expression in the discussions which arose relative to the Revised Version...What special claim King James's translators possessed, that they should be regarded as specially qualified by God for the work that they undertook...that they had been inspired of God...But it is nothing less than this which is claimed on their behalf...There may be those to whom matters like this constitute no difficulty. They have been accustomed to regard every word of Scripture as of equal authority...they shrink from dealing with their writings as they would with any other productions of human literature. To them the Bible occupies a position absolutely unique. None of its statements are to be challenged, no features of its composition to be minutely examined...Biblical criticism is in their view, therefore, little more than an act of daring sacrilege, full of menace to

the highest interests of the soul itself. The scientific spirit, as applied to the Bible, savours of blasphemy and revolt..."
(James Guinness Rogers, *Present-day Religion and Theology: Including a Review of the Down Grade*, 1888)

1889: "We refer to the Revised Version of the New Testament. It can not be made to supersede the old King James translation. It came with a great flourish of religious trumpets. For ten years it was in the hands of scholars said to be in every way exalted. When the work was done, the cry went up from orthodox lips that it marked a wonderful epoch in religious history. It was to fasten the attention of the world upon it, and thereby bring about such an upheaval as had never been known in all the long record of spiritual movements, uprisings and revivals. Multitudes of those who professed to be theologians and Scriptural commentators praised it to the skies...The gudgeons were baited with an edition without a hell, and the new orthodox revolution, as far as any sort of an insight could be got from the surface, was an accomplished fact...Tabooed, spurned, a failure from the beginning, it has now passed almost completely out of sight and out of mind...And what is the reason for it all? Mr. John Fulton attempts to give the reason in the June number of 'The Forum.' He says in substance that too many changes were introduced to suit some and not enough to suit others. He also thinks that the poetry of many passages was impaired...Mr. John Fulton does not go deep enough. He does not get down to the real bone and sinew of the subject. The translated New Testament, or rather the revised edition of the New Testament, was the work of a lot of intellectual duds. They refined away poetry, pathos, rugged Saxon, quaint forms of expression, old landmarks, verses that had been lived and died by for centuries, old texts, old promises and old prophecies. **One thing the people as a mass will never permit to have taken away from them, and that is the old-fashioned Bible. They never asked for any revision. They never for a moment considered that a revision was necessary...The old**

King James version was venerated. Since its publication it has been a household book, the one sacred record of the births, marriages and deaths in a family for a generation. Its teachings had brought solace in sorrow...[The common man is] only solicitous to know that it is his father's Bible, and that the refiners, the agnostics, the tweedle-dum and tweedle-dee fellows of the last half of the nineteenth century have not laid their hands upon that...Anchored fast to his old-fashioned Bible, even the **very gates of Greek** shall not prevail against his old-fashioned belief in fire and brimstone."
(J. Edwards, *John N. Edwards*, 1889)

1890: "That by reason thereof the King James version of the Bible, only **received as inspired and true by the Protestant religious sects**, is regarded by the members of said Roman Catholic Church as contrary to the rights of conscience..."
(*The Weekly Wisconsin*, March 22, 1890)

1890: "...the practice of reading the King James version of the Bible, commonly and only received as inspired and true by the Protestant religious sects..."
(*Decision of the Supreme Court of the State of Wisconsin Relating to the Reading of the Bible in Public Schools,* 1890)

1890: "The critical prefer it [the Revised Version], but the people still cling to the King James Version."
(*The Chautauquan*, Volume 11, 1890)

1891: "Upon all such questions as Inspiration, the Deity of Christ, the Atonement, an educated layman, with the English Bible in his hands, is just as capable - perhaps more so - of giving an intelligent opinion as a German critic. The critic has access to no sources of information shut out from the layman. All information possible on all such questions is within the four corners of our English Bible."
(*The Theological Monthly*, Volume 5, 1891)

1892: "Of course there were great difficulties in the way. **There was the veneration and love which had gathered for so many years around the Old Version, and which regarded any attempt at revision with as much horror as the dissection of the body of some dear friend**...a good man got up, and in a voice trembling with emotion, **deprecated laying any hands on the Sacred Ark** [i.e. the AV]...The revisers [the RV translators], who, with one exception, were all Trinitarians, declare unanimously that this celebrated passage [1 John 5:7] is no part of the Bible at all...and like honest men they have ruthlessly cut it out. But what are we to say to those who assert that its omission makes no difference to orthodox doctrine? It is the only text in the Bible which clearly states the doctrine of the Trinity: in no other place is it declared that '*these three are one*'; it is the one unmistakable proof text from which thousands of sermons have been preached. The doctrine is only inferred from other texts; in no other place is it explicitly taught. Does it make no difference to the scripture proof of a doctrine that the one and only text which plainly declared it is now pronounced a forgery? It is only childishness and folly to say everything is as it was, and revision has made no difference. Our Baptist friends have been accustomed to justify their refusal of baptism to children, and their doctrine of believers' baptism only, by the requirement of Philip and the confession of faith on the part of the eunuch of Candace before his baptism: and Philip said, '*If thou believest with all thine heart thou mayest* (be baptized). *And he answered and said, I believe that Jesus Christ is the son of God.*' But now when the Baptist turns to the New Testament he cannot find his favourite passage: it has no place in the best manuscripts, and the revisers have expunged it as an interpolation. No other text so clearly upheld the Baptist position, and yet we are told that its excision leaves the question untouched! Our evangelical friends have for ages made much of the words, '*Without shedding of blood is no remission*'...But is not their favourite doctrine shaken to its foundations by the new rendering of the whole verse?...Or look at some of the well-known and often quoted proof texts of the doctrine of Christ's Deity. Here is the famous one, '*God manifest in the flesh.*' The revisers tell us that the word God 'rests on no sufficient ancient evidence,' but that the passage should read, '*He who was manifested in the flesh.*' Does this make no difference to the proof of the Godhead of Christ? It is a great difference. One striking proof text is now admitted to be no proof at all, having no bearing on the question. One other instance will suffice. Here are the words: '*Hereby perceive we the love of God, because he laid down his life for* us.' According to this rendering it was God who laid down his life for us and died on the cross, and in this sense it has been triumphantly used as proving that Christ is God. But how does this Revised Version run? '*Hereby know we love, because he laid down his life for us*'...The Revised Version is of great doctrinal significance. **It tends to break down the rigidity of orthodoxy, and it justifies that Liberal Christianity which we, in this place, hold and teach. We, at any rate, have every reason to be grateful...[We] welcome with the deepest thankfulness the Bible which the revisers have placed in our hands...What are the people who have held the Infallibility of the Authorized Version of the New Testament to say to the fact I mentioned last Sunday, that the Revised Version contains 36,000 changes?** I have shown you that there is no Greek and no Hebrew text free from error, and that no two of those ancient MSS. absolutely agree."

(Joseph Wood, *The Bible: What It Is and Is Not,* American Unitarian Association, 1892)

These words from this Unitarian (infidel), not only prove that many believed the infallibility of the King James Version in 1892, they also show the great use that infidels have made (and do make) of the new, revised versions. The Revisers merely *revived* the ancient infidelity in modern times! They based their translations upon manuscripts that were long ago corrupted through the same unbelief (2 Corinthians 2:17). By 1892, it was apparent that the sound warnings from decades earlier had proved true:

"...the stronghold of the anti-revisionists is, that any interference with our Bible would unsettle men's faith, and give an advantage to infidelity."
(*The Journal of Sacred Literature*, Volume 3, 1849)

1893: "The King James' Version was **regarded by many as too sacred** to admit of revision!...In opposition to all this Alexander Campbell taught that the Bible, while an inspired volume, must be interpreted according to the same common-sense rules which we apply to other literature..."
(*New Christian Quarterly*, Vol. 2, 1893)

1893: "...up to the latter end of the present century, it practically amounted, as we have seen, to the most rigid theory of verbal inspiration - **an inspiration usually attributed by the people at large, and even sometimes by their ministers, to the Authorized English version**."
(John James Lias, Eyre and Spottiswoode, *Principles of Biblical Criticism*, 1893)

1894: "There is a class of ignorant people to whom **the King James version of the Bible is the inspired word of God in all its language.** They regard a revision as a tampering with the **sacred text**, and as an essential **profanation**. The forms of language in which sacred truth has been presented to them are quite as sacred as the truth itself...To this class belonged the bigoted fool who declared that the new revision would make more infidels than all the Bob Ingersolls in the world, simply by its admissions that there had been some mistakes in the English Bible hitherto preached to the world...We fear that there is a leaven of this kind of dishonesty pretty widely scattered throughout the church - a feeling, or a fear, at least, that the exact truth in a new revision will remove some of the props from under old dogmas

that had become precious, or that are regarded as fundamental in their accepted schemes of belief..."
(Harriette Merrick Hodge Plunkett, *Josiah Gilbert Holland*, 1894)

Jude 1:10 But these speak evil of those things which they know not: but what they know naturally, as brute beasts...

John 7:48 Have any of the rulers or of the Pharisees believed on him?
49 But this people who knoweth not the law are cursed.

1895: "...was it [the AV] not for every Protestant an absolute, infallible rule of faith?...So this book, the infallible voice of God revealing His ways, **this sole rule of faith for millions of Englishmen**, and by which millions had lived and sworn and died during more than two centuries, had to be revised...It appears, then, that **the King James Bible of some years ago has not been as most Protestants of necessity claimed for it - the pure, authentic, unadulterated Word of God**. And if not, what guarantee have we that the promiscuous body of recent translators, however learned, withal not inspired, have given us that pure, authentic, unadulterated Word of God?...So **far Protestant revisions have done Catholics a service**...thus demonstrating the correctness of the old Vulgate; but they have also **led Protestants** to reflect seriously, and to realize that **the 'Bible only' principle** is proved to be false and dangerous."
(Herman Joseph Heuser, *Chapters of Bible Study,* 1895)

Again, we see that Roman Catholics (like the Unitarians and other infidels) rejoiced when these so-called scholars attempted to replace the King James Version. However, they also gave us one more testimony to the vast number of Christians who considered the Authorized Version to be infallible. Quotes could be multiplied showing the praise that Catholics heaped upon the RV for justifying the readings in the Catholic versions (e.g. Cardinal

Wiseman; Thomas S. Preston, the priest of St. Anne's Catholic Church in New York; Tobias Mullen, Bishop of Erie, Pennsylvania; etc.). Even Dr. Benjamin Warfield admitted that the RV (etc.) was largely a return to the Catholic bible:

"...a careful comparison of these new translations with the Rhemish Testament, shows them, in many instances, to be simply a return to this old [Catholic] version...."
(*Collection of Opinions and Reviews*, Vol. 2)

1896: "...**the public** has long since weighed the Revised Version in the balances and found it wanting...**They have turned away from the new** with a conviction that it could be no substitute for that which still forms the moral and spiritual backbone of the English people...The Authorized Version is the outcome of faith and zeal that have never been excelled. How is this to be accounted for?...After their [RV] NT was issued, Ciasca lighted upon an Arabic translation of Tatian's Diatessaron. This takes us back to the text of the year 150, and decides in favor of the Authorized readings against those of the Revised...Those preachers who confide in them, and who give their congregations 'the more correct reading,' are not airing their knowledge but revealing their ignorance."
(*Word and Work Magazine;* quoted in *The Truth,* 1896)

1896: "I can imagine the indignation with which these radical suggestions will be read...by **people to whom the Authorised Version is sacrosanct** and irreproachable."
(*The Contemporary Review*, Volume 69, 1896)

"Sacrosanct" means "sacred; inviolable."(*Webster's*, 1828)

1897: "At a recent meeting of the **Methodist preachers in and around New York city**, Dr. Buckley (editor of *The Christian Advocate*), in discussing a paper read by Dr. Curtis, took occa-

sion to say that there were not four men in the room who **believed in the infallibility of *the English version*** of the Scriptures. **The statement being challenged**, he called for a vote; but the meeting adjourned without its being taken."
(Andrew Edward Breen, *A General and Critical Introduction to the Study of Holy Scripture*, 1897)

"At a recent meeting of ministers at the Methodist headquarters, Boston, Mass., Prof. O. A. Curtis of Drew Seminary read a paper intended to combat the views of Rev. Lyman Abbott, that the Bible sometimes errs. Dr. Curtis skilfully and clearly maintained the infallibility of the Bible teachings. The *Transcript* says: - There were present one hundred and fifty members of the clergy; and they all, with one exception, applauded his views. The exception was Dr. Buckley. The doctor is editor of the New York *Christian Advocate*...In replying to Prof. Curtis, he said: 'I am sorry to disagree with my friend Curtis. I don't believe in the **infallibility of the English version of the Bible**, and I think there are **scarcely four men** in this meeting who do.' **There was immediately a chorus of protests**."
(*The Unitarian*, Volume 12, 1897)

"Dr. James M. Buckley, editor of *The Christian Advocate*, in the discussing the paper afterward, said: 'I do not believe that there are four men present who believe **absolutely in the infallibility of the English version** of the Bible...'...There was a stir in the meeting...Before Dr. Buckley could continue his remarks, the Rev. J.N. Shaffer of Newburg...got to the floor and said: **'If you don't believe it, doctor, we can do without you.'** 'Do you believe it?' retorted Dr. Buckley. **'Yes - substantially,' replied Mr. Shaffer**...The incident would probably have ended here but for a proposition by Dr. Buckley to put the question to a vote of the meeting...The Rev. Dr. Francis H. Smith of the Seventh Street Church, who was also present, said: 'The **discussion involved the authenticity of the translations more than any-**

thing else. Fifty years ago there were Christians who believed that everything about the Bible, down to the commas, was inspired...'"
(*The New York Times*, February 16, 1897)

"It **may be** that there are advanced professors in the University of Chicago who have **their doubts about the infallibility of the English version of the Bible**...But, **if so, they keep their doubts to themselves**...Even more surprising than the remark [by Dr. Buckley] was the reception with which it was met...It seems clear, however, that **there is a considerable number of Methodist ministers in New York and its neighborhood who do not believe absolutely in the infallibility of the English version of the Bible.** Inasmuch, however, as the Bible is held up by all these ministers to their congregations as in some sense infallible, and as the English version is the only one the majority of their congregations ever read, it seems proper that they should explain in what sense they regard it as infallible, and what parts of it their congregations are at liberty to reject as uninspired ...They are told to search the Scriptures, which are infallible. If this infallibility is, in the belief of many Methodist ministers, only partial, it seems that they owe their people the duty of pointing out which are the fallible and therefore negligible parts."
(*The New York Times*, February 17, 1897)

"As one purpose for which this paper was founded is to take glad and thankful note of the progress of the world in **liberal thought and deed**, we call attention to the free manner in which the Methodists are at present tackling the question of the verbal inspiration of the Bible. Dr. James M. Buckley, editor of the 'Christian Advocate'...tells his clerical brethren that the time has passed for holding to many of the old fashioned notions as to the Bible. **One of these is the belief in the infallibility of the English version. He does not quarrel as yet with the original text, but with the King James translation...**"
(*The Pacific Unitarian*, Volumes 4-5, 1895)

Notice, there were some American liberals in 1897 that did not believe in the infallibility of the King James Version! But this certainly shows how many people, even ministers, *did* embrace the doctrine of its infallibility! It also shows how this doctrine was opposed by Unitarians, liberals, infidels, etc., as a barrier to what *they* deemed to be *progress*. But their *progress* is called in the Bible, the "falling away" in preparation for the coming of the Antichrist.

1897: "A remark of Jowett's [Regius Professor of Greek at Oxford] on the work of the [RV] committee when it appeared is perhaps worth recording here...[He stated]: 'They seem to have forgotten that, **in a certain sense, the Authorised Version is more inspired than the original.**'"
(Evelyn Abbott, Lewis Campbell, *The Life and Letters of Benjamin Jowett*, 1897)

1897: "...the decided probability is that the King James version will be the Bible, not only of this generation, but of several generations to come."
(*Des Moines Daily News*, October 27, 1897)

1897: "What, in truth, is inspiration? and in what sense and degree is the Bible an inspired book? Such are questions heard all around us, and the answers given range from a claim to a verbal inspiration, almost, of the King James' Version..."
(*The Churchman*, Vol. 75, 1897)

1897: "A hundred years ago the Authorized Version, which had been in our fathers' hands for nearly two hundred years, **was no longer a version. It had come to have all the significance of an original book.** Outside the pulpit and the university no one dreamed that it was translated from another language…**When our fathers, as they did, stoutly maintained the doctrine of verbal inspiration, the inspired words they really had in**

mind were not Hebrew or Greek, but English words; the words of that version which Selden called 'the best translation in the world,' and of which the late Master of Balliol once remarked, 'In a certain sense, the Authorized Version is more inspired than the original'...The Bible was read in those days, as it is not read now; it was committed to memory by the children, and trodden in by catechizing, as is not done now...[Before long, interpreters] felt it increasingly necessary to make their own translation of the book on which they were commenting. All these things gradually wrought in the ordinary religious mind a feeling of unrest...If the foundations are destroyed, what will the righteous do?...while the Revised Version stands on the library shelf as a much-valued commentary, the book that gathers the dog's-ears, that is read and cherished as a closet companion, is still the venerable version of King James. Nor can I see signs of its displacement...Here is a book [the KJV] that is more than a version...A severe blow the theory of verbal inspiration had already received...The most obvious initial step to [making the Bible an ordinary book in people's minds]...is to print the Bible like another book...A step toward this result was taken by the Revised Version by dividing into paragraphs instead of verses..."

(*Minutes of the Annual Meeting*, General Association of the Congregational Churches of Massachusetts, 1897)

1898: "No pains were spared by the translators, and in 1611 they published that which has since been considered the greatest treasure of English literature; known to us as the *authorised version* of the Bible; which is still used by Churchmen and nonconformists alike as the pure Word of God...**many persons now, forgetting that all English versions are merely translations from the ancient Hebrew and Greek, imagine each word and letter of the 1611 translation to be inspired by God**..."

(Charles Arthur Lane, *Illustrated Notes on English Church History*, 1898)

1898: "...and they even stretch the mantle of Divine authority to cover the English words selected in making King James' version..."
(Dr. Frank Crane, *Is the Old Book True?*, 1898)

1898: "It is said of Bishop Lee, that he considered every word of the English Authorized Version inspired, and an absolute belief in it to be necessary to Salvation, as in every particular whether History, Chronology, Geography, or Physical Science the Book is infallibly accurate...This may seem an extravagant statement, but **it represents a view held unconsciously by simple-minded, earnest, sincere Christians...**"
(Robert Needham Cust, *Linguistic and Oriental Essays*, 1898)

1 Corinthians 1:20 Where is the wise? where is the scribe? where is the disputer of this world? hath not God made foolish the wisdom of this world?

1898: "There are some who insist on the Divine inspiration ...and they even stretch the mantle of Divine authority to cover the English words selected in making King James' version. It is needless to say that I do not hope to allay this timid fear which is the child of ignorance..."
(*Our Day,* Volume 17, Chicago, 1898)

1899: "...thousands who have come to regard the very phrasing of the King James version as sacrosanct..."
(*Record of Christian Work*, Volume 18, 1899)

1899: "We doubt whether any new translation, however learned, exact, or truly orthodox will ever appear to English Christians to be the real Bible. The language of the Authorized Version is the perfection of English, and it can never be written again, for the

language of prose is one of the few things in which the English have really degenerated. Our tongue has lost its holiness."
(Ellis Yarnall, *Wordsworth and the Coleridges: With Other Memories, Literary and Political*, 1899)

CHAPTER 10

1900-1949

1900: "Most disappointing of all, his citations are from that work of scholarship, not of inspiration - the Revised Version! It was of the King James Version, however, that Coleridge and Saintsbury and Addison and Arnold and Ruskin were speaking. It is the King James Translation that is the monumental work of literature, - a work wrought from the heart by inspired men."
(*Harvard Illustrated Magazine*, Volume 1, 1900)

Quotes such as this are praising the *literary* inspiration of the KJV; and they could be multiplied. For example, as noted earlier, Benjamin Jowett, Regius Professor of Greek at Oxford, claimed that, "in a certain sense the Authorized Version was more inspired than the original." Likewise, Professor William Lyon Phelps, of Yale, believed:

"...our English translation is even better than the original Hebrew and Greek. There is only one way to explain this; I have no theory to account for the so-called 'inspiration of the Bible,' but I am confident that the Authorized Version was inspired."
(*The Biblical Review*, Volume 7, Biblical Seminary in New York, 1922)

At the very least, these scholars recognized that there is a great difference between the Authorized Version, and the newer translations!

1901: "An effort to beat the King James version has recently

been made, with the usual unsatisfactory result. Some of these attempts to improve upon the Holy Book as it is commonly accepted have proved interesting and instructive, but for the most part they can hardly be said to have been otherwise than diverting."
(*Pella Chronicle*, Iowa, October 11, 1901)

1902: "The speaker said that **many people** seemed to have a very strange idea about the Bible. There were those who seemed to think that it was written in heaven...That it came just as we have it now...with every dot of an 'i' and every cross of a 't'...just as we find it in the King James translation."
(*Dubuque Telegraph-Herald*, January 6, 1902)

1902: "An old lady asked how she liked our Revised Bible replied, 'If St. James version was good enough for St. Paul, it is good enough for me.'"
(Joseph Packard, Thomas Jones Packard, *Recollections of a Long Life*, 1902)

Reports concerning these KJV Only ladies, etc., are endless. See the history under "1966."

1902: "And yet, alas! there are teachers and leaders and officers in the churches who are so orthodox that they will not give up the King James Version, nor will they accept **any change** in the English translation. There are teachers and officers in the churches today who seem to think that God and the Holy Spirit spoke English, and that the King James is the original language of Jehovah."
(*Baptist Missionary Magazine*, Volume 82, 1902)

1903: "The excellency of the King James Bible is attested by the single fact that nearly three centuries passed before the concerted effort to revise it....Then came the hints of corruptions in

the text of Scripture, of later interpolations, of wrong translation, of inaccurate renderings...Men could no longer be induced to **accept it as the fathers did**, as **absolutely perfect and not to be improved**..."
(W.H. Lindemuth, *The Sunday School Journal*, Volume 35, Methodist Pub. House, 1903)

2 Timothy 4:3 For the time will come when they will not endure sound doctrine; but after their own lusts shall they heap to themselves teachers, having itching ears;

1904: "Preachers and old people...insist on the young using the King James Version as if it were an inspired version..."
(*The Park Review,* Volume 5, 1904)

1904: "The interpolations and mistakes made by the translators in this connection, enable...persons who believe - **as the Christian world generally does - in the correctness and inspiration of the King James translation**...to accept such statement as a fact..."
(*Young Men's Mutual Improvement Association*; Mormon, 1904)

1905: "When one comes to think of their undertaking [i.e. *The Twentieth Century New Testament*] as an undertaking to supplant the authorized version, it becomes an undertaking of 'stupefying impudence.' For it is an undertaking to displace not only an English classic, but the English classic...Whoever reads the King James version is cultivating his literary taste...The presumptuous person who attempts to destroy such a literary landmark for the purpose of setting up in its place a specimen of the style of last evening's newspaper should be told that the judicious look upon his undertaking with impatience and disgust."
(*The New York Times*, February 11, 1905)

1906: "I am requested again to explain Matt. 25:46. This verse

seems to be a stumbling block in the way of **many who are inclined to accept the King James version of the Bible as inspired, infallible Truth**."
(*Life: A Monthly Magazine of Christian Metaphysics*, 1906)

1906: "The same spirit is shown in this country **by many who hold that the Authorized Version of 1611, the old St. James Bible, is inspired of God in every word and point,** and that to modernize its language is sacrilege. The old deacon stated the position of the people of this class in a way that cannot be bettered: 'I don't want to hear of your Hebrew and your Greek, the language that Moses and Paul spoke is good enough for me'...This superstitious reverence for words...The fetishism of words, the belief that words have some mysterious power and meaning dependent on their form, has prevailed from the earliest times and is not yet extinct."
(*The Independent,* Volume 61, 1906)

2 Chronicles 36:16 But they mocked the messengers of God, and despised his words, and misused his prophets, until the wrath of the LORD arose against his people, till there was no remedy.

2 Timothy 1:13 Hold fast the form of **sound words**, which thou hast heard of me, in faith and love which is in Christ Jesus.

John 6:63 ...the words that I speak unto you, they are spirit, and they are life.

1907: "In 1629 a company, projected by the Rev. John White, of Dorchester, obtained a charter from King Charles I. granting them the rights of settlement in the country along the Massachusetts shore...**They carried their English Bible as the ancient Hebrews bore with them the Ark of the Covenant**."
(Josiah Quincy, *Dorchester Day*, Dorchester Historical Society, 1907)

1908: "And this infallibility is, in practice, claimed for the Bible as printed in the English tongue and read in our churches. And only to breathe a question like this is fatal to **the popular dogma of the infallibility of the English Bible**..."
(*Appleton's Magazine*, Volume 12, 1908)

1909: "The people are conservative. True, some are radicals, but the masses are conservative...they do not say the New is better, but in the most emphatic manner say: 'The Authorized Version is the one for me!'"
(*Herald of Gospel Liberty*, Oct. 14, 1909)

1909: "After mature reflection it was determined to use the Authorized Version. None of the many Revisions have commended themselves **to the people at large**. The Revised Version, which has now been before the public for twenty-seven years gives no indication of becoming in any general sense the people's Bible of the English-speaking world."
(C.I. Scofield, *The Scofield Reference Bible*, *Introduction*, 1909)

Although Scofield was not what we would call "KJV Only," his words do alert us to the general views of the public. In his day, the King James Version was "the people's Bible."

1909: "It is within the memory of some now living that a certain professor in Edinburgh was suspended from his office because he would not subscribe to a form of Bibliolatry which implied that the Bible came down from heaven, with its scientific and historical facts...headings to chapters and all. **It is not so long ago that considerable opposition was shown to the Revision of the text of the Bible on like grounds**...to them every word of the Bible was divinely inspired and equally infallible...The spirit of Bibliolatry is far from dead amongst us even now, and the belief that the Bible, 'from cover to cover,' is verbally inspired, and 'came straight down from heaven,' is not con-

fined to simple-minded pious souls."
(J.R. Cohu, *The Gospels in the Light of Modern Research*, 1909)

1909: "This was called the Authorized Version of the Bible, and has been in use by Protestant Christians since 1611, and **has been accepted as authoritative and correct by the masses**, though critics have been assaulting its authenticity ever since it was issued. But **the pulpit called it the 'Infallible Word of God,'** and it had been the rule of faith for almost three hundred years."
(George Henry Walser, *The Life and Teachings of Jesus*, 1909)

1910: "Now, as to your religious talks, as I said above, they do me good in that they cause me to read and to search the Scriptures and **to be more deeply grounded in my faith in the King James version of the Bible as the inspired Word of God**..."
(*The Medical World*, Volume 28, Letter by C. C. Cochran, 1910)

Mark 12:37...And **the common people heard him gladly**.
38 And he said unto them in his doctrine, **Beware of the scribes**...

1910: "The merit of the King James Version is so great that some have even thought it better than the original in places."
(*The Princeton Seminary Bulletin*, Volumes 4-6, 1910)

1911: "*Is the King James Version of the Bible Infallible?* A clipping has been sent to us for consideration, according to which the Rev. A. W. Bond, of Vancouver, declared from the pulpit...that the King James version of the Bible could not be considered infallible. Here is what he said: 'I believe that **thousands of Christians** have been changed into infidels through an effort to **take the whole of the Bible as it stands in this version**, or none of it at all."
(*The Flaming Sword*, Volume 25, 1911)

1911: "After the Reformation, the Puritans had substituted for a belief in an infallible Pope, **a belief in an infallible Book, and had invested the King James Version of the Bible with a sacredness, which, to them, included the very punctuation and paragraphing**...When the German scholars applied to the study of these manuscripts the same laws which governed the study of other early literature, the Christian world was aghast."
(*The Records of Christ Church, Poughkeepsie, New York*, 1911)

1911: "As the years went on, **the great body of Protestant Christians** came to have for the Authorized Version a feeling which was almost that of bibliolatry. They did not go to such extremes of book-worship as the Jews went...But doubtless there were good people who thought that the *textus receptus* was verbally dictated, and that the very punctuation and verse-divisions of the Authorized Version were inspired."
(*The Sabbath Recorder*, Volume 70, American Sabbath Tract Society, George B. Utter, 1911)

1911: "*Pastor Russell Points Out More Deceptive Additions to the Word of God Contained in Our Common Version Bibles, But Shown to Be False Because Not Found in the Oldest Greek MSS*...Not long ago I pointed out that the last twelve verses of St Mark's Gospel in our Common Version are spurious...Today I invite attention to some other dead flies, some other additions to God's Word, which have had much to do with twisting the theology once delivered to the saints. Take, for instance, the closing words of the Lord's Prayer: 'Thine Is the Kingdom and Power and Glory.' These words, if uttered by our Lord, should be found in the old Greek MSS. But they are not found therein. They are therefore, to be rejected...We cannot on this occasion make further investigation, take out more of these dead flies: but, the Lord willing, at some future time I John v, 7, 8 will have our attention. It is worthy of it. It has caused the ointment to stink and has confused the minds of many of God's dear saints by the way in

which the error in this case has been interwoven with the Truth...Nor should I be considered as fault-finding with our Common Version of the Bible. While it is not without its faults, it has so many excellent qualities and beautiful translations that I prefer it to any other and generally use it...**Published by kingly authority, it is now venerated by English and American Protestants as though it had come direct from the finger of God**. This is a mistake...The basis for our Common Version was the Latin Vulgate...There is, therefore, a difference between reverencing and loving the Word of God and reverencing and loving a particular translation, errors and all..."
(*Raleigh Herald*, West Virginia, June 8, 1911)

Not only does this founder of the (so-called) Jehovah Witnesses (Charles Taze Russell) reveal that the KJV Only view was strong in his day, he also argues in the exact manner, with the same errors, as modern promoters of the new versions! Along with Catholics, Universalists, Unitarians, Rationalists, and other infidels, who praised the new version, we can also add the *Watchower* organization. What will it take for God's people to awaken from their slumber (Jeremiah 6:17)?

1911: "...it is a fine version for its day, and its influence has been immeasurable for religion and character, and, what is of some importance, for the conservation of the English language. Our English speech cannot get far away from the words, forms and idioms of the Bible which every one knows. Shakespeare has done much to fix our speech, but the accepted Bible has done a hundred times more...**If there is a certain standard of recognized personal and social duty, praised, accepted, and the failure to reach it condemned by public censure, it is the English Bible which has made the standard. So sacred has the inspired Word been held to be that the very words of our old English translation have been regarded as too sacred to be used lightly, and its very style has become a standard of**

speech, beautiful and stately and musical, because we have from our childhood attached to its words something of the virtue of the inspiration back of them. Doubtless the Bible is less read than it was in the days of our grandfathers, when newspapers were few, and there were no magazines loading their tables, and the Bible was almost the only book in the house; but even yet it is the one book which is more quoted, more known, than any other book or all other books in the language..."
(*The Independent*, Volume 70, 1911)

1912: "There was a time when men believed everything taught by students of divinity...**They did not question the infallibility of King James' version of the Bible, from the first chapter of Genesis to the last verse in Revelation, and interpreted literally the text: 'If any man shall take away from the words of the book of this prophecy God shall take away his part out of the book of life and out of the holy city, and from the things which are written in this book'**...The superstitious reverence for the English Bible has been a stumbling block in the way of individual thought, and has helped to hold the orthodox churches together."
(*The Word: Monthly Magazine Devoted to Philosophy, Science, Religion; Eastern Thought, Occultism, Theosophy and the Brotherhood of Humanity,* Volume 15, 1912)

What a statement from this New Age magazine! These worshippers of Lucifer argue that the common belief in the infallibility of the King James Bible is a hindrance to their goals!

1912: "[There are those] who identify loyalty to constitutional government with veneration, not for the spirit, but for the letter of our ancient Constitution, just as **some very worthy people** identify pure religion and undefiled, with a **fervent belief in the verbal inspiration of the King James version** of the Bible."
(George H. Haynes, *The Election of Senators,* 1912)

1913: "Again, apart from the dogma of the superhuman (i.e. essentially non-human) origin of the Scriptures, our reverence for the Prophets and Apostles...might lead us to say that their views of God and Christ and salvation must have been right, and that it is very presumptuous for us to set up our views against theirs. This feeling is sometimes manifested in ludicrous ways, as in the case of the woman who, when the minister began to read from the Revised Version of the Bible, indignantly left the church, saying that if the King James Version was good enough for Saint Paul it was good enough for her."
(*The Harvard Theological Review*, Volume 6, 1913)

Matthew 22:29 Jesus answered and said unto them, Ye do err, not knowing the scriptures, nor the power of God.

Jude 1:10 But these speak evil of those things which they know not: but what they know naturally, as brute beasts, in those things they corrupt themselves.

1914: "In [Alexander Campbell's day] **it was a hazardous thing to call in question the infallibility of the King James version**..."
(Charles Clayton Morrison, *The Meaning of Baptism*, 1914)

1914: "To an American generation now rapidly disappearing, there was one great Book, King James' translation of the English Bible. For a certain body of religiously-minded people of that passing generation, it contained a closed and fixed system of knowledge human and divine. It was literature, history, science, philosophy and religion, the guide and precept for life and the pathway to the skies. **The physical Book itself was a sacred incarnation**...It was spiritualized until it mounted to the throne of the eternities. Whatever may have been the limitations of their basic philosophy, who would place small estimate on the culture

values of these old time Bible worshippers?..."
(*Report of the Proceedings by Pennsylvania State Educational Association*, 1914)

1914: "Whatever else our own Revised Version has done or failed to do, it has broken down the superstition which **had erected the Authorized Version, with its titles, headings, and marginal chronology, into a more sacrosanct original than the Greek and Hebrew** themselves."
(*Church Quarterly Review*, Volume 78, 1914)

1914: "I was brought up by my father to **believe that every word in the English Bible was inspired by the Spirit of the living God. There was not one word in it but had the power and authority of God behind it**."
(Edgar Simmons Buchanan, *The Search for the Original Words of the Gospel*, 1914)

1915: "One School Board passed a resolution that the original Bible must be read in the schools under their jurisdiction, not knowing that they were asking the teachers to read the Bible in Hebrew, Greek and Aramaic. A director holding King James' Version in his hand exclaimed: 'The Bible that was good enough for St. Paul is good enough for me.'"
(*The American Educational Review*, Volume 36, American Educational Co., 1915)

See the history listed under "1966."

1915: "About a hundred years after Tyndale, there was published an English version of the Bible which for nearly three centuries was destined to be in a peculiar way **'the Bible,' and the only Bible**, of the vast majority of English-speaking Christians. This was the King James Version or the so-called Authorized Version."
(Harold Bruce Hunting, *The Story of Our Bible*, 1915)

1916: "In the case of the English, this became (**what it remains in some instances to this day**) a conviction of **the direct divine inspiration, the finality and infallibility of the King James Version** of 1611."
(Horace James Bridges, *Some Outlines,* 1916)

1916: "The belief that **every word in the English Bible was inspired by the spirit of God**, and the hard system of dogma that condemns to eternal torment every soul that does not believe in a vindictive God who has prepared an eternal torture for millions of his creatures could not be accepted with satisfaction by the writer."
(*The Biblical World*, Volume 47, 1916)

1917: "Is the King James version absolutely inerrant? On this point we are inclined to think that **even unto comparatively recent years, such a theory has been entertained**..."
(William B. Riley, *The Menace of Modernism*, 1917)

1917: "Let us turn our attention to the first point under discussion for a moment, namely: That the occult scientist does not believe in or accept the Bible in its entirety, as it stands today. Before we begin to draw any conclusions, however, as to who is right on this subject; **the orthodox student who insists that the English text of the King James version of the Bible is absolutely correct from cover to cover, as though it had been originally written in the English language**, or the occult scientist who makes no attempt to vindicate the Bible in the form in which it is commonly known to us today, as the only true and inspired Word of God..."
(*Rays from the Rose Cross, A Magazine of Mystic Light*, Volumes 7-8, Rosicrucian Fellowship, 1917)

Sadly, too many Christian scholars in our day sound more like these "occult scientists" of 1917.

1917: "Those good people who have faith in the literal **inspiration of the English Bible** have, perhaps, more justification for their faith than those who scoff..."
(Grant David Yeats, *The Sword*, 1917)

1918: "But first of all the truly sincere investigator must rid himself of many of his preconceived ideas, chief among which is the belief that either the Bible as we now have it, is the 'Word of God' from cover to cover...**it is** a deplorable fact as stated in the Cosmo, page 318: **'There is a large number of people in this country who insist that the English text of the King James version is absolutely correct from cover to cover, as though the Bible had been originally written in English, and the King James version were a certified copy of the original manuscript.'**"
(*Rays From the Rose Cross: A Magazine of Mystic Light,* Volumes 9-11, Rosicrucian Fellowship, 1918)

These occult writers are contending against a "large number" of KJV Onlyists in 1918, and earlier. The *Cosmo,* that is quoted within the quotation above, was written in 1910 (i.e. Max Heindel, *The Rosicrucian Cosmo-Conception: or, Mystic Christianity*, 1910).

1919: "If you start, as these men did, **with a belief that the King James version is the verbally inspired word of God**, and you desire to be saved, the meaning of the Bible becomes a thing of immense importance."
(Jacob Piatt Dunn, General William Harrison Kemper, *Indiana and Indianans: A History of Aboriginal and Territorial Indiana and the Century of Statehood,* Volume 2, The American Historical Society, 1919)

1919: "*Is the Doxology of the Lord's Prayer Genuine?* - The Catholic priest said it is not...the words are wanting in the... English Revised...Of course, the words are wanting in the Vulgate - hence the belief of your Catholic priest in their spuriousness...I believe that they are genuine, in spite of this traditional attitude of textual critics...The rejection of these words dates from 1514, when the editors of the Complutensian Polyglot, while admitting that the words were found in their Greek copies, banished them from the text solely in deference to the Latin version. In a marginal annotation they started the hypothesis that the doxology is a liturgical interpolation. But how is this possible, seeing that the doxology is commented on by Chrysostom?...When such codices as Bezae, Vaticanus, and Sinaiticus were discovered, which do not contain the words, the critics grew more and more confident...Since 1514 scholars have become acquainted with the Peshitta version (the Syriac translation dating from ca. A. D. 400, and representing a much older text), which in all extant copies contains the words. Then came the ancient Coptic version (third century), and now the *Didache* (of the first or second), both containing the Doxology. Note also that in the fourth century the Gothic translation has it, later the Ethiopic. *Every uncial MS. except the three mentioned,* and *nearly all cursives,* many of them representing a very ancient text, have the verse as it stands in our Textus Receptus!...The Authorized Version still holds its own in the book market. Even since the publication of these revisions it has increased in sales to enormous figures. No version of the Bible in any language, and no other book, has ever approached in circulation the King James Version. I could not recommend to you any of these revised Bibles for use with classes or in the pulpit. The revisers have marred their work by adopting, in some notable instances, a phrasing which rests upon faulty exegesis, and which plainly shows a New Theology bias...A Unitarian, Dr. Ezra Abbot, was an influential member of the American Revision committee...Another of the revisers, and one of the few who lived to see the American Revision published, Dr. Thayer, was closely associated with Dr. Abbott, and edited the Unitarian theologian's *Critical Essays,* in which the deity of Christ is consistently denied. A revision sponsored by men of such New Theology bias can hardly be expected

to serve the purposes of an evangelical denomination..."
(*Homiletic Magazine*, Volume 43, Evangelical Lutheran Synod, 1919)

The Doxology refers to the concluding words of Matthew 6:13, "For thine is the kingdom, and the power, and the glory, for ever. Amen." New versions remove these words, or place them in brackets, casting doubt upon their inspiration. The views of these early Lutherans alone refutes the common, misinformed objection that these textual arguments began with Seventh-Day Adventists in 1930.

1919: "As far back as I can remember, I understood the Bible to be the word of God, every word of it...that it was all divinely inspired, *verbatim et literatim,* **just as it appeared in the old King James version**; that it was God's revelation to mankind, **beside and outside of which there never was, and never would be any** other; that every word of it was literally, and infallibly true, just as it read. Such a thing as figurative, or allegorical interpretations I never heard of until I was a grown man, as we shall see later. This, of course, meant a literal six-day Creation, an anthropomorphic God, a literal physical heaven, and likewise a literal, physical hell, a personal devil, the absolute, literal, truth of the story of Eden, the original perfection and fall of man, total depravity of the race, vicarious atonement and the eternal damnation of all mankind...my parents were members of the Baptist Church...I was brought up in the country districts...I felt that the greatest thing in the world a man could do would be to devote his life to warning men of their danger and pointing the way to safety...While I did not feel that I would be 'lost' if I failed in this...yet I felt that my future happiness in heaven would be diminished just in proportion as I failed to do my best in this behalf...In due course of events I went to college to 'prepare for the ministry'...Here in a 'school of the prophets,' where I was supposed to be thoroughly trained, rooted and grounded in the faith of my church, **I was to learn the first lessons that ulti-**

mately led me entirely out of the orthodox faith, into a broad, rational liberalism!...The first shock I got was in the study of Geology...The professor...explained that the story of creation in Genesis was to be interpreted 'figuratively'...**this was thirty-six years ago**...My idea had always been...that the Bible was inspired word for word, just as it reads. But I found the more progressive and better educated class among both students and professors had abandoned this idea...in a few months I found myself a 'circuit rider' in the Louisiana Conference of the Methodist Episcopal Church, South...I was born and reared in the 'pine hills' of Mississippi...All orthodox Christianity is based upon the doctrine that the Bible is the supernaturally inspired, infallible word of God...Take away this doctrine of Biblical infallibility, and orthodoxy crumbles to dust...**I had naturally supposed that not only the original text was divinely inspired and infallibly correct, but that by some sort of divine supervision, it had been so preserved and kept down thru the ages.** And now I was not only disappointed, but alarmed. I wondered what would come next...I was studying a thoroughly orthodox author, a distinguished professor in one of our leading colleges...if this was what I was getting from such a source...what might I expect from a Biblical scholar and critic [?]...It was years later before I learned to interpret [religious experiences] from the scientific standpoint of psychology... If man was never lost, kidnapped or stolen from God, he needed no *redeemer*...These conclusions I reached...the New Testament, like the Old, is just literature,- no more...The Bible is not the supernaturally inspired, infallible word of God...superstition made of them [i.e. the Books of the Bible] a fetish...I have shown how I was born in the bondage of orthodoxy; and how I was ultimately driven to abandon, not only it, but religion altogether..."
(George Thomas Ashley, *From Bondage to Liberty in Religion*, 1919)

In the above autobiography, Ashley explains how he went from a belief in the infallibility and inspiration of the King James Bible (which was common in his day) to become a modernist Unitarian! He describes how so-called "conservative" schools and textbooks taught him to first doubt the preservation of the Bible. It is too bad that no one ever taught this man as a child that one of the primary proofs of the Bible's inspiration is its supernatural prophecies and amazing scientific foreknowledge (Isaiah 42:9, 41:21-24). And God preserves these inspired Scriptures. He keeps His Word (Psalms 12:6-7). He promised that He would preserve His words, and He cannot lie (Titus 1:2).

1920: "The less intelligent among the Christians tell us that their scriptures are directly inspired by the Holy Ghost...I am sorry to say that they sometimes make themselves ridiculous by carrying it further still, and **saying that every word of the English translation must necessarily also be directly inspired by God**. In fact, I fancy that many of the people who hold that view believe that the original messages were given in English! The nearest approach to rationality along this line is the theory that the same Holy Spirit who inspired the original writers also descended upon the translators and made them do their work with verbal accuracy..."
(Charles Webster Leadbeater, *The Monad: and Other Essays Upon the Higher Consciousness*, Theosophical Publishing House, 1920)

The above writer is a Theosophist (i.e. a New Age, worshipper of Lucifer, etc.). We may therefore be confident that any views he deems to be "less intelligent" are actually worthy of serious investigation! It is extremely common for occult writers to attack the Authorized Version, and praise the Revision.

1920: "Some ministers even speak of the 'St. James Bible,' and think of it as if the medieval version had originated with the Hebrew apostle of the first century, instead of with the British monarch of the seventeenth. I heard a minister in the American capital deprecate 'all this meddling with the Bible,' and declare

that its revision had been a curse..."
(*Homiletic Review*, Volume 79, 1920)

1921: "Unthinking Christians assume that the particular text familiar to them [KJV] is itself the inspired Word, rather than a translation into their living language [ASV]..."
(*Daily Times*, Arkansas, October 18, 1921)

John 7:49 But this people who knoweth not the law are cursed.

1921: "One may say without offence that in the religion of Protestant England there has always been a tendency to an unintelligent Bibliolatry. The very perfection and finality of the Authorized Version was conducive to this."
(R.L. Gales, *Old-World Essays*, 1921)

1922: "The general and well-founded belief that Scripture was the Word of God was stretched until it became a new legalism, until it covered every word of the Authorized Version, and, **in the minds of many**, every comma of the splendid translation."
(John Huston Finley, *Christianity and Problems of Today,* 1922)

1922: "We are thinking now of a letter we received a few days ago from a most sincere Christian who attacks the use of any other than the King James Version, on the ground that this version was, as he declares, **'authorized by God.' This conception of the King James Version is more or less general in many communities**...They attach to it a **God-endued sanctity and authority** different from other versions; and hence they look with much suspicion upon all other versions - and upon those folks who prefer other versions."
(*Herald of Gospel Liberty*, Volume 114, Issues 1-26, March 2, 1922)

1922: "One writer boldly declares that **the King James version is 'a perfect translation'**...Perhaps he would refer for his au-

thority to the statement of Professor William Lyon Phelps (in the introduction to 'Human Nature and the Bible') that, whether the original was inspired or not, the King James version certainly is."
(*The University of Chicago Magazine*, Volumes 15-16, 1922)

1922: "*King James Bible Barred in Schools*...The King James version of the Bible cannot be used in the public schools of California...The opinion of the Appellate Court...holds...that the King James Bible is really the 'book' of the Protestant religion."
(*The New York Times*, November 2, 1922)

1923: In 1923, Edgar J. Goodspeed published his *American Translation.* It received a storm of protest, even by much of the media:

"*Monkeying with the Bible*. The title is not irreverent. It is a statement of fact and a protest. Dr. Edgar J. Goodspeed of the University of Chicago is adding another modern version of the New Testament. There is the *Twentieth Century*, the *Moffatt*, the *Weymouth*, the *Ballantine*, and now there is to be the *Goodspeed* translation. The King James version contains the rarest beauty of the English language. **Tampering with it is chipping a cathedral**. For centuries generations of people speaking the English language and worshipping in Protestant churches have been raised upon its texts. It was expounded to them in childhood before they could appreciate the beauty which was joined to religion. They have not stumbled their way through it. They have not been perplexed by the words the translators used even where words and phrases have lost currency in the modern language. Thousands of people who read very little read this book. It has been what it was intended to be, a guide and consolation and inspiration. It **is a perfect version**, and tampering with it not only spoils the beauty but creates confusion in text. It makes rents in the fabric...It is substituting a signboard for a

work of mural art. It is tearing down a temple to build a warehouse. It is worse than putting Shakespeare into the modern English of the streets..."
(*Chicago Tribune*; quoted in, *Alton Evening Telegraph*, October 12, 1923)

"Not a few of the editors of [daily newspapers]...praised [the KJV]...and ridiculed any effort to improve upon that translation...One editor referred to [Dr. Goodspeed's translation]...as 'Monkeying with the Bible.' Another thought it was tearing down the Bible. Others were sure that the common people could understand every word and every phrase [of the KJV]..."
(*The Pella Chronicle*, Iowa, July 3, 1924)

"Monday morning I was awakened from a troubled sleep by a friend calling, 'Have you seen the *Tribune*?'...the *Tribune's* tribute, entitled 'Monkeying with the Bible'...spoke strongly for the King James version. 'Tampering with it,' it declared, 'is chipping a cathedral.' It regarded the King James version as a seamless coat, a perfect version."
(Edgar Johnson Goodspeed, *As I Remember*, 1953)

1923: "According to **the 'Fundamentalists'** the Bible is inerrant, verbally inspired, the final authority in all matters...the atonement involves an actual cleansing of the sinner by the real blood of Jesus; Jesus is soon coming to set up his kingdom on the earth; the end of the world is near...**Every letter, syllable, word, phrase, clause, sentence, chapter and book is perfect as these now stand in the King James Version of the English Bible**."
(*The Universalist Leader*, Volume 26, 1923)

1924: "The idea of the divine inspiration of the King James Version is still **strongly held** in some quarters..."
(*The Atlantic Monthly*, Volume 133, 1924)

1924: "...some people think that Divine Inspiration was not confined to the writing of the various books but that the King James translation was also divinely inspired...[The] majority of those calling themselves fundamentalists...[believe] every word of the King James Version is infallibly correct."
(*The Universalist Leader*, Volume 27, Issues 1-26, 1924)

1924: "Those who favor the modern Version [RV] will point to the fact that, during the three hundred years that have elapsed since the AV was translated, much material has been discovered whereby additional light is thrown upon the Text. How comes it then that the King James Version has not only maintained its place of supremacy, but of late years has forged further and further ahead of its rival? This surely is a matter worthy of our thoughtful consideration...Briefly then, to sum up the matter thus far, we observe: 1. That the most important and deplorable of the departures of the New Greek Text from the Received Text have been made with the support of less than one percent of all the available witnesses...2. That the two Mss. which had the controlling influence in most of these departures are so corrupt upon their face as to justify the conclusion that they owe their survival solely to their bad reputation...we are justified in believing that it was through a providential ordering that the preparation of that Version was not in anywise affected by higher critical theories in general...For when we consider what the AV was to be to the world, the incomparable influence it was to exert in shaping the course of events, and in accomplishing those eternal purposes of God...when we consider that this Version was to be, more than all others combined, 'the Sword of the Spirit,' and that all this was fully known to God beforehand, we are fully warranted in the belief that it was not through chance, but by providential control of the circumstances, that the translators had access to just those Mss. which were available at that time, and to none others. What shall we then say to these things? Shall we accept the RV (either the English or American) as a substitute for the AV? That

question, we take it, has been settled by the almost unanimous rejection of the modern Versions…We say that the question whether or not the RV should supplant the AV has been **settled by the people themselves**..."
(Philip Mauro, *Authorized or Revised?* 1924)

Philip Mauro (1859-1952) was a believer in stern accountability for Christians at the Judgment Seat of Christ. He knew well the warnings in the Bible about adding to, or taking away from, the words of God:

"As far as twentieth century Christian figures are concerned, Philip Mauro [1859-1952] stands out as one of the most captivating. After coming to a saving knowledge of the Lord in 1903, at the age of forty five, Mauro, a member of the bar of the Supreme Court of the United States and one of the foremost patent lawyers of his day, began his 'Testimony' of what was to him the most important event in his life...Perhaps one of the most important occasions where his legal work was requisitioned was in connection with the famous Tennessee-Scopes trial in 1925. The brief or argument which Bryan used, and thereby won the case, was prepared by Philip Mauro."
(www.schoettlepublishing.com/biographies/pmauro.htm)

1924: "...there has arisen the latest modern religious movement, which is settling down upon the human race like a dense fog. I refer to the popular, apparently insatiable craze to undertake the seemingly insignificant task of correcting the Bible by revision ...Constantly we hear...that, 'such and such' a word is in the original and should be translated 'so and so.' The strange, inexplicable point of it all is that many of these do not know...that the original manuscripts are not in existence, and have not been seen by anyone in modern times. Think of it! All this in the face of God's Definite Warnings [Deut. 4:2; Prov. 30:6; Rev. 22:18-19]...Solemn warnings indeed are these...How

quickly Satan can get people to bow down to scholarship...Let us be warned. Conditions are fast becoming as they were in France just previous to horrible Infidelity and Revolutionary period... Are we blind to the force of a statement such as this: 'You have many different Bibles and no two are alike'? Can you estimate the effect upon the rising generation to have nothing settled? Will our children not soon begin to think that Holy Scripture is a nose of wax to be twisted hither and thither? No wonder the Roman Catholics smile as they say, 'Where does the infallibility of your Bible come in?' What a fog!...'If the foundation be destroyed, what can the righteous do?'...If we grant Modernism the authority to revise and correct our Bibles, we must be prepared to grant...That the translators of the Authorized version were not guided by the Holy Spirit...That, considering the number of modern attempts that have been made, each claiming to be the best rendering, the correct form of translation must be very difficult to ascertain...That, after all is said and done, we can never have an infallible guide upon which to base our faith...I can still believe the Lord Jesus Christ, when he said: 'For verily I say unto you, Till heaven and earth pass, one jot or one tittle shall in no wise pass from the law, till all be fulfilled' (Matt. 5:18). 'Heaven and earth shall pass away, but my words shall not pass away' (Matt. 24:35). If these words mean anything, they inform us that the Lord Jesus intended to see to it that the Bible, His Word, would be preserved for us in a perfect, infallible state..."
(William Aberhart, *Prophetic Voice*, "The Latest of Modern Movements," Oct., 1924)

William Aberhart (1878-1943) was a pastor, popular radio preacher, and statesman in Alberta, Canada. He built a Bible college (the Prophetic Bible Institute). He was the founder of the Bible Institute Baptist Church. He became the seventh Premier of Alberta between 1935 and 1943:

"One of the most prominent, Canadian fundamentalist leaders

during the time of Pankhurt's ministry was William 'Bible Bill' Aberhart. He went so far as to claim that the Authorized Version was inerrant."
(Timothy Larsen, *Christabel Pankhurst: Fundamentalism and Feminism in Coalition,* Boydell Press, 2002)

While Aberhart may not have believed in the *absolute* perfection of the AV (at least as early as 1924), he surely came close! Men like Mauro and Aberhart, in the early 1920s, certainly rebuke the desperate fable that the KJV Only viewpoint, with its various arguments, grew out of Benjamin Wilkinson's book, *Our Authorized Bible Vindicated* in 1930! (Wilkinson was a Seventh-Day Adventist).

1924: "*Bible Re-Writers. In vanity and egotism,* ***some would 'improve' inspired words of King James Version***. These are times when standards, long accepted as forever enduring, are being tossed aside into the discard. It is a heyday for pretenders...This change has come about through the influences of Judaism and Jesuitism. It is found in music. The new, witless, jazz composition speaks for itself...[It] panders to the primitive, bestial, sensual. Likewise in art. Also in most forms of expression of thought and emotion. It is strikingly noticeable in the urge which many have to change the Bible. New versions of the Holy Writ are flooding the bookshops almost as rapidly as new jazz dance pieces and best-selling novels. The King James version of the Bible has been accepted as authoritative for 300 years. But here come a crop of alterers, tamperers, chippers, re-writers who would turn it into a different work. Each of these differ among themselves, as much as they disagree with the King James version. It is confusion worse confounded, a modern tower of Babel. Most of those who are busy in revamping the King James version **do not regard it as the divinely inspired Word.** They do not see in it a message concerning Life, written by those of greatest spiritual elevation in their respective eras. They regard it

as a literary classic and not as the living Word of God. The aim of these is to recast the Bible into 'everyday English.' This gives them free rein to chop and slice as they see fit...American readers do not desire a syncopated Bible, and they turn away from these new versions. Such variety of vanities is the direct result of Jesuit and anti-Christian Jew mental manipulation. It is the work of the anti-Christ. It should be recognized for what it is and be guarded against."
(C. Lewis Fowler, *The American Standard*, Volume 1, New York City, 1924)

Fowler, like many in his day, was able to discern the higher motives behind the new version movement.

He has been accused of racism (a charge he denied). However, those who would attempt to associate the KJV Only position with racism because of Fowler would be wrong for at least two reasons. Fowler is only one of a vast number of examples in this history. Furthermore, a far more sinister racism is associated with modern textual criticism, love of the new versions, and hatred of the King James Bible!

For example, Westcott and Hort were the men behind the Revised Version (and the new versions that have been derived from their Greek text). They believed in evolution (a racist theory, especially at the time). And notice the following racist quote from Hort:

"...everywhere (not in slavery only) they [blacks] have surely shown themselves only as an **immeasurably inferior race**, **just human and no more**, their religion frothy and sensuous, **their highest virtues, those of a good Newfoundland dog**..."
(Arthur Fenton Hort, *Life and Letters of Fenton John Anthony Hort*, Volume 1, 1896)

Hort's wicked views concerning the races were similar to those of H. P. Blavatsky, an open follower of Lucifer, in her *Secret Doctrine* (she likewise despised the King James Bible).

Furthermore, notice the words of Duren James Henderson Ward (1851-1942), a Unitarian minister, concerning the Authorized Version:

"The **White Race** is facing its third Crisis...Protestantism is practically doing what its founders would have called 'giving up the Bible'...the old-time preacher is still here threatening Divine retribution upon all who yield to the new...Although the whole Jewish literature was virtually adopted...yet the Aryan thinkers have always been against it...**Aryans** [are] now developing their own faith...To [science]...belongs the future...**As it stands, the 'Authorized Version' is the worst hindrance now menacing civilization**...Bibliolatry is getting supplanted by Rationality."
(Duren J. H. Ward, *A Receivership for Civilization*, 1922)

Like Margaret Sanger, Hitler, and other "Nazi" types, Duren J. H. Ward viewed the discarding of the old, Bible-based Christianity, as "progress." And like all of these infidels, he hated the KJV-Only doctrine as a menace and hindrance to civilization!

Therefore, Fowler's KJV Onlyism was not due to any racism, any more than his constant defense of the right for every man to read the Bible and have freedom of religion was racist. As seen from this history, these convictions were discernable to a great number of Christians from all walks of life.

1925: "The popular attitude toward this question of translations varies very widely. There is the reader utterly indifferent; [and] **there is the one to whom any departure from the King James version is unpardonable sacrilege**...it seems clear to me that some admirers go past reason to an almost fanatical worship of

the King James translation."
(*The Lethbridge Herald*, Canada, January 10, 1925)

1925: "The efforts of those who desire to 'improve' on the Bible by revising the King James version have not been very successful as measured by the majority-mind....Nobody has yet improved upon the inspired stylists of the King James version. The Bible cannot be syncopated without something not far from sacrilege, any more than the lily can be painted or refined gold gilded..."
(*Bluefield Daily Telegraph*, West Virginia, January 11, 1925)

1925: "...you have the King James' version, and a revised version and there are 30,000 differences between the King James' version and it...Who is to say that the King James version is the Bible?...***Stewart Claims St. James Version standard in Tennessee*****...the St. James Version of the Bible is the recognized one in this section of the country**...The defense counsel, of course, disclaims any knowledge on the subject...but this witness would testify that the King James version is not an accurate translation...Indictment was based on the King James Version of the Bible...Catholics claim there are examples of wilful perversion of the Scriptures in the King James' translation..."
(*The World's Most Famous Court Trial*, The Lawbook Exchange, Ltd.,1925)

The above record of the famous Scopes Monkey Trial reveals that infidels and Catholics rejected the King James Bible; but the good, Christian people of Tennessee saw it as *the standard* (see the history under "1931").

1926: "Very well; let me say to you as the young curate did to his astonished congregation: 'If the King James Version was good enough for Saint Paul, it is good enough for me.'"
(Alfred Edward Newton, *The Greatest Book in the World*, 1926)

1926: "It might be held to be sacrilege, tampering with divine things, to discard a word used in the King James Bible."
(Ethan Allen Cross, *Fundamentals in English*, 1926)

1926: "There are, of course, some persons to whom a new English translation of any part of the Holy Scriptures seems a sacrilege...The old version is regarded as faultless and something more."
(*Saturday Review,* Volume 3, 1926)

1927: "Many of them also hold strong views upon election and predestination; basing these upon rigid belief in the verbal inspiration of the 'Authorized Version'..."
(Frank Ballard, *Twentieth-century Christianity*, 1927)

1928: "...the English Bible, and specifically the King James version, is losing, or has already lost, a power over the imagination almost unexampled in history. It was couched in a prose so rich with the genius of a great language, and **so invariably read with reverence, love, or fear, that there is perhaps no equivalent instance of the style as well as the substance of a single book influencing and sometimes dominating the mold of thought and form of expression of a whole people**. The Bible, for English speakers from the seventeenth century on, was the Word...The Logos, for English readers, was neither reason nor the Divine expression as such, but the Word of a sacred Book...The most sophisticated megalopolitan can not read Isaiah today, or Paul, without yielding to the spell...Enter to scoff and you remain to be stirred and exalted...It is as the Word, in the sense which English readers understood, that the English Bible is dying...Whatever statistics may show as to the sales and distribution of the English Bible, it is not read as it once was. Our daily conversation, our writing, and our speaking prove this too readily. *Ye shall know them by their fruits* applies to books as well as to men. Even fundamentalists are modern...if the Bible is read

weekly in churches, it is clear that neither preacher nor congregation listen as they once listened to the Word."
(Henry Seidel Canby, *Saturday Review*, 1928)

1929: "...public opinion had been left undisturbed for two-hundred and fifty years to settle its faith undisputedly upon one version of the English Bible as the sacred Word of God...to the people at large the inspiration of the words of Scripture meant the words of their English Bible. To revise it meant to them to tamper with something sacred...Dr. Hoare tells of a young deacon who argued that if the Authorized Version was good enough for St. Paul, it was good enough for him."
(Laura H. Wild, *The Romance of the English Bible*, 1929)

1929: "...if he means by that a retranslation of the King James' Bible into Twentieth Century English he is wanting something he cannot get. When the Bible is presented in any other form than the Authorized Version it ceases to be the Bible...This [new translation], of course, would be the end of the English Bible. The language of the Authorized Version is the authentic gold of English speech..."
(*Winnipeg Free Press*, Canada, January 29, 1929)

The above writer appears to be arguing from a literary viewpoint. Even Pilate and his wife knew that Jesus was just, and that He was being accused by the chief priests and elders because they envied Him (Matthew 27:18-19). Pilate even called Jesus "the King of the Jews" (John 19:14-15, 19-22). In like manner, it is tragic when some outside of Christian circles appear to have more faith in the preserved Word of God than many Christian leaders!

1930: "...a man of North Carolina, named David F. Jones... proposed to come to Japan for two hundred dollars a year...**His faith in the verbal inspiration of the English version** of the Bible

was unique. But he made converts..."
(*The Missionary Herald*, 1930)

1930: "To tamper with such majesty of phrase would seem a sacrilege second only to tampering with that literary as well as spiritual foundation stone of our people, the King James version of the Bible. The elemental cannot be improved upon..."
(Quincy Sharpe Mills, *Editorials, Sketches and Stories*, 1930)

1931: "As a facetious liberalist once wrote, **fundamentalists believe** that one fair morning God dispatched to this planet a corps of angels bearing a copious edition of King James Bibles freshly printed and neatly bound in black leather with gilt-edged pages...it would be very difficult for him to show that this is not the view of the matter **implicitly held by a vast majority of orthodox Christians in England and America**. As an actual matter of fact, such persons will make their belief explicit on this point under questioning. Such was the case with the **Tennessee legislator, Mr. Butler**, who drafted the law under which Mr. Scopes was tried in 1925. He told Charles Francis Potter quite frankly that **he thought God used the language of the King James version when dictating the Pentateuch to Moses.** He saw nothing wrong with such a conviction. Here was a far more than averagely well informed member of Mr. Gaebelein's fold. **Such notions have been found universal in extensive samplings of orthodox belief on this point which it has been my privilege to make in many parts** of the United States."
(*The North American Review,* Volume 232, 1931)

John Washington Butler (1875-1952) was the writer of the *Butler Act* (prohibiting the teaching of the Evolution Theory in public schools). He (like so many of his neighbors) raised his family on the letter of the King James Bible:

"...expressing the view that the Bible had been dictated by God

in the English of the King James version. The bill passed by the astounding majorities..."
(Willard Thorp, *A Southern Reader*, 1955)

"...many of the members of which [the Tennessee legislature of 1925] actually believed that God had dictated this revelation to Moses in the faultless English prose of the King James version of the Bible."
(Harry Elmer Barnes, *Living in the Twentieth Century*, 1932)

1931: "...so long as the Bible is a fetish, the King James version will be THE WORD."
(George Amos Dorsey, *Man's Own Show: Civilization*, 1931)

1931: "...the multitude of English-speaking Christians who... know only the Bible of King James' translators and believe that any verbal changes in it constitutes a tampering with the inspired Word of God. To such as these, brought up in the atmosphere of the 'old time religion,' the Revised Version...was looked upon with suspicion as the work, perhaps, of unsanctified men, careless how they undermined the foundations of faith...the Revised Version is not generally read..."
(*San Antonio Express*, October 25, 1931)

1932: "In all these instances the Bible means the translation authorized by King James the First...they made a translation so magnificent that **to this day the common human Britisher or citizen of the United States...accepts and worships it as a single book by a single author, the book being the Book of Books and the author being God**."
(George Bernard Shaw, *The Adventures of the Black Girl in Her Search for God*, 1932; from his explanatory notes at end of the play)

1932: "The Chicago University is announcing its new edition of the Bible, of which Drs. Edgar Goodspeed and J.M.P. Smith are

the authors...There is the Jefferson Bible with all of the miracles of the Lord left out, and Moffat's translation which many 'nomodidaskaloi,' teachers of the law, or doctors of divinity like so much, and all the sacredness seems to be sifted out of it. Well, the King James Version is still good enough for me and shall continue to be **my only book**."
(J.M. Fleming, *The Robesonian,* North Carolina, January 4, 1932)

1932: "It is high time, therefore, that the superstitious reverence with which this version [KJV] has been regarded should be challenged."
(Arthur Evill Overbury, *The People's New Testament,* 1932)

1933: "Adam Liked It Too...The preacher was reading the Scripture when an old lady broke in, 'What kind of a Bible are you using parson?' 'I'm reading from the revised version,' he answered. [She replied,] 'The King James version was good enough for St. Paul and it's good enough for me."
(*Hope Star*, December 19, 1933)

Statements such as these continue to reveal the many people who believed the King James Bible is a duplicate of the Originals. (See 1966 in this history).

1934: "One grows a little weary of the continual laudation of the Authorized Version for any and every purpose. That attitude is summed up in the answer of an old patriarch when he was offered one of the newer translations of the Bible: 'If the Authorized Version was good enough for Jesus it is good enough for me.' The Authorized Version has become sacrosanct..."
(*Amherst Graduates Quarterly*, Vol. 24, 1934)

1935: "It reveals the colossal ignorance of the people who think that **God authorized** the **King James version** and no other."
(*The Christian Leader*, Volume 38, Part 2, 1935)

Matthew 21:26 But if we shall say, Of men; we fear **the people**; for **all** hold John as a prophet.

Mark 12:37...And **the common people heard him gladly**.

1935: "But there are queer notions held by people about the King James version...Another impression is that the King James version is 'the authorized Bible.' In fact it is the third authorized English version. Other versions have been authorized since. But, as Goodspeed says, 'the tragic thing is that **the people** who still call it the authorized version, mean by it **divinely authorized**'...**Sometimes the statement is made that 'the King James version is the sole, unique, divine Bible, untouched by human hands**'...Instead of honoring God the dogma of Bible infallibility has dishonored some of the noblest sons of God ..."
(*The Universalist Leader*, Volume 38, Issue 44, 1935)

John 7:46 The officers answered, Never man spake like this man.
47 Then answered them the Pharisees, Are ye also deceived?
48 Have any of the rulers or of the Pharisees believed on him?
49 But this people who knoweth not the law are cursed.

2 Corinthians 2:17 For we are not as many, which corrupt the word of God...

1936: "Unfortunately the King James Version came finally to be considered as itself divinely inspired, and **the idea is not entirely gone**...People who so venerate the King James Version imagine that what they have today is an exact duplicate of that which appeared originally."
(Paris Marion Simms, *The Bible in America*, 1936)

1936: "For all his Fundamentalism, Evangelist [Harry] Ironside handsomely admits: 'I know the King James's Version didn't fall from heaven bound in morocco.'"
(*Time Magazine*, December 14, 1936)

The fact that Ironside felt that he had to make this statement, and the apparent surprise in the writer of the article, reveals the great extent that Fundamentalism was identified with belief in the inspiration and infallibility of the King James Bible.

1936: "He [John Wesley] is far removed from those of his followers who worship the letter of the authorized version..."
(The *Christian Student*, Vol. 37, 1936)

1937: "Not many people would agree with the deacon who said 'the King James Version was good enough for Paul and it's good enough for me,' but **large numbers do seem to regard that version as verbally inspired**."
(*Bulletin*, Volumes 10-11, Colgate Rochester Divinity School, 1937)

1937: "...[my parents] firmly believed in the direct and infallible inspiration of the Authorised Version of the English Bible."
(*The Congregational Quarterly*, Volume 15, 1937)

1938: "The King James Version has a rare distinction. As a translation of two great languages in antiquity...it has given to the world a literature greater than that of the original tongues."
(Wilbur Owen Sypherd, *The Literature of the English Bible*, 1938)

1939: "Some people seem to think that God handed down the Ten Commandments to Moses in perfect King James English. One student refused to learn Greek because he felt that if English was good enough for Jesus Christ, it was good enough for him."
(Wayland Farries Vaughan, *General Psychology*, 1939)

1 Corinthians 1:20 Where is the wise? where is the scribe? where is the disputer of this world? hath not God made foolish the wisdom of this world?
27 But God hath chosen the foolish things of the world to confound the wise; and God hath chosen the weak things of the world to confound the things which are mighty;

1940: "Their minds are in the grip of the hydra-headed monster of tradition, ignorance and prejudice...A religious woman went to purchase a Bible. The shop-assistant set before her copies of the Authorized Version, the Revised Version, Dr. Ferrar's *Bible in Modern English* and Dr. Moffatt's *The Bible: A New Translation*, and politely asked, 'Which version, madam, do you require?' **The woman replied heatedly, 'I don't want any of your versions. I want the Bible as God gave it to us.**'"
(Graeme Maurice Elliot, *Spiritualism in the Old Testament,* The Psychic Book Club, 1940)

These necromancers mock KJV Onlyism. It is no wonder; the new versions they praise are derived from the fathers of modern necromancy! Nevertheless, Elliot reveals one more unnamed woman to add to the growing list of KJV Onlyists in history.

1941: "...holding in his hands perhaps a copy of the King James version in limp leather binding to add to his oratorical effect...**to the vast majority it remains 'the Word of God' in some 'infallible' or 'supernatural' sense**..."
(*The Universalist Leader,* Volume 123, 1941)

1942: "We knew an ancient brother in Iowa who held stoutly that the King James translation of the Bible was verbally inspired, and that all other translations were, therefore, heterodox..."
(*Encounter*, Volume 3, Christian Theological Seminary, 1942)

1943: "Manning quickly placed his own imprint on his men-

tor's [Aberhart's] radio ministry when he inherited it in 1943...*Back to the Bible Hour* and its brand of fundamentalist religion translated across Alberta's borders with **the central message of the inerrant King James Bible** and dispensationalism...**Manning was most concerned over the status of the King James Bible; he was firmly convinced that only the King James Version was 'the verbally inspired and divinely preserved infallible word of the living God.'** Any other translation was a 'corruption.' He rejected the pragmatic position of many evangelicals that the new translations of the Bible should be supported if they made it easier to understand...The only result of the explosion of biblical translations that Manning could see was widespread confusion and doubt...Manning was in the same camp as the most committed and perhaps militant fundamentalists...the low status of the Bible...the rising apostasy within the churches...as well as the fact that the Jews had never been so persecuted and were on an exodus to Palestine were all clear signs that 'Christ's personal return must be very near at hand.'"
(Marguerite Van Die, *Religion and Public Life in Canada*, University of Toronto Press, 2001)

Ernest C. Manning (1908-1996) was the premier of Alberta for 25 years. Manning was the first graduate of Aberhart's Calgary Prophetic Bible Institute in 1927.

1944: "...we will have to undo much that is cherished error. The problem of revising the Bible shows how difficult it is to do this. For the last hundred years, we have been trying to get out an edition of the Bible that is reasonably correct; but nobody wants it. What's wanted is the good old King James version, every jot and tittle of it, because **most people are convinced that God dictated the Bible to King James in English**."
(Manly P. Hall, *Horizon*, "Asia in the Balance of the Scales," Volume 4, No. 1, 1944)

Many P. Hall was one of the most influential occult writers. He was also a 33° Mason. In the above quote, this occultist is complaining that their "plans" were being hindered by KJV Onlyists! It is clear from such testimonies that there were enough KJV Onlyists around to trouble men like Hall:

"The **enthusiastic jot and tittle worshipper will insist that the words of the King James version are the words of God Himself**...every statement contained in the Bible should be checked with the Greek and Hebrew originals...The oldest existing codices of the New Testament reveal considerable change and amendment. The King James version omits a number of passages...the Bible student is not justified in accepting the King James version as an infallible production..."
(Manly P. Hall, *How to Understand Your Bible*, 1942)

Too many "conservative" scholars and teachers today share the views of this Lucifer-worshipping occult leader concerning the King James Bible and textual criticism.

1944: "But there will be others who feel that it is a sacrilege to alter a word of the 1611 'authorized' version of the Bible."
(*The University of Chicago Magazine*, Volumes 37-38, 1944)

1945: "The book itself was holy. Nothing might be laid upon it ...The *Authorized Version* was itself sacred, and talk of revision or correction was blasphemy..."
(Henry Wood Nevinson, *Visions and Memories*, Oxford University Press, 1945)

1945: "...so far as the generality of English-speaking people was concerned, the King James Version was the Bible...its every comma sacrosanct. Its cadences became the warp and woof of common thought."
(Lawrence Emerson Nelson, *Our Roving Bible*, 1945)

1945: "The King James version of the Bible is the best there is or ever has been or will be, and you get a bunch of college professors spending *years* working on it, and all they do is take the poetry out of it."
(President Harry S. Truman, quoted in, Merle Miller, *Plain Speaking: An Oral Biography of Harry S. Truman,* 1985)

Truman made this statement during a meeting in his office with Rabbi Stephen S. Wise in April 20, 1945.

1946: "**Many** religionists of the English-speaking realm...have a hazy notion that [the Bible] was written in heaven, in English, of course...They skittishly shy away from the *American Standard Version* and other modern translations of the Bible, thinking that their religiously venerated King James Version Bible is **the only** true Bible."
(*Equipped for Every Good Work,* Watchtower Bible and Tract Society, 1946)

The so-called Jehovah's Witnesses had to contend with the King James Bible Only movement in 1946. They love the textual criticism behind the new versions (e.g. they use the Greek text of Wescott and Hort in their *Kingdom Interlinear Translation of the Greek Scriptures*):

"...the earlier the manuscript the more likely it is to be correct...Many other translations have followed after the King James Version, keeping pace with the evolving languages. Older manuscripts have been found and knowledge of Greek and Hebrew has been increased, making possible more accurate translations. A noteworthy illustration of this is the *American Standard Version* of 1901."
(*Ibid.*)

In the above book (and other publications), they constantly attempt to "correct" the King James Bible with the American

Standard Version; and they praise the Vatican and Sinaiticas manuscripts. For example, notice their praise for the new versions in regard to 1 John 5:7:

"Next looms up that text so often quoted by the trinitarians, 1 John 5:7, according to the King James Version Bible. It does not appear in the old manuscripts Vatican...Sinaitic, and Alexandrine...all modern versions rightly omit this spurious text...The modern and accurate American Standard Version Bible correctly renders this portion of the epistle..."
(*Ibid.*)

1946: "'It could almost be predicted,' Dr. [Edgard Franklin] Romig said, 'that some people would criticize the new translation [RSV] from the Greek on ground that **the King James version could not be improved.** As literature it cannot be improved upon..."
(*The New York Times*, February 18, 1946)

1946: "Mr. Gilbert claims that the King James Version of the Bible contains 20,000 errors. This version has so long held undisputed sway that **most of its readers scarcely think of any other as the true Bible.**"
(*Council Bluffs Nonpareil*, Iowa, April 25, 1946)

1946: "When a Bible teacher refers to the original languages of the Bible, there is a danger of giving a wrong impression about the authority and true value of the standard King James Version. Too many are ready to say that they have a better rendering, and often in such a way as to give an impression that the King James Version is faulty, or that other versions are much better. We believe that God overruled His gift of the King James Version of 1611, so that we have in it the very Word of God."
(Le Baron Wilmont Kinney, *Acres of Rubies*, Loizeaux, 1946)

1947: "But perhaps more harm is done by extreme 'fundamentalists' who make a fetish out of the Bible...I have actually met people who seem to think that the King James Version of the Bible was written by the hand of God, with every punctuation mark and every chapter heading divinely certified."
(Walter Dewey Ferguson, *Journey Through the Bible*, 1947)

1948: "She would ban all teachings of the Scriptures...And she objects to **teaching that the King James version of the Bible 'is called the Christian's Guide Book, the Holy Writ and the Word of God'**..."
(*America*, Volume 79, America Press, 1948)

Vashti McCollum was the mother of a student enrolled in the Champaign, Illinois public school district. She was an avowed Atheist. The school (like many at the time) was setting aside "release time" in classrooms for religious instruction. McCollum protested, among other things, the King James Bible being called the Word of God, etc. Her case, *McCollum v. Board of Education*, 333 U.S. 203 (1948), was ruled upon by the U.S. Supreme Court in 1948.

2 Timothy 2:9...but the word of God is not bound.

1949: "The exact words of the Bible were believed to have been dictated by God...In more recent times, **many laymen** have mistakenly thought that the King James version was the original Bible..."
(Edgar Monroe McKown, Carl J. Scherzer, *Understanding Christianity*, 1949)

CHAPTER 11

1950-2011

1950: "My people, especially my father, had believed in the literal **inspiration of the English Bible**."
(James Henry Cousins, Margaret E. Cousins, *We Two Together,* 1950)

1951: "In popular practice fundamentalists have claimed infallibility for a particular version of the Bible: the King James Version of 1611!"
(Bernhard W. Anderson, *Rediscovering the Bible,* 1951)

1952: "Some people think **the King James is the original**...[But so] far as is known today, there is not one word of the original Bible in existence. It was lost during the era of early Christian persecution."
(*Gastonia Gazette*, North Carolina, December 3, 1952)

1952: "Various ministers I have heard over a period of years seem to refer to the King James Bible as the Bible..."
(*Oakland Tribune*, October 23, 1952)

1952: "I don't think I would care to replace it with any modern book. I have all my life heard it preached from the pulpit of many denominations that the King James version is the word of God revealed to man through spiritual inspiration...None of the so-called modern translators have had any fear of being burned at the stake, and it would seem they have more desire for popularity than to be trying to save the soul of humanity. The new [version] that is now coming out has the earmarking of trying to establish a

profitable publishing business."
(*Austin Daily Herald,* Minnesota, December 11, 1952)

1953: "...the King James Version, which is the Bible. It not only contains truth about God - it came from God...But some perhaps will wonder whether the King James Version is completely beyond improvement. **This writer holds the conviction that the Book is inspired; that it has its origin from above**...It was the King James Version of the Bible, based on the Received Text, which was the foundation of all the great evangelical Protestant churches...This God-given Book has lost nothing either of its value or its power. It has been assailed before...But it carries on and is always victorious. It has strength and an inherent power which derives from its eternal author...it yields a spiritual power to him that reads and practices its teachings...the modernist reviser has been taught to doubt. So he doubts."
(Elton A. Jones, *Which Bible?,* California, 1953, 1960)

Elton A. Jones appears to be a Seventh-Day-Adventist; however, he quotes numerous Christian writers in his day that reproved and exposed the new versions. It is commonly asserted that KJV Onlyism began with a Seventh-Day-Adventist named Benjamin G. Wilkinson (*Our Authorized Bible Vindicated*, 1930). This history documents the absurdity of that claim. Bible believing Christians no more gleaned KJV Onlyism from Seventh-Day-Adventists, than they gleaned premillennialism from them. Unlike Jones, above, Wilkinson did not even believe in the inspiration and/or infallibility of the King James Bible! He wrote:

"The original Scriptures were written by direct inspiration of God. This can hardly be said of any translation."

But he did strongly advocate that the new versions were rooted in modernism.

The fact that the KJV Only position is embraced by a few Adventists, etc., is nothing compared to the innumerable multitude of infidels, modernists, liberals, Unitarians, Roman Catholics, Universalists, free-thinkers, Theosophists, Russellites, etc., who believe the KJV is faulty, and in need of revision based on the modern findings of textual criticism, etc.

1953: "A hundred years ago **most Christians** believed that the Bible was an infallible book, verbally inspired by God. In the case of English-speaking Christians that Bible was our familiar King James version. This belief still survives..."
(Willard Learoyd Sperry, *Sermons Preached at Harvard*, Harper, 1953)

1953: "A United Presbyterian upbringing that hued mighty close to the fundamentalist lines in a consistent fashion impressed us with a firm conviction the King James Bible was a perfect literary work divinely inspired."
(*Carroll Daily Times Herald*, February 27, 1953)

1954: "One young woman of my acquaintance...exclaimed, 'The King James Version was good enough for St. Paul and it's good enough for me.'"
(Louis Booker Wright, *The British Tradition in America*, 1954)

1954: "...the King James Bible has become the Bible for the pious. It seems to have its own aura of oracular inerrancy. Modern translations are viewed with alarm by the ultra-traditionalists..."
(Phillips Endecott Osgood, *Religion Without Magic,* 1954)

1955: "...fanatical fundamentalists, **believing the King James Version of the Bible to be infallible**, have burnt the Revised..."
(William Hordern, *A Layman's Guide to Protestant Theology*, 1955)

1955: "In common with other Christian bodies, the Disciples have their fundamentalists and their liberals. The literalists, or fundamentalists, **accept every word of the Authorized Version of the Bible as a final and infallible word of God.** The liberals believe that newer translations of the original tongues, and the studies of inspired scholars, have thrown new light upon many passages of the Scriptures."
(Leo Calvin Rosten, *A Guide to the Religions of America: The Famous Look Magazine Series on Religion*, Simon and Schuster, 1955)

1955: "This Old Time Religion is but another of the variant forms of American Protestantism...The adherents of this faith apparently look upon the Bible as a book dropped down from heaven, already translated into **the King's English, correct and infallible down to every dot and comma**. They oppose new translations..."
(*Liguorian*, Volume 43, 1955)

1956: "When I heard one...**insist on the absolute literal infallibility of the King James version of the Bible**, I usually maintained a respectful silence..."
(Rockwell Dennis Hunt, *Mr. California: The Autobiography of Rockwell D. Hunt*, 1956)

1956: "In practice most Englishmen believed in the inspiration of the Authorized Version (hence the alarm over textual criticism and revision)..."
(L. E. Elliot-Binns, *English Thought, 1860-1900*, 1956)

1956: "...the beloved King James Version of our day and time! **Today millions** worship this version with a positive idolatry! ...Those who figure that if the King James Version was good enough for Paul and Silas it is good enough for them and, therefore they'll have no truck with the new Bible!"
(*Beckley Post Herald*, October 31, 1956)

1956: "...the King James Version is the historic Bible of English-speaking Protestants. Upon it God, working providentially, has placed the stamp of His approval through the usage of many generations of Bible-believing Christians. Hence, if we believe in God's providential preservation of the Scriptures, we will retain the King James Version, for in so doing we will be following the clear leading of the Almighty."
(Edward Hills, *The King James Version Defended*, 1956)

Edward Freer Hills (1912-1981) was a distinguished Latin and Phi Beta Kappa graduate of Yale University. He completed his doctorate at Harvard in New Testament textual criticism. Hills apparently believed the KJV was "practically perfect." He believed that those who defend it are providentially used by God to preserve His Holy Scriptures.

1957: "...this book [RSV] is not the Bible, but a misconception of the Scriptures to make merchandise of the Bible and to destroy the Christian Faith. God has always preserved His word and He will continue to do so."
(*The Gastonia Gazette*, October 12, 1957)

1957: "*King James Bible Still Outsells Revised Standard*...The 'RSV' has been a phenomenal success...But it has NOT taken the place of the 346-year-old King James Bible. And it begins to seem doubtful that it will ever do so. The King James Version still outsells the RSV by a ratio of about 8 to 1..."
(*Lebanon Daily News*, Pennsylvania, October 26, 1957)

1957: "To the Fundamentalists faith is coextensive with the Bible, the King James' version of the Bible."
(Gail Kennedy, *Evolution and Religion*, 1957)

1957: "I believe that the King James edition of the Bible is holding first place in the hearts and minds of our people. I for

one believe it is the true word of God and nothing will ever replace the word of God. It will stand when the world is on fire (II Peter, 1-21)...Man cannot understand it other than by the Holy Ghost, which the Revised Standard Version doesn't accept...J.M. Western."
(*The Anniston Star*, Alabama, October 31, 1957)

1958: "There are devout Christians who suppose that the King James Version of the Bible is infallible, and any departure from it is a betrayal of the faith..."
(Millar Burrows, *More Light on the Dead Sea Scrolls*, 1958)

1958: "The Authorized Version of King James, the translation counted as 'the' Bible by the great mass of English-speaking Christians across the last two centuries..."
(Harold L. Phillips, *Translators and Translations*, 1958)

1959: "As for me, I will take the King James translation as the very Word of God for the English people. I believe it is without error. It is 100 percent correct...people who do not know a word of Greek can become real Bible scholars. Many times their understanding is far greater than the Greek scholars."
(B.F. Dearmore, *The Message*, "Greek Versus English," May 28, 1959)

Benjamin F. Dearmore was the founding pastor of South Fort Worth Baptist Temple; he also founded such institutions as Worth Bible College.

1959: "..the fundamentalist...identifies the Word of God with the seventeenth-century language forms of the King James Version...he concludes that someone is tampering with the Word of God..."
(Edward John Carnell, *The Case for Orthodoxy*, 1959)

1959: "...the preacher read from the American Standard Ver-

sion...'That was interesting, but prefer the Bible.' For him and thousands like him, the King James is the only form in which the real Bible ever appeared."
(Fred Gladstone Bratton, *A History of the Bible*, 1959)

1960: "I note your Bible quotes are taken from the Revised Standard version. Why not the King James version? When one reads that Pro-Communist 'revised' it should make us all aware of what is happening to our churches."
(*Hutchinson News*, December 2, 1960)

1960: "The movie [*Inherit the Wind*] will surely stir up fundamentalist Biblical defenders who regard the King James version as being the literal words of the Nazarene and who insist they must, therefore, be taken literally."
(*Charleston Gazette*, West Virginia, August 20, 1960)

1961: "...the King James 'Authorized' Bible...Many Christians cling to it as inspired and therefore sacred."
(Frederick Clifton Grant, *Translating the Bible*, 1961)

1961: "'I have read the series on Bible translations in the Lutheran *Witness* (Nov. 29 and Dec. 27, 1960, Jan. 24, 1961). I am sorry to say that I cannot help but resent the inference that the King James Version is obsolete. The general tone of the articles seems to sell the RSV, and I can never accept this translation for two reasons. The first is the translation of Isaiah 7:14, which in my humble interpretation rejects the divinity of Christ. The second reason is that the National Council of Churches collects a royalty on every RSV copy sold. I am a member of the Missouri Synod, not only because it has upheld the fundamental Christian truths but because I am a fugitive from the social doctrines of the NCC. Please let's stand by the eternal truths and not be taken in by modernism.' Dearborn, Mich., Mrs. J. W. Mason...'I have been thoroughly shocked by the articles pertaining to the RSV

and King James Versions. **To me, the King James is the inspired Word of God and always will be**. We have no business trying to translate it into the modern-day language to suit certain men. I know that I am not the only one who is not in favor of the RSV. Why not print a few of these letters that come to you and let the people know that not everyone is in favor of it?' Taylor, Mich. Mrs. Margaret Theis...'There must be someone down in Saint Louis who still loves the King James Version as we do, who would write an article *for* **our Bible**. When people are continually picking apart and changing **our Bible** they are certainly undermining the very foundations of our faith.' Taylor, Mich., Alton F. Sell...'Have our people fallen to such intellectual depths that they can no longer understand beautiful English when they read it? Someone has rightly said, 'The King James Version is the product of an age of faith.' Most of today's translations are products of a new age of unbelief.' Taylor, Mich., Theodore Smithey...'I have two children, one a teen-ager and the other eight years of age. They each received a Bible (King James Version)...They seem to have no trouble reading and understanding it....'"
(*The Lutheran Witness*, Volume 80, 1961)

1961: "One elderly lady gave coin to the feeling that all other translations of the Bible are heretical. 'Give me the good old King James Bible,' she said, 'exactly like the Apostle Paul wrote it'...there are **hundreds of thousands** of readers by whom this (KJV) is accepted as 'The Word of God' in a sense which no other version would be so accepted..."
(*Big Spring Daily Herald,* March 26, 1961)

1961: "...the King James is preferred of course by the literary people, by the orators, and by the masses. It might surprise you to know how **many** otherwise intelligent people there are in this world who believe that the 'King James Version' is the only 'inspired' version and that only 'heretics' use the revised...**the**

majority of people believe that the King James Version is the only 'inspired' version..."
(Billy James Hargis, *Christian Crusade*, Volumes 13-14, 1961)

1962: "Raymond A. Horn, Mooresville, NC, said he came up believing in the verbal **inspiration of the King James Bible**."
(*Presbyterian Outlook*, 1962)

1962: "In this view the King James Version of the Bible becomes infallible, a paper pope, as contrasted to the living Pope in Rome. Those who hold it believe that the Bible as God's Word is not only definitive, but terminal."
(Leonard Griffith, *What is a Christian?,* 1962)

1962: "Now some among us seem to assume the King James Version is inspired."
(*The Lutheran Witness,* Vol. 81, 1962)

1962: "I have known sincere Christians who believed that every word of the 'Authorized Version' was divinely inspired."
(Victor Paul Wierwille, *Receiving the Holy Spirit Today*, 1962)

1963: "These revisions were most disturbing to those who believed in the verbal **inspiration of the King James version**..."
(Clifford Merrill Drury, *San Francisco YMCA: 100 Years by the Golden Gate, 1853-1953*, 1963)

1963: "If anything in our literary past is held sacrosanct...it is the King James version. Merely to lay hands on it with a view to alteration raises the hackles of **thousands** of readers..."
(James Donald Adams, *The Magic and Mystery of Words*, 1963)

1963: "...a group that is no longer interested in the Greek or Hebrew...but who profoundly believe that the King James Version is an inspired translation..."
(Margaretta K. Bowers, *Conflicts of the Clergy*, 1963)

1963: "In this country there are those who blast any version save the King James Version as false, heretical..."
(*The Lutheran Standard,* Vol. 3, 1963)

1964: "It would be difficult to state more clearly the case for the divine inspiration of translators. Moreover, this view has certainly not died out. For example, **people not infrequently** ask the Bible societies whether they publish the King James Version in Japanese or the King James Version in Spanish, **implying that they regard the King James Version as in a special sense divinely inspired**...In contrast to the views of St. Augustine and his present-day successors, Jerome was completely opposed to the idea of the divine inspiration of translators."
(Eugene Albert Nida, *Toward a Science of Translating*, 1964)

1964: "But there are still some who hold to the conservative view of the Bible, chiefly because they have not been instructed otherwise. **They think that every word is inspired**, forgetting that our English Bible is a translation from Hebrew and Greek... The story of Genesis they accept as history."
(Dr. Robert Harvey, *Winnipeg Free Press*, Canada, November 7, 1964)

1964: In this year, Dr. Peter Ruckman published his first book, *Bible Babel,* on the Bible translation controversy. He is well-known for his numerous books, articles and sermons defending the infallibility of the AV. He is also the author of *The Creed of the Alexandrian Cult* which he prints in his *Bible Believer's Bulletin* to expose the "Originals only" advocates. The following are some excerpts from this *Creed*:

"There is no final authority but God. Since God is a Spirit, there is no final authority that can be seen, heard, read, felt, or handled. Since all books are material, there is no book on this earth that is the final and absolute authority on what is right and what is wrong: what constitutes truth and what constitutes error. There

WAS a series of writings one time which, IF they had all been put into a BOOK as soon as they were written the first time, WOULD HAVE constituted an infallible and final authority by which to judge truth and error. However, this series of writings was lost, and the God who inspired them was unable to preserve their content through Bible-believing Christians...The most inaccurate translations were those that brought about the German Reformation (Luther, Zwingli, Boehier, Zinzendorf, Spener, etc.) and the worldwide missionary movement of the English-speaking people: the Bible that Sunday, Torrey, Moody, Finney, Spurgeon, Whitefleld, Wesley, and Chapman used. But we can 'tolerate' these if those who believe in them will tolerate US. After all. Since there is NO ABSOLUTE AND FINAL AUTHORITY that anyone can read, teach, preach. or handle, the whole thing is a matter of 'PREFERENCE.' You may prefer what you prefer, and we will prefer what we prefer; let us live in peace, and if we cannot agree on anything or everything, let us all agree on one thing: THERE IS NO FINAL, ABSOLUTE, WRITTEN AUTHORITY OF GOD ANYWHERE ON THIS EARTH."

1965: "Eventually, however, the intrinsic worth of the King James Bible came to be widely acknowledged, and many people came to accept it as 'the Word of God' in a sense in which no other version would be so accepted."
(Bruce M. Metzger, *The New Testament*: *Its Background, Growth and Content*, 1965)

1965: "There are large groups of fundamentalist Protestants who are emotionally attached to the King James Version (KJV). Despite its critical shortcomings, **the KJV is for them the Bible**; and attempts to replace it with the Revised Standard Version (RSV) led to book-burnings in the Bible Belt."
(Raymond Edward Brown, *New Testament Essays*, 1965)

Raymond E. Brown was a Roman Catholic priest. He was a

leader in higher-criticism. Brown praised Vatican II for vindicating many of his views. He denied the inerrancy of Scripture.

1966: "For three-and-a-half centuries the King James Version... has been the only Word of God known by millions of believers ...many Christians even today cannot feel at home with any other translation, and they read the Authorized Version as though the very English words have been given immediately by God."
(George Eldon Ladd, *New Testament and Criticism,* Wm. B. Eerdmans Publishing, 1966)

1966: "...the Rev. Thomas Miller of Seattle and the Rev. Harold Webb of Tacoma...are members of the Bible Presbyterian Church, which is not related to the huge Presbyterian Church. They classify themselves as 'Fundamentalists,' persons who believe that the King James version of the Holy Bible is the unquestioned word of God. Christians who disagreed with this point of view they consider as 'liberals' and not true believers..."
(*El Paso Herald-Post*, June 16, 1966)

1966: "*My Answer, By Billy Graham...*'Our minister says that the modern translations of the Bible were compiled by liberal theologians, and that they are unreliable. Is this true?...' [Answer]: 'I realize that your minister's view is held by some. However, I have many modern translations of the Scriptures such as Williams, Philipps, Moffat and the New English Bible, and I have found these to be most helpful in studying the Bible, and comparing Scripture with Scripture...But let's not be like **the dear old lady** who said: **'I'll stick with the King James version; what was good enough for St. Paul is good enough for me.'** I **like** the King James version and **use** it in the pulpit, for it is the most familiar translation..."
(*Syracuse Herald-Journal*, New York, March 29, 1966)

Billy Graham was greatly financed and marketed in order to assault fundamentalism and promote new versions. He commonly cited this story in order to mock people that believed in the infallibility of the King James Bible (John 7:49, 52). But in doing so, he testified that the KJV Only viewpoint is not new:

"*My Answer, By Billy Graham*...QUESTION: 'I am concerned about so many of the new translations of the Bible. The Word of God says that nothing is to be taken from, or added to it. I don't believe any translation is an improvement on the King James. Am I just too old fashioned? L.D.' ANSWER: True, the Word of God is not to be altered by man. But, working toward clearer translations does not necessarily alter the content of the Bible. While I like the King James translation, and use it in the pulpit because more people are familiar with it, I find that some of the newer translations like Philips and Living Letters make some passages clearer...**I heard of a lady years ago who said: 'I'll use nothing but the King James. What was good enough for the Apostle Paul is good enough for me'**..."
(*Winnipeg Free Press*, Canada, February 14, 1969)

This story of the dear old lady (or sometimes an old deacon, etc.), was used years before Graham by modernists in order to mock fundamental Christianity itself! This type of mockery was used against Jesus (Psalms 69:12, Mark 10:34). Notice the following words of William M. Southern, Jr. (a well-known Mason and newspaper editor):

"I think [the song] is entitled 'The Old Time Religion.' I do not remember much about it except the assertion that it was good enough for father and good enough for mother and it is good enough for me. I do not go along with this sentiment at all. It reminds me of the man who was protesting against the Revised Version of the Bible and said that the King James version was good enough for Paul and was good enough for him."
(Wm. Southern, Jr., *Moberly Monitor-Index*, Missouri, June 24, 1932)

A similar story is also found in the *Dubuque Telegraph-Herald*, (January 6, 1902), and in several other places (as seen throughout this history):

"The phrase 'gospel truth' is important to every Christian. **Typical of the attitude of many immovable fundamentalists is the view that 'what was good enough for Jesus is good enough for me.'** Authorities who have worked on the new version are quick to point out they are not tampering with theology in any sense."
(*Galveston Daily News*, September 3, 1952)

"I recall one hot-eyed woman with the hard, thin mouth of the born sin-spotter, who flipped through a Revised Standard, sniffing all the while before she laid it down with a thud. **'I'll keep my King James,' she said. 'If it was good enough for Jesus, it's good enough for me.**'"
(*Amarillo Globe-Times*, April 4, 1961)

All of these nice ladies (and good old deacons) were not as "ignorant" as their accusers believed. Most of them simply believed that God is able to *preserve* His Word according to His promises. The liberal Sadducees in the days of Jesus thought that believing in Christ and the resurrection was ridiculous. They were likewise proud of their questions and absurd, hypothetical scenarios that they used to mock the truth (Matthew 22:23-29). But Jesus rebuked them with the following words:

Matthew 22:29 Jesus answered and said unto them, Ye do err, not knowing the scriptures, nor the power of God.

When we rightly understand and believe the promises of the Scriptures concerning preservation (Psalms 12:6-7, Isaiah 40:8, Matthew 24:35, etc.), and we have faith in the power of God to fulfill these promises, we can likewise say with John Bunyan (and the many faithful ladies and deacons down through the ages), "so do I believe our English Bible is a true copy of the original."

Nevertheless, the liberal mockers will never tire of using these stories as propaganda in an attempt to make believers in preservation appear uneducated or silly. For example, notice the following news report from 1995:

"The New Testament gets a major facelift next month with a new English translation eliminating references to God the Father, turning the Son of Man into 'the human one' and removing accusations that Jews killed Christ. The new translation says children should not 'obey' their parents but heed them. Wives are no longer 'subject' to their husbands but committed to them...the 'Lord's Prayer' now begins 'Our Father-Mother in heaven.' References to the right hand of God are also deleted, eliminating possible embarrassment to lefthanded people. It now becomes God's mighty hand. The editors of 'The New Testament and Psalms: An Inclusive Version' deny they have spent the last five years producing a 'politically correct' Bible but admit that a legion of traditionalists are waiting in the wings to 'cast the first stone' and begin one of the biggest Bible debates in years...'The book will be published Sept. 11...' This translation is aimed at churches and Christians who are thoughtful about the way the Bible includes everyone...' said Susan Brooks Thistlethwaite of the Chicago Theological Seminary, who is one of the six editors. **'I have had people say to me: 'If the King James version of the Bible was good enough for Jesus, it's good enough for me,'** she added."
(*Daily Herald*, Illinois, September 1, 1995)

It is no wonder that these publishers and advocates of modern versions use this commonly repeated story. Philip Schaff, one of the earliest, well-known promoters of new versions (and unbiblical ecumenism), often told the same story! (See the history about Schaff's associations with Theosophists, and such like in Chapter 17):

"...even in the enlightened State of Massachusetts **a pious deacon** is reported to have opposed the revision of 1881 with the conclusive argument, **'If St. James's Version was good enough for St. Paul, it is good enough for me.'** There are also not a few ...[who] if they had the power, would gladly commit the Westminster Revision, Greek and English, to the flames..."
(Philip Schaff, *Companion to the Greek Testament, and the English Version*, 1883)

"A certain kind of **popular** prejudice, expressed **in the words which Dr. Schaff often laughingly repeated, 'that if St. James' Version was good enough for St. Paul, it is good enough for me,'** he was prepared for...He expressed himself in this confident way, a few years before the New Testament appeared..."
(David Schley Schaff, *The Life of Philip Schaff*, 1897)

In 1926, A.T. Robertson (another well known critic of the KJV), used the same propaganda:

"But there were others more like **the old preacher** who said that the King James Version was good enough for the Apostle Paul and it was good enough for him...They felt that some scholars were trying to rob them of parts of the New Testament. Drs. Burgon and Miller made a vigorous protest against the text of Westcott and Hort..."
(A.T. Robertson, *Studies in the Text of the New Testament*, 1926)

Either all of these new version advocates perverted their personal history in the same manner as they did the Word of God, or else Christian history has been literally *filled* with multitudes of dear old ladies, dear old deacons, and good old preachers, who believed the King James Bible is the preserved, infallible Word of God, and should not be replaced or changed in this generation!

1966: "In 1946 **the King James Version of the Bible, the rock on which fundamentalism rested**, was abruptly shaken [by the RSV]."
(Curtis Mitchell, *Billy Graham: The Making of a Crusader*, 1966)

And where is the RSV, today? It had its head cut off, like all of the other "champions" (1 Samuel 17:51). Like Dagon, it has fallen, defeated, before the AV (1 Samuel 5:3).

1967: "Some fundamentalists object to any change whatsoever in the sacrosanct King James version."
(*Arizona Republic*, May 14, 1967)

1967: "At one end of the scale an appeal is made to the verbal inspiration of the Bible in which every 'jot and tittle' is inspired by God who crossed every 't' and dotted every 'i' in the King James Version, of course."
(William R. Clarke, *Pew Asks, Pulpit Answers*, 1967)

1968: "Coming from fundamental churches in the Bible belt, we soon learned not to use any Biblical text except the King James version. The modern translations had to be the work of the devil..."
(*Alton Evening Telegraph*, February 24, 1968)

1968: "For **many English-speaking Christians** the King James or Authorized Version is the Bible. They regard most other translations with disfavor and often with suspicion."
(Carl Hamilton Morgan, *The Layman's Introduction to the New Testament*, 1968)

1969: "...I saw a church bulletin board that advertised: 'Bible-Burning Ceremony Tonight!' Upon inquiry I found that the pastor of this church was conducting a one-man war against the Re-

vised Standard Version of the Bible because he opposed any 'tampering with the Word of God.' I have heard others loudly denounce this version or that on the grounds that 'to depart from the singular beauties of the King James version is blasphemous'..."
(*Ada Weekly News*, May 8, 1969)

1970: "The Rev. H. Lloyd Walters, a Baptist minister, officiated at the burial of a copy of 'Good News for Modern Man' ...The Rev. Mr. Walters is **one of those people who holds that the King James version of the Bible is the only 'true word of God.'** For weeks he has been carrying on a campaign against the 'Good News for Modern Man' translation..."
(*Florence Morning News*, July 1, 1970)

1971: "**Many** go so far as to believe that the Bible was first communicated to man in English or at least to teach that the translators of the King James Version were miraculously safeguarded from error or uncertainty..."
(George Finger Thomas, *The Vitality of the Christian Tradition,* Ayer Publishing, 1971)

1972: "But first, let us ask a few pointed and practical questions: We as evangelicals believe the Bible to be the Verbally Inspired Word of God, Inerrant - namely, without error. THEN - we ask, is there one version extant among the multiplicity of versions which is without error today? If there is not then we worship a God who is either careless or impotent to keep His Word pure thru the ages."
(Dr. David Otis Fuller, *Is the King James Version Nearest To The Original Autographs?*, 1972)

Dr. David Otis Fuller 1903-1988) was a Baptist pastor and author of books defending the KJV such as, *Which Bible?* (1970), *True or False?* (1973), and *Counterfeit or Genuine?* (1978). He was saved in 1916, and was baptized in the First Baptist Church of New York City by Dr. I. M. Haldeman (a fiery, premillenial fundamentalist of the early decades of the twentieth century). Fuller was co-founder of the Dean Burgon Society with D.A. Waite (author of *Defending the King James Bible,* 1992). Notice some other quotes from Fuller on the KJV:

"There are two objects of Faith I have held for **well over fifty years** which I find so many scholars, and laymen too, just do not have. **I believe I have the true, pure, inerrant Word of God found in the KJV** which this Sovereign God has kept and used and honored and blessed for the past 375 years...I also believe I worship a God Who KEEPS HIS WORD intact and pure through the ages...I never would have attended, let alone graduated from Princeton, if I had not been absolutely certain I had such a Book to rest my weary soul upon for Time and Eternity...I fear friend Lewis, that we are re-enacting the sad tragedy of the golden calf by worshipping the golden calf of scholarship...Keep looking UP! It's MUCH, MUCH later than we think and THAT is the understatement of ALL understatements for the year."
(Dr. David Otis Fuller, A letter to A. Allison Lewis, October 2, 1986, www.christianbeliefs.org/kjv/fullerkjv.html)

"Dr. David Otis Fuller of the 'Which Bible Society' of Grand Rapids. Mich., asked for and was denied the right to speak on the floor about 'the most critical issue ever to come before this association in its (45-year) history.' Between conference sessions he met with those who wanted to hear about the issue. Not only are the original words divinely inspired and infallible, he said, but one English translation - the King James version of 1611 - is 'the true, infallible, inerrant Word of God.' He called the development and acceptance of newer translations 'the greatest crisis in the perversion of the Word since the Garden of Eden.'"
(*Des Moines Register*, July 2, 1977)

1973: "The theology of the people by 1901 was very largely...what official theology had been in 1837. It depended on a

conscious or unconscious belief in the inerrancy of the King James Bible..."
(Lewis Charles Bernard Seaman, *Victorian England*, 1973)

1973: "For the average black West Indian Christian the words of the Bible as used in the *King James* Version, are the exact words of God and are therefore absolutely infallible..."
(Idris Hamid, *Troubling of the Waters*, 1973)

1973: "I believe we have an infallible Bible. I believe that Bible to be the Authorized Version, or the King James Version."
(Bruce Cummons, *The Foundation and Authority of the Word of God*, 1973)

1973: "...we now have an infallible Bible in our language. By infallible I mean 1. Free from error 2. Absolutely reliable; sure; that cannot be mistaken."
(Herbert Evans, *Dear Dr. John: Where is my Bible? A Written Dispute with John R. Rice*)

1973: In this year, Foy Esco Wallace (1896-1979) published, *A Review of the New Versions*, which was a mammoth work advocating the King James Only position. Wallace was a popular Campbellite preacher (i.e. of the so-called "Church of Christ" movement, which believes in baptismal regeneration). Interestingly, the Campbellite movement was founded by Alexander Campbell (1788-1866) who was a relentless critic of the King James Bible (see the history under "1828" and "1893"). In 1826, Campbell published a new version called, *The Living Oracles* (the first modern translation!). It certainly anticipated the NIV and the NAS, etc., in many places, deleting or diminishing the same verses (e.g., Matthew 6:13, Acts 8:37, 1 John 5:7, etc.). When the RV was published in 1881, Campbellites welcomed it as the final fruit of their own labors:

"More than half a century ago, Mr. Campbell was busily sowing Revision seed all over this continent and some of that seed fell on English soil, whose ripened fruit is seen today in the volume I hold in my hand [i.e. the RV]."
(*Gospel Advocate*, "The New Revision," July 1883)

1974: "Support Lutheran Reformation Hour...We regard the King James Bible to be the trustworthy, faithful word of God in the English language."
(*Neenah-Menasha Northwestern*, December 21, 1974)

"Wayne A. Popp, Pastor of St. Mark's Ev. Lutheran Church, Sauk Village, Ill., and Richard W. Shekner, Pastor of Gloria Dei Ev. Lutheran Church, Tinley park, Ill., were suspended from the Lutheran Heritage Hour radio broadcast for publicly upholding the integrity of King James Version (1611) of the Bible over against various modern erring translations...In 1971 the Lutheran Reformation Hour began broadcasting over radio station WYCA, Hammond, Indiana, with Pastors Popp and Shekner as the speakers."
(www.illinoislutheranconference.org)

1975: "...its victory was so complete that its text acquired a sanctity properly ascribable only to the immediate voice of God; **to multitudes of English-speaking Christians it has seemed little less than blasphemy to tamper with the words of the King James Version.**"
(Stanley Lawrence Greenslade, *The Cambridge History of the Bible*, Volume 1, 1975)

1975: "Accept and preach the King James Bible as the inspired and preserved Word of God..."
(Donald Clarke, *Bible Version Manual*, 1975)

1975: "And a fearful result has come in the minds of **many peo-**

ple. They think the King James Version is inspired and that inspiration in the Bible has to mean perfection in our language...For thousands of these, if anybody shows that one word in the King James Version is not the best word, then you have proved that the Bible isn't true...And now to have many, many common and rather ignorant people...writing that Westcott and Hort, St. Augustine, any Catholic who had any part in the translation, anybody who now raises a question about the proper wording of some passage in the King James, are perverts or modernists or hypocrites or ignorant fools...is a sorry business..."

(John R. Rice, *The Sword of the Lord*, A letter to Dr. David Otis Fuller on the KJV, November 28, 1975)

1 Corinthians 1:27 But God hath chosen the foolish things of the world to confound the wise; and God hath chosen the weak things of the world to confound the things which are mighty;

1975: "Some of these same sincere folks have told me there is no other version, 'The King James is the only real Bible,' they say."

(Robert E. Lind, *Titusville Herald*, April 26, 1975)

1976: "The world contains but one volume of scriptures, authorized by a reigning monarch. This volume is universally recognized as the King James version of the Holy Bible. Accept no substitutes, and please avoid the Scofield folly. The King James Bible has been cursed by the pope, denied from the pulpit and condemned by the Jews. Yet multitudes have died believing in it and for many years, I have been prepared to [live] that way. One outstanding quality of the King James Bible that I have noted over the years is its unfailing ability to separate the men from the boys..."

(*Daily Review*, July 19, 1976)

1976: "His technician fades out the gospel hymn, Old-Fashioned Meeting - the program's opening theme for 29 years - and the pastor welcomes the radio audience to another People's Gospel Hour. 'This is Pastor Perry F. Rockwood speaking'...His sermon is uncompromisingly fundamentalist - the Second Coming is at hand...ecumenism and the United Nations are harbingers of the antichrist; **all Bibles except the King James version are corrupt and incorrect...But especially he preaches that the King James Bible is the infallible word of God, has all the answers for mankind and must be believed literally and totally.** He belongs to no creed except the independent church he founded, but he considers his beliefs about the same as those of a Baptist. Above all, he is no longer a Presbyterian. His bitter feud as a fiery young minister within that church shook the foundations of Canadian Presbyterianism in 1946 and 1947...The doctrinal sickness was liberalism which, he said, was teaching men to be proud, rather than to know they are sinners, and was changing the meaning of the Bible. 'The pulpits of our land are manned by men who are upholding the liberal point of view, which at its best is unchristian,' he said...Today, his radio ministry is a booming success. The weekly 12-minute People's Gospel Hour reaches 114 radio stations in Canada, 74 in the United States and four overseas. Since 1968 he has also been preaching an 11-minute daily program, Prophecy for Today, which reaches 316 stations. That puts many millions of people into his potential radio audience...Mr. Rockwood has always been nearly as harsh with Catholicism as with liberalism..."
(*The Brandon Sun,* November 3, 1976)

1977: S. Franklin Logsdon (1907-1987) was a pastor and Bible conference speaker. He believed there will be chastisement at the Judgment Seat of Christ for some unfaithful believers. This holy fear of God, no doubt, played a big part in his willingness to hear the truth concerning the new versions, regardless of the cost. He renounced his connection with the New American Standard Version and converted to the KJV-Only position. In 1977, he explained how he changed his view:

"When questions began to reach me [about the translation controversy], at first I was quite offended. However, in attempting to answer, I began to sense that something was not right about the NASV. Upon investigation, I wrote my very dear friend, Mr. Lockman, explaining that I was forced to renounce all attachment to the NASV...The product, however, is grievous to my heart and helps to complicate matters in these already troubled times."
(Logsdon, a letter to Cecil Carter of Prince George, British Columbia, June 9, 1977)

The extent of Logsdon's involvement with the NASV is revealed in his following testimony:

"Two questions were handed me tonight which if I could answer them would take care of almost all the other questions: 'Please tell us why we should use the Authorized Version and why the New American Standard is not a good version, and the background from which it came.' 'What is your opinion of the 1881, 1901 and other variations of the Bible in relation to the Authorized Version?' May I point out to you very specifically, not that you do not know but to stir up your pure minds by way of remembrance, we are in the end time. And this end time is characterized by a falling away, and of course that is apostasy...So you can understand why the archenemy of God and man would want to do something to destroy this Book...Nevertheless, getting back to this, the devil is too wise to try to destroy the Bible. He knows he can't. He can't destroy the Word of God. But he can do a lot of things to try to supplant it, or to corrupt it in the minds and hearts of God's people. Now he can only do it in one of two ways: either by adding to the Scriptures or by subtracting from the Scriptures...When people speak of the oldest manuscripts, they usually mean the A and the B, the Codex Siniaticus and the Codex Vaticanus...I'm just going to ask, 'On what manuscript or manuscripts is this version based?' And if it's based upon a manuscript that came down through this Roman stream, I don't want anything to do with it...Friends, you can say the Authorized Version is absolutely correct. How correct? 100% correct!...I tell you, I used to laugh with others when a person would try to slander the intelligence, perhaps, of some who say, 'Well, if the Authorized Version was good enough for Paul it's good enough for me.' You get a lot of ha, ha's. Say, that perhaps is true. If this is the Word of God, and Paul had the Word of God, then things equal to the same thing are equal to each other...Back in 1956-57, Mr. F. Dewey Lockman of the Lockman Foundation [contacted me. He was] one of the dearest friends we've ever had for 25 years, a big man, some 300 pounds...Well, up to that time I thought the Westcott and Hort was the text. You were intelligent if you believed the Westcott and Hort....Mr. Lockman got in touch with me and said, 'Would you and Ann come out and spend some weeks with us, and we'll work on a feasibility report; I can pick up the copyright to the 1901 [ASV] if it seems advisable.' **I'm afraid I'm in trouble with the Lord, because I encouraged him to go ahead with it. We laid the groundwork; I wrote the format; I helped to interview some of the translators; I sat with the translators; I wrote the preface. When you see the preface to the New American Standard, those are my words**...some of my friends across the country began to learn that I had some part in it and they started saying, 'What about this; what about that?' Dr. David Otis Fuller in Grand Rapids...I've known him for 35 years, and he would say (he would call me Frank; I'd call him Duke), 'Frank, what about this? You had a part in it; what about this; what about that?'... You know how you justify yourself the last minute. But I finally got to the place where I said, 'Ann, I'm in trouble; I can't refute these arguments; it's wrong; it's terribly wrong; it's frightfully wrong; and what am I going to do about it?' Well, I went through

some real soul searching for about four months, and I sat down and wrote one of the most difficult letters of my life, I think. I wrote to my friend Dewey, and I said, 'Dewey, I don't want to add to your problems...but I can no longer ignore these criticisms I am hearing and I can't refute them....I must under God renounce every attachment to the New American Standard'...I tell you, dear people, somebody is going to have to stand...If we could hear His voice we would have no trouble learning His Word from the Authorized Version...And besides this, we've had the AV for 362 years...It's God's Book."
(Transcribed by David Cloud, Way of Life Literature; printed in *O Timothy* magazine, Volume 9, Issue 1, 1992)

1977: "Although there had been two other new English versions before, the RSV was the first major challenge to the preeminence of the King James Bible, first published in 1611 and **still believed** by some to be the way God really wrote the Bible."
(*Simpson's Leader-Times*, Pennsylvania, December 30, 1977)

1977: "Many Christians today still believe that King James is the only translation to be used. On this point, any other translation is heretical..."
(*West Coast Review of Books*, Volumes 3-4, 1977)

1978: "So securely has it established its place in the affections of the English-speaking peoples, that **to most of its readers the Authorized Version is The Bible.** Although it is often called the Authorized Version, it was never authorized by any official action on the part of any church or state. On the contrary, **its universal reception by the common people** of all denominations seems clearly to be another instance of the providence of God."
(John Wahnert, *America's Priceless Heritage: The King James Version of the Bible,* 1978)

1978: "The exact wording of this version [KJV] was prized as if

it were the holy of holies...for fundamentalist society as a whole the Authorized Version functioned as the direct and immediate expression or transcript of divine revelation."
(James Barr, *Fundamentalism,* Westminster Press, 1978)

1978: "Fundamentalists ordinarily view the scriptures as literal truth and the King James version as sacrosanct..."
(Justin Scott, *The Turning*, 1978)

1978: "Some believe that the verse about inspiration means that every word and sentence of the King James Version was individually directed by God."
(*The Disciple*, Volume 5, Christian Board of Publication, 1978)

1979: "...there are people who fanatically insist that the King James Version was perfectly translated with no errors; if there is a single error in the translation we have no trustworthy Bible. They say God is obligated to have such a perfectly translated Bible which is exactly true to every word of the original autographs..."
(Dr. John R. Rice, *The Sword of the Lord*, March 30, 1979)

1979: "The defenders of the KJV are beginning to get their message across, at least to some...If the only infallible Bible was the originals, then anyone would know that no mortal man that ever lived saw them at one time here upon the earth...I am utterly worn out with all of the corrections, better translations, better renderings, etc., that we are forced to listen to when we hear the average preacher preach or teach. It is doing untold harm to the cause of Christ, by destroying the faith of people in the Word of God...Here is an example of a fundamental Baptist Church amending their Church Constitution to read: 'We accept the Authorized Version of 1611 (commonly called the King James Version) as the Word of God, preserved in accordance with Psalms 12:6,7 and Matthew 24:35...'..."
(E. L. Bynum, *"King James Fans"?,* 1979)

1980: "Some men hold that the King James English Bible is inerrant just as the original autographs. They teach that God guided the translators of the King James Bible, even in the words they used, to preserve them from all error and from all omission."
(Dayton Hobbs, *The Projector*, May, 1980)

1980: "The error being referred to here is that of saying a lot of nice things about the King James Bible without believing that it is inerrant. Many a true Bible believer has been deceived into thinking that every person who says or writes good things about the King James Bible believes that it is without error."
(Gary Ferkel, *The King James Contender*, May, 1980)

"There is no need to revise, update, correct, better explain, or change in any way, the present King James Bible."
(John Phillips, *King James Contender*, April, 1980)

1980: "If the King James Version is not a valid and authoritative translation that God has used to preserve the Word of God, then where is the Word of God? Where can I obtain a copy? The King James Version is a staunch defense against the trend of liberalism today. I don't know of a liberal preacher today that admits that it's God's Word."
(Pastor Ben Sanders, Bethlehem Baptist Church; quoted in, *Plains Baptist Challenger,* Edited by E.L. Bynum, March, 1980)

1981: "Our position is that there are no 'errors' or 'mistakes' in the King James English Version of the Bible."
(Homer Massey, *Where is the Word of God Today?*)

1981: "The Bible is the most-read Book that has ever existed...There are **undoubtedly many** who do not realize that the 'Authorized Version' (the 'King James Bible')...is in fact a translation, and who therefore believe that every one of its words is

inspired and infallible...It is the one I am using in this book, because, even today, it is the Bible **in the minds of almost all** English-speaking people."
(Isaac Asimov, *In the Beginning,* 1981)

1982: "...sacrosanct, as the King James Version of the Bible is to some Christians - the version itself, in addition to the central truth of the Bible, is made sacred."
(Elaine Dickson, *Say No, Say Yes to Change,* 1982)

1983: "We believe that the Bible (KJV) is the Word of God, and we also believe that God has preserved it perfect for us today. It was not just perfect in the original autographs."
(Barry Burton, *Let's Weigh the Evidence*, Chick Publications, 1983)

1983: "...there never was a book of 66 originals of the Bible...no one living today would know or recognize any one of the 66 originals if they saw one...to flee to the supposed sanctuary of the originals is unreal, hypocrisy, a fetish, and worse than the proverbial ostrich hiding its head in the sand and thinking it is covered and out of sight."
(Ralph I. Yarnell, *A Fresh Look At The King James Bible*, 1983)

1984: "...the AV 1611. It is the pure, perfect, inerrant and infallible word of God."
(Norman Ward, *Famine in the Land,* 1984)

1984: In 1984, Jack Hyles preached a sermon titled, "Logic Proves the King James Version," (April 8, 1984). Hyles (1926-2001) was a fiery, Baptist preacher who built one of the largest churches in America. In 1993, Hyles also published the following words:

"In order to live as a child of God, I must have a perfect Bible...This preacher believes that those preserved words are in the

Bible that I hold in my right hand at this very moment - the King James Bible!...I have more respect for the person who says that one of the false Bibles contains the very words of God than for the person who says only the original contains the very words of God. At least he believes, though wrongly, that we still have the words of God which are pure. For many, many reasons I believe that the King James Bible has been preserved in the English language word-for-word."
(Jack Hyles, *Enemies of Soul Winning*, 1993)

1984: "'We don't need that other stuff! No sir, we've got all we need. We've got the Bible. It's right here. We don't need the Greek – we've got the Bible, the King James Bible and it says it all. Woe to you if you don't pay attention. Remember the flood. Remember what happened to Sodom and Gomorrah. Remember the fires of hell are burning. The flames of hell are hot, brothers and sisters. They are hot,' said the sweating preacher, hoarse from his exhortations. 'Amen,' said some of those listening. 'That's the truth...' There they were sitting on wooden chairs in a tent, sawdust on the ground...They listened and they believed. Then there's Robert Schuller, he of the Crystal Cathedral. No tents, no wooden chairs, no sawdust, and no hell fire and damnation. The Rev. Robert Schuller preaches an upbeat, 'I'm OK, you're Ok' kind of sermon that emphasizes the positive. He doesn't sweat. His voice is well-modulated...Different strokes for different folks..."
(*Chronicle Telegram*, September 1, 1984)

1985: "In time, the Jesuits got into the Bible departments to teach the young impressionable men who would become future Protestant pastors. 'Let's see how accurate the King James is against the 'original Greek.' The Greek they used from was Satan's Alexandrian manuscript (Vaticanus)...the students didn't know they were being deceived...Daily in their classes the Word of God was criticized and cleverly put to ridicule. Young men

who came believing the King James Bible was the Word of God were soon turned against it...Pastors and radio preachers are constantly correcting the Word of God and recommending other translations...'The Vatican is busy secretly pouring millions of dollars into multitudes of new Bible translations...'"
(Jack T. Chick, *The Attack,* Chick Publications, 1985)

1986: "One attack which is receiving quite a bit of attention these days is a direct attack upon the Word of God as preserved in the English language: the King James Version of 1611...Our authority for the infallible words of the English Bible lies in the power and promise of God to preserve His Word!"
(David R. Reagan, *The King James Version of 1611: The Myth of 'Early Revisions,'* 1986)

1987: "...we hear people saying that the English wording used by the KJV translators was chosen by God...they believe the King James translation is perfect."
(Eric Pement, *Gimme the Bible that Paul Used*, 1987)

1987: "I am in favor of intensifying our reading time in the only authority we have, the Authorized Version!...Today it is widely taught and accepted that God wrote the originals perfectly, but that there is no perfect translation. Yet, there is no scripture that teaches any such thing! This teaching is based on logic, man's logic. Christian educators of today say that it is absurd to believe that God could use sinful men to translate His Word perfectly. Such a supposition of a perfect translation is no more absurd than the teaching that God used sinful men to write the Bible perfectly in the originals! *Every* argument *for* inerrant, infallible inspiration applies also for inerrant, infallible *preservation.* It is the same God!...I personally believe that God has perfectly preserved His Word in the King James or Authorized Version. I can at least produce a King James Bible to show what I believe in. Any person who claims that God inspired the original autographs

perfectly, cannot produce those original manuscripts to prove it! I do not believe that the King James Bible is a new inspiration..."
(Samuel C. Gipp, *An Understandable History of the Bible*, 1987)

1988: "Those learned men that our Lord providentially put together to give us our Authorized King James Bible were better qualified than was Scofield to deal with the text. Do not be fooled by anything in print that takes issue with the text of our Bible. Change not a paragraph, not a sentence, not a word."
(Bob Steward, *Removing the Landmarks,* 1988)

1989: "It is amusing yet appalling that a King James Bible believer, who BELIEVES the Bible to be inerrant, is called a 'heretic' by people who claim to believe that the Bible is inerrant...Critics of the King James Bible believe that the 'Bible' is the inerrant word of God. BUT, ask them to hand you a copy of that inerrant Bible that they 'believe' in, and you will find that it doesn't exist anywhere on this earth!...Actually the 'heretic' label is designed more to scare young adherents away from the inerrant Bible, than to honestly define the name caller's feelings."
(Samuel C. Gipp, *The Answer Book*, 1989)

1989: "...the King James translation is the only one acknowledged by certain fundamentalists...Some fundamentalists organized book-burnings of the Revised Standard Version, a.k.a., 'The Bible of Antichrist'..."
(Kathleen C. Boone, *The Bible Tells Them So*, 1989)

1990: "...the King James Version of 1611, which remains the standard text for many evangelical Christians, **some of whom regard it as the inspired word of God**."
(Ari L. Goldman, "New Bible," *The New York Times*, September 28, 1990)

1990: "Fundamentalists, who oppose the changes, continue to embrace as their standard text the King James Version of 1611,

which many evangelicals regard as the inspired word of God."
(*Huntingdon Daily News*, October 6, 1990)

1991: "We learned that **a large number** of Bible readers (or at least Bible owners) thought that the King James Version was 'the original' Word of God and that anything else was an untrustworthy counterfeit. Some pastors really believe that only the King James Version is the inspired Word of God. A pastor from Texas, however, was a bit extreme when he declared that since the King James Version was good enough for Abraham and Noah, it was certainly good enough for him."
(Kenneth Nathaniel Taylor, Virginia J. Muir, *My Life: A Guided Tour*, 1991)

Kenneth Taylor (1917-2005) was the creator of the so-called *Living Bible* (1971). Taylor states that he made his paraphrase from the *American Standard Version* of 1901. Roman Catholics adored the *Living Bible*, and it even received an official *Imprimatur*, and *Nihil Obstat* (a stamp of approval from the Catholic Church)!

Did Taylor lose his voice as a judgment for tampering with the Bible?:

"Mysteriously half way through the paraphrase Taylor lost his voice and still speaks in a hoarse whisper. A psychiatrist who examined him suggested that the voice failure was Taylor's psychological self-punishment for tampering with what he believed to be the word of God."
(*Time*, Volume 100, 1972)

Interestingly, other textual critics were afflicted in a similar fashion (e.g. S.P. Tregelles, Philip Schaff, B.F. Wescott, J.B. Phillips, etc.). The Bible warns of such a judgment:

Luke 1:20 And, behold, thou shalt be dumb, and not able to speak...**because thou believest not my words**...

Psalms 31:18 Let the lying lips be put to silence...

Psalms 63:11...the mouth of them that speak lies shall be stopped.

1992: "I believe that the Authorized Version is the inspired, infallible, inerrant, immutable, pure word of God to English speaking people..."
(James Son, *The New Athenians*, 1992)

1992: "45 years on air and Perry Rockwood is still going strong...Rockwood is 75 but there's not a wrinkle in his face. His white hair is thick. His face is round but there's no fat on him. He strides like a man half his age...His deeply fundamentalist message hasn't changed: The Bible is absolute literal truth. Modernist churches that preach otherwise are doing Satan's work. All translations other than the King James version are perversions."
(*The Lethbridge Herald*, Alberta, Canada, November 14, 1992)

1993: In 1993, Gail Riplinger published her book, *New Age Bible Versions.* It soon became one of the most influential books encouraging and defending the KJV Only view in recent times.

1993: "From the material above (and more like it) and the witness of the Holy Spirit, we are firmly convinced that any edition of the Authorized King James Version of 1611 (apart from typographical errors, of course) is God's pure, inerrant, infallible word."
(Timothy Morton, *Which Translation Should You Trust?*, 1993)

1993: "*...the King James Bible has been preserved by God to be propagated by man!*...Until we hear His trumpet sound (1 Thes-

salonians 4:16), we must not only believe the King James Bible is the preserved Word of God, but we must also win every man, woman, boy, and girl to Christ while there is still time...We must 'get the seed out of the barn.'"
(William P. Grady, *Final Authority: A Christian's Guide to the King James Bible*, 1993)

1994: "Last year, Dr. Mickey Carter sent me a book entitled *Things That are Different are not the Same*. It was in defense of the King James Bible as the preserved Word of God for English speaking people...we believe the King James Bible is the preserved Word of God..."
(Dr. Curtis Hutson, "Things that are Different are not the Same," preached at Southwide Baptist Fellowship, Northside Baptist Church, Charlotte, North Carolina, Oct., 1994)

The above words were from Curtis Hutson's (1934-1995) last major preaching opportunity. He was a dynamic evangelist, pastor and editor of the *Sword of the Lord*. Like Jack Hyles, his change to KJV Only views disgruntled some new version advocates. One Christian bookstore owner fumed:

"Dr. Rice's successor, the late Dr. Curtis Hutson...with Jack Hyles...jumped-on the Gail Riplinger bandwagon, and reportedly bought and mailed a thousand copies of Riplinger's book to preachers affiliated with the Sword."
(Bob L. Ross, *Dr. John R. Rice's Reply to Dr. David Otis Fuller on the KJV, with an introduction and analysis*)

1994: "...among Fundamentalist circles in America...religious leaders of our day...had/have reached the conclusion that only one translation of the Scriptures was/is needed and that whoever promoted/promotes or used/uses any other translation was/is a heretic and must be exposed...If I should ask what that one translation is, chaos might break out. Immediately, someone from the 20th century would say, 'It has to be the Authorized King James

1611 Version.'"
(Estus Pirkle, *The 1611 King James Bible*, 1994)

1995: "'I would like a *real* Bible,' she says. 'A real Bible?' the salesclerk asks. 'Yes,' she replied, 'a *real* Bible, the Bible God honors, the King James Bible, the AV 1611.' Scenes like this are repeated almost daily across the English speaking world."
(James R. White, *The King James Only Controversy*, 1995)

James R. White is an advocate of modern versions. But like so many others, his attempt to refute the King James Only movement calls attention to the vast number of men and women who believe the KJV is the infallible Word of God:

1 Corinthians 1:19 For it is written, I will destroy the wisdom of the wise, and will bring to nothing the understanding of the prudent.
20 Where is the wise? where is the scribe? where is the disputer of this world? hath not God made foolish the wisdom of this world?
26 For ye see your calling, brethren, how that not many wise men after the flesh, not many mighty, not many noble, are called:

John 7:31 And **many of the people** believed on him, and said, When Christ cometh, will he do more miracles than these which this man hath done?
32 The Pharisees heard that the people murmured such things concerning him; and the Pharisees and the chief priests sent officers to take him.

1995: "Until you come to realize that we have an absolute authority, perfect and settled in the King James Version, you are not prepared to serve the Lord! It is a basic essential to Christian service."
(Raymond Blanton, *Perilous Times*, June, 1995)

1996: "...the King James Version is the book of choice among many groups such as fundamentalists, Baptists and traditional churches in the Bible Belt, said Philip Comfort, professor of New Testament Literature and Interpretation at Wheaton College and senior editor at Tyndale House Publishers Inc. in Carol Stream. Many people take their King James very seriously, said Comfort, author of 'The Complete Guide to Bible Versions,' sort of the bible on various Bibles. 'There are very strong, what I call King James fanatics or King James-only people,' Comfort said."
(*Daily Herald*, Illinois, May 28, 1996)

1996: "Like a delinquent carving on the Mona Lisa, those who use Greek and Hebrew aids are theological delinquents...No Greek or Hebrew text will be as pure as the English words in your KJV."
(Roy Branson, *KJV 1611: Perfect! A Conviction, Not a Preference*, 1996)

1997: "To the Editor: Scott Herrmann comments in the Sept. 26 issue that his Bible is 'jam-packed with vague symbolism, gross inconsistencies, mistakes and out-and-out lies.' This, of course, is the source of his, and many others' problem with Christianity. They have no absolute source they can consult to learn the truth, and they are upset when someone else does. However, he does have a valid point because of the variety of bibles on the market today. The only Bible I have read that does not have errors or contradictions is the Authorized King James Version of 1611. My suggestion to Herrmann is to discard his present bible and to read one without errors so he can speak with authority...John T. Banewicz, Cortland."
(*The Post-Standard*, New York, October 9, 1997)

1998: "The King James, Authorized Version of 1611 is the seventh major English translation of the Bible, 'purified seven times' in the English language. Seven is God's number of completion and perfection. When the seventh major English translation of the Bible was published, the Word of God in English was complete; it was perfect. Seven years were spent from the inception of the project till the first copy was handed to King James I...In verse seven of Psalm Twelve we find God's promise of divine preservation. 'Thou shalt keep them, O Lord, thou shalt preserve them from this generation for ever.' 'The words of the Lord are pure words: as silver tried in a furnace of earth, purified SEVEN times.'"

(Bill Brady, *Purified Seven Times: The Miracle of the English Bible*, 1998)

1998: "Personally, I cannot find anything 'Godly' about changing even one word in the King James Bible."

(Charles Perkins, *Flaming Torch*, April-June, 1998)

1998: "Old-style 'fundies' have a great reverence for seventeenth-century English Protestantism: for them, the King James bible is the only inspired translation..."

(Damian Thompson, *The End of Time: Faith and Fear in the Shadow of the Millennium,* 1998)

1999: "Thoreau said more than 100 years ago that the Bible would be replaced in people's homes in a short time. He was wrong. While the influence of God's Word has lessened, **there is still a great number of people who believe that the King James Bible is the word of God**...When I really, really compared the versions, the unmistakable conclusion is that the King James Version is how God wanted His word said in English. Which brings me to the 20th century distracters. Satan's plan of replacing the Bible with naturalism or existentialism having failed, the world's system turned to 'improving' the word...To date, there have been about 50 'new' Bibles this century...And the KJV lives on. Why? Because when one believes, studies, rightly divides, and applies the KJV he has a power in his words

and message that cannot be withstood..."
(Jerry Lockhart, *New Braunfels Herald-Zeitung,* September 10, 1999)

1999: "The Authorized Version, (AV), King James Bible (KJB) is without error."
(Solomon Aordkian, *Honoring the King James Bible*, 1999)

1999: "The Authorised King James Version on the other hand, is the inspired, preserved, and infallible Word of God for today; just as it has been for generations of Protestants for nearly 400 years."
(David B Loughran, *The New International Version: Is This the Word of God?*, Stewarton, Scotland, 1999)

2000: "Many fundamentalists favor the King James Version, claiming it is the authentic, inspired Word of God."
(*The Chronicle Telegram*, Ohio, January 12, 2000)

2000: "I thought it might be interesting to relate to you why I have taken the position that the King James Version of the Bible is not my Bible of choice, the Bible I prefer, but is instead to me, the Living Word of God!...The same year I was converted I went to study for the ministry at a good Christian college. The course in Bible required me to take many hours of Greek...A little thought kept occurring in my mind that armed with this superior knowledge of Greek and the way it should be translated, made me, in some way, superior to the common layman and even some of the less educated preachers I had come across. Statements like, 'I have the same Bible the Apostle Paul had, the KJV!,' would just make me chuckle about their ignorance! Imagine them actually trusting a Book, calling it inspired, when we all knew it was filled with errors that should be corrected...I answered myself that the King James Version had been sufficient to cleanse my soul, teach me doctrine, convict me of the separated life! This Bible (the KJV) was what called me to preach

and to soul-winning! The more I studied, the more I compared, the more I checked out the translators, the more I became convinced that the KJV was the inspired and preserved Word of God that God had allowed the English-speaking world to have for hundreds of years! I began to suspect that there was something (or one) far more sinister behind the translations that were being ground out by the score, than just the money motive."
(Walter S. Beebe, "Why Did I Become a KJV Fan? Again!," *The Flaming Torch*, 2000)

2001: "At present there is **a widespread and enthusiastic movement** among conservative Christians, especially among Baptists, that claims that the King James Version (KJV) of the Bible is the only legitimate translation of the Bible in English. Many of these enthusiasts further affirm that the KJV is an infallible, error-free translation..."
(Article by Douglas K. Kutilek, quoted in, Roy E. Beacham, Kevin T. Bauder, *One Bible Only?: Examining Exclusive Claims for the King James Bible,* 2001)

2001: "The church members...tend to interpret the King James Version of the Bible as 'God's unalterable Word to humanity.'"
(Vincent L. Wimbush, Rosamond C. Rodman, *African Americans and the Bible*, 2001)

2001: "*King James Only movement divides U.S. fundamentalists*...Hard-liners among the KJOs believe only the King James is the Word of God...The KJO phenomenon underscores the difference between 'fundamentalism' and the similar but more moderate 'evangelical' movement..."
(*The Daily Globe*, Michigan, July 21, 2001)

2002: "A similar issue involved English translations of the Bible. Fundamentalists, at their most conservative, were (and are) apt to trust only the Authorized Version...and to view all others

as liberal distortions."
(Timothy Larsen, *Christabel Pankhurst: Fundamentalism and Feminism in Coalition,* Boydell Press, 2002)

2003: In 2003, Gail Riplinger's mammoth book, *In Awe of Thy Word: Understanding the King James Bible Its Mystery and History Letter by Letter*, was published.

2004: "If we believe that the Bible is *still* the inerrant Word of God, we must then deal with the problem of determining which version is the true Word of the Living God...two contradictory 'Bibles' cannot both be the inerrant Word of God. This author proclaims from the outset that the 'King James,' or 'Authorized Version' is the Word of God translated into the English language to the extent that it is the final authority in all matters of conduct and faith."
(Floyd Nolen Jones, *Which Version is the Bible?,* 2004)

2005: "Even when you ask a lost person if he believes the Bible, they say 'Which bible?' They don't know. We used to believe the Bible. Now we believe anything that says B-I-B-L-E on it (except the KJV). Why? Because we've allowed men with titles after their names to say, 'In the original…' and change what it says. But, every one of these so called 'brilliant scholars' who write a different version, disagree with everybody else. So, who's right?...When I stand before God, I do not want to be accused of changing one Word, or of believing one word other than what He says. *'Every word of God is pure, he is a shield unto them that put their trust in him.'"*
(Rick Wilder, "Why I Believe the King James Bible Only!," *The Flaming Torch*, 2005)

2005: "At the level of popular belief, it was commonly held that the King James version of the Bible of 1611 was divinely in-

spired or dictated."
(John D. Buenker, Joseph Buenker, *Encyclopedia of the Gilded Age and Progressive Era*, Volume 1, 2005)

2006: "We believe that we have the perfectly preserved words of God in our 1611 King James Bible, also called the 'Authorized Version' or KJV...God warns us not to add to or take away from His holy words. But the Devil does, all the time! Satan does everything he can to corrupt the word of God, especially through modern Bible versions. But 'modern Bibles' are not truly modern. They really come from ancient corrupted manuscripts...they were later used to make the perverted Roman Catholic Bible."
(Gary Miller, *Why the King James Bible is the Perfect Word of God*, 2006)

2006: "Every verse, chapter and book is inspired, inerrant, impeccable, irrefutable, indestructible, invincible...It is powerful, perfect, priceless, pure, productive and preserved for us in our own language in the 1611 King James Bible."
(Raymond Barber, *Walking in Wisdom*, 2006)

2006: "Many of my fundamentalist brothers have adopted a 'KJV Only' position..."
(Robert Israel, *Glasgow Road*, 2006)

2006: "In the second stage of Bhakti Yoga, then, the connection with God is a little bit closer...The King James Bible is such a complete departure from the Aramaic...Isn't that interesting that the King James is the *Bible* that is most referred to now?...it's difficult for them when I say, 'Well, that's not really a good translation.' And they want to come back really quickly and say, 'Well, it's God speaking...It's the word of God.'"
(Sean Thomas Forrester, Yogi Sean Thomas, *Dancing in the Fire of Transformation*, 2006)

Eastern mystics are trying to realize their own godhood. And notice that they are having trouble recruiting people because of

KJV Onlyism. They must first deceive them into believing that the King James Bible is an erroneous translation (Genesis 3:1). Once there is no faith in the infallible, objective standard that God has given, people are then left to their own subjective feelings or experiences. Satan first tempted Eve to doubt God's Word; then he tempted her with godhood once the foundations of the Word, and the fear of God, were removed.

2007: "The rank-and-file believers, however, still frequently maintain - as they have been taught - that the King James translation, for one, is inerrant and its translators inspired. Regardless of whether or not trained apologists believe this..."
(D.M. Murdock, *Who Was Jesus?,* 2007)

2008: "Which text of Scripture are we to use?...The fundamentalists normally resolved this question by arguing that the Authorized (King James) Version (KJV), is the only one that should be used...This argument is **still maintained by many fundamentalists today**...Those who held to this position argued that no other English translations are either possible or desirable because God had given His church, once for all, an inerrant English Bible."
(A. T. B. McGowan, *The Divine Authenticity of Scripture: Retrieving an evangelical Heritage*, 2008)

2008: "...there are hundreds of US churches listed in telephone and website directories as 'King James Only'..."
(Lori Anne Ferrell, *The Bible and the People*, 2008)

2008: "Distinctions between fundamentalists and evangelicals - [Fundamentalists] believe the Authorized (King James) Version of the Bible as the only inspired translation [and] have a literalistic approach to interpreting the Bible..."
(Harriet A. Harris, *Fundamentalism and Evangelicals*, 2008)

2009: "Among very many English-speaking Protestants on both sides of the Atlantic, **there remained (as there still remains today)** a sturdy belief that the team of forty-seven scholars convened by King James I of England brought forth in 1611 the Scriptures as God Himself would have dictated them in our tongue...the popular presumption has been that God authorized it and that attempted alterations represent tampering with His Word."
(David Rooney, *The Wine of Certitude: A Literary Biography of Ronald Knox*, 2009)

2009: "...the King James Version is *the* Bible for millions of Christians around the world."
(David G. Burke, *Translation That Openeth the Window,* 2009)

2009: "A North Carolina pastor says his church plans to burn Bibles and books by Christian authors on Halloween to light a fire under true believers. Pastor Marc Grizzard told Asheville TV station WLOS that the King James version of the Bible is the only one his small western North Carolina church follows. He says all other versions, such as the Living Bible, are 'satanic' and 'perversions' of God's word."
(*Southtown Star*, Illinois, October 15, 2009)

2009: "Some Christians today believe that the King James Version (KJV) of the Bible is the only legitimate and trustworthy English-translation Bible. Further, like the original writings of Scripture, they believe that only the KJV is inspired and inerrant (without error)."
(John Ankerberg, Dillon Burroughs, *Taking a Stand for the Bible*, 2009)

2009: "I believe that the Holy Spirit inspired every word of the King James Bible and that it should not be replaced by these so called revisions."
(Colin K. Duncan, *Ministries of the Holy Spirit*)

2010: "A Fundamentalist pastor would probably not participate in ecumenical services or activities, particularly if Catholics were involved. They generally accept only the King James Version (KJV) as the inspired and infallible word of God and insist on scriptural inerrancy, even in the English translation."
(Doug Gonzales, *Steps of Grace*, 2010)

Conclusion

Psalms 68:11 The Lord gave the word: **great was the company** of those that published it.

The arrogant prediction of Philip Schaff, in 1883, is laughable in light of this history:

"King James's Version can never recover its former authority...It is slowly but surely declining, and **doomed to a peaceful death** and honorable burial..."
(Philip Schaff, *A Companion to the Greek Testament and the English Version*, 1883)

The common claim that KJV Onlyism is of recent origin is also exposed as an old wives' fable:

Psalms 2:4 He that sitteth in the heavens shall laugh...

2 Timothy 2:9...the word of God is not bound.

CHAPTER 12

CAN TRANSLATIONS BE INFALLIBLE?

"...the English Bible has brought and still brings home the knowledge of God's revealed truth to myriads more of minds, than ever received it through the original tongues."
(Isaac Ferris, *Jubilee Memorial of the American Bible Society*, 1867)

"Oh, the exquisite English in many parts of our version of the Scriptures! I sometimes think that the translators, as well as the original writers, must have been inspired."
(Samuel Rogers, *Recollections of the table-talk of Samuel Rogers*, 1887)

Modern-version-scholars (to justify their constant publishing of new versions) must maintain that translations cannot ever be infallible. If we already have an infallible translation, what need is there of a new version every few years? For this reason (and others), the false teaching that only the original manuscripts of the Bible were inspired and infallible is promoted. The view that a translation could be the inspired Scriptures is mocked and derided with the greatest scorn. To further maintain their propaganda, these advocates of the new versions often claim that no "true scholar" ever believed that a translation was the infallible, inspired Scriptures, etc. They then define the meaning of "true scholar" so that anyone who teaches anything contrary to their great assumption does not qualify!

The historical quotes in this book reveal that many great and wise men did/do believe that the Authorized Version is the infallible, inspired, preserved Word of God in English. Earlier Christian history is also filled with writers who believed that translations could be infallible. Almost all of the so-called "early fathers" believed that translations could be inspired and infallible. Augustine even wrote that God could say some things differently to translators, that He did not say to the original writers (*City of God*, 18:43)! Jerome, in the fourth century, testified that "the common people" believed that translations could be infallible:

"When the Bishop of Rome, Pope Damasus, in the fourth century, told Jerome to revise the Latin Version of the Bible, he positively refused. 'They will kill me,' he said, 'or curse me for meddling with it': for it was their Bible, the only Bible..."
(Anson D.F. Randolph, *The Presbyterian and Reformed Review*, Volume 7, 1896)

"The old Italic version into the rude Low Latin of the second century held its own as long as Latin continued to be the language of the people. The critical version of Jerome never displaced it, and only replaced it when Latin ceased to be a living language, and became the language of the learned."
(Fulton, *Forum*, June, 1887)

It is not necessary at this time to debate the legitimacy of these early views in regard to the particular translations they endorsed. The point is that new version advocates often attempt to paint KJV Only believers as outside the mainstream of Christian history for believing a translation could be infallible. Yet, they are the ones embracing a fringe view of God's ability or willingness to preserve His Scriptures. In fact, they are practical Deists in regard to this issue; they practically believe that God fell asleep, and left His perfect, pure words to be scattered, never again in this age to be absolutely or perfectly recovered in one Book! They hold a doctrine that maintains that God must preserve His inspired words only in the original languages in which they were first written. There is not one word of support for such a view in the Bible. And the advocates of this view (who do not believe that we possess any Greek manuscript today that is infallible in every word) do not even know for certain that the Greek copies they possess have been copied from Greek!

But we are not dependent upon early, post-Biblical writers. The folly of the new-version-scholars is also plainly revealed in the Scriptures themselves. Was there ever a time when all of the *original* manuscripts of the 66 Books of the Scriptures were gathered together into one book called "the Bible"? Timothy certainly did not, at any time, hold in his hand all of the original manuscripts of the Holy Scriptures - not even of the 39 books of the Old Testament. Yet, notice what the Holy Ghost, through Paul, said unto him:

2 Timothy 3:13 But evil men and seducers shall wax worse and worse, deceiving, and being deceived.
14 But continue thou in the things which thou hast learned and hast been assured of, knowing of whom thou hast learned them;
15 And that **from a child thou hast known the holy scriptures**, which are able to make thee wise unto salvation through faith which is in Christ Jesus.
16 **All scripture is given by inspiration of God**, and is profitable for doctrine, for reproof, for correction, for instruction in righteousness:
17 That the man of God may be perfect, throughly furnished unto all good works.

"All *scripture* is given by inspiration of God." And Timothy had heard and read the *Holy Scriptures* from a child. But Timothy did not read these Scriptures from the original manuscripts. Therefore, the Bible does not teach that *only* the original manuscripts are inspired. Timothy read a translation, or at least a copy, of the originals. God's providential power was sufficient to preserve these correct copies so that Timothy, and others, could hear the inspired Scriptures in their age.

After God inspires the writing of the original manuscripts, no new inspiration is needed. God then performs the miracle of preservation. But this act of preservation keeps the inspired Scriptures from expiring! As we have seen, Paul did not even write many of his Epistles with his own hand (Romans 16:22). The same God who kept Paul's scribes from error, can also keep subsequent copiers and translators from error as He pleases. He has promised to do so, throughout the ages (Matthew 24:35, Psalms 12:7, Isaiah 40:8). What good is inspired Scripture that is not preserved?

When Jesus read from the Scriptures, in the synagogue, He was not reading from an original manuscript:

Luke 4:17 And there was delivered unto him **the book** of the prophet Esaias. And when he had opened the **book**, he found the place where it **was written**,
21 And he began to say unto them, This day is **this scripture** fulfilled in your ears.

Jesus called what He read in the book "scripture." And He affirmed that Scripture "cannot be broken" (John 10:35). Yet, it is not likely that He was then reading from the original manuscript of Isaiah! Jesus also challenged others to read the "scriptures":

Matthew 21:42 Jesus saith unto them, Did ye never read in the **scriptures**...

John 5:39 Search the **scriptures**...

He believed they possessed these scriptures, even though they did not have the original manuscripts.

Likewise, the Holy Ghost calls the Book of Isaiah that the eunuch of Ethiopia was reading “scripture”:

Acts 8:27 And he arose and went: and, behold, a man of Ethiopia, an eunuch of great authority under Candace queen of the Ethiopians, who had the charge of all her treasure, and had come to Jerusalem for to worship,
28 Was returning, and sitting in his chariot **read Esaias the prophet.**
32 The **place of the scripture which he read** was this, He was led as a sheep to the slaughter; and like a lamb dumb before his shearer, so opened he not his mouth:
35 Then Philip opened his mouth, and began at the same **scripture**, and preached unto him Jesus.

Paul reasoned out of the “scriptures”; and he commended the Bereans for searching the “scriptures” as their final authority:

Acts 17:2 And Paul, as his manner was, went in unto them, and three sabbath days reasoned with them out of **the scriptures,**
10 And the brethren immediately sent away Paul and Silas by night unto Berea: who coming thither went into the synagogue of the Jews.
11 These were more noble than those in Thessalonica, in that they received the word with all readiness of mind, and **searched the scriptures daily**, whether those things were so.

The Bereans did not possess the original manuscripts. And if the copies they possessed were in error, then how could they be used to test the teachings of the Apostle Paul? The Holy Spirit has written that all Scripture is given by inspiration, and that it cannot be broken. The words of the Lord are pure words (Psalms 12:6):

1 Peter 1:25 But the word of the Lord endureth for ever...

Samuel P. Tregelles (1813-1875) was a British scholar and textual critic. He produced a revised Greek text (1857-1879) that preceded and influenced the Westcott-Hort text (1881). He assisted Tischendorf at the Vatican in transcribing Vaticanus B (one of the manuscripts that new versions are based upon). He often scorned those who would use verses such as 1 John 5:7 or Acts 8:37 to prove doctrine. It is obvious that he was no friend to the KJV Only viewpoint! However, he actually argued that translations can be inspired! His lengthy quotes below are worth reading carefully:

"But it is *asserted* that St. Matthew wrote in Greek: this assertion is believed by many; and I have now to examine the grounds on which the opinion is considered to be true...They seek to show that the Greek Gospel which we possess is not a translation... They maintain that the Greek original is more in accordance with the principles of the dealings of God, and thus they endeavour to give a *dogmatic* sanction to their opinion...The evidence of Papias [b. 70 A.D.] is treated as though it had but little weight, because of what Eusebius says of *the smallness of his understanding*...One ground on which the *understanding* of Papias has been assailed, has been his belief in the doctrine of a Millennium: but if *this* be a ground for treating his testimony as unworthy of credence, what shall we say of Justin Martyr, Irenaeus, Hippolytus, and many others in ancient times, and also not a few in the present day?...Indeed there are many who would rather regard Eusebius to have been in error in denying the pre-millennial advent of our Lord, than Papias in asserting it...this was what the Christians knew about the matter; it was as much a point of common information amongst them that St. Matthew wrote in Hebrew, as that he wrote a Gospel at all...It is granted that St. Matthew's Gospel in Greek does not seem like a translation; that the language does not seem less original than the other New Testament writings; and that, unless we had external testimony, we should, probably, not have imagined it to be a version: but all this does not *prove* the contrary. Are there no works which we *know* are translations, which bear no internal impress of the fact? ...A book was actually written by inspiration on one occasion, which was almost immediately *lost* beyond recovery. I mean that book of Jeremiah's prophecies which the king ordered to be burned [Jeremiah 36]. It is true that he dictated the prophecies again to Baruch, but 'many like words' were added; so that this was not a reproducing of the identical book which had been destroyed. Can proof be more plain than this, that **God acts according to *His own* wisdom in the inspiration and preservation of Scripture? As, then, I know nothing of God's actings except what he has revealed**, I deny that this dogmatic point of view is valid in itself, or is a ground for rejecting the evidence to the Hebrew original of St. Matthew's Gospel. It has been asked, what opinion can we form of the care of the early Christians over their sacred books, seeing they did not transmit a Hebrew original? If they believed in a Hebrew original, is it credible that they should have lost it? Whether *credible* or not, here are the facts: they *did* believe that St. Matthew wrote in Hebrew, and yet they did not transmit the Hebrew document. Greek was the language they *used,* and they preserved to us the copy which they *used,* though they avowed it to be a version...they transmitted the Greek Matthew as *authoritative*...If we possess an *authoritative* Greek gospel, why need the most timid shrink from believing, with all the ancients, that it is translated from the Hebrew which Matthew wrote? **Some have, indeed, thought the idea of an *authoritative translation* self contradictory. But this is only one form of dogmatic a *priori* argument: it is said that God may inspire an original writing; but an *inspired translation,* an authoritative version, is supposed to involve some incongruity. But why so? Can any of us say that he has penetrated into the Divine mind? Can we tell *how* God acted in the inspiration of Scripture? Can we say how it becomes Him to act? Unless we can affirm these things, we must not hastily reject the possibility of authoritative, inspired translation. Now we**

do possess inspired translations: the Scripture abounds with them. Are not the discourses of our Lord parts of inspired Scripture?...Sometimes the pen of inspiration expressly tells us that words were spoken in Hebrew, and then gives them in Greek: is not this a pretty plain intimation that inspired translation is not inconsistent with the ways of God?...**We may hold the highest views of inspiration, and yet admit that a version may be inspired. St. Paul rarely wrote with his own hand; and yet we do not doubt the full authority of all his Epistles; we do not say that Tertius and others may have erred in writing down his words.**"

(Samuel Tregelles, *The Journal of Sacred Literature*, Volume 4, 1850)

It is not necessary to enter into the debate as to whether Matthew originally wrote in Hebrew or Greek at this time. The important thing at hand is that one of the principle fathers of "modern" textual criticism (i.c. Tregelles) argued so well that he sawed off the very branch upon which his brand of textual criticism hangs. His goal was to prove that the Greek version of Matthew's Gospel was a translation - yet still authoritative and inspired. However, his powerful words leave him little room to argue against the common view that God has indeed preserved His Holy Scriptures, in these last days, in English, in the Authorized Version.

Tregelles writes:

"I know nothing of God's actings except what he has revealed..."

Amen! And what has He revealed concerning the subject of preserving His words? When Moses broke the tablets of the Law, God *preserved* them by rewriting them. Resurrection! When the king cut up the roll of Jeremiah and burned it (Jeremiah 36), God gave them again. When Jesus Christ (The Word) was crucified and buried, God resurrected Him. As one international language fades in its usefulness, and another takes its place, God is well able to insure that an authoritative, inspired translation is available.

It is readily acknowledged that English is the international language in these modern times. Notice the following testimonies concerning the English language:

"Sudan needs English to build bridges between North and South ...In the North, Arabic is and will remain the primary language, coexisting with English as the international language of the internet, trade and international engagement....Even in today's globalised world with the rise of other languages such as Chinese, English still remains the language of business."
(Martin Davidson, *Guardian Weekly,* January 11, 2011)

"There is no denying that English is the only official international language spoken and understood in most places all over the world and is very important for higher education."
(www.newsformatics.com)

"*How English evolved into a global language*...The need for an international language has always existed..."
(www.bbc.co.uk, December 19, 2010)

"Half the world's population is expected to be speaking English by 2015. Interest in English teaching positions abroad has mushroomed. That is because English is the international language of business, technology and academia."
(www.lemongrove.patch.com)

"*To Raise Its Global Profile, a Korean U. Shakes Up Its Campus* ...Postech this year became only the second Korean university to begin the transition to an all-English system. Undergraduate classes are to be conducted in English, and the university's entire administration would be bilingual...'But English is the global

language. We have a responsibility to train our students in a language that will be understood anywhere in the world'..."
(http://chronicle.com, January 5, 2011)

"English is the international language that is used worldwide. In this era of globalisation, you cannot afford to be left out by not mastering English...Many blogs or online journals are mushrooming everywhere which are being posted in English...English is the main mode of communication with the global audience... As English is the lingua franca, many countries using native languages have decided to switch to English so that the people have a better chance to do business internationally. Primary schools and secondary schools are using English as the main media of knowledge in the textbooks and exams. Many parents are also speaking to their toddlers in English and buying English books or encyclopedias for them to read and to improve on their written English...To sum up, in order to get ahead in this fast pace world that embrace technology, you need to master English well..."
(Mike Novik, *English is the International Language*, www.buzzle.com)

"Carried around the world by missionaries, it [the King James Bible] provided the base by which English is about to become the lingua franca of the world in the next century."
(Charlton Heston, *In the Arena: An Autobiography*)

Quotes could be endlessly multiplied. The fact that English is the main international language is indisputable.

As a side note, it is very interesting that English is largely derived from the Hebrew language. Robert Govett (1813-1901), who is known for writing one of the first commentaries on the Book of Revelation showing that its prophecies are literal and future, also penned a book titled, *English Derived from Hebrew* (1869). He writes:

"...having gone into this matter to some extent, I now believe that *English is derived from the Hebrew*...there are not five percent of Saxon words which cannot be traced to Hebrew. I wish, however, not to theorize, but to present the reader with examples..."

In conclusion, it is often maintained that something is always lost in translating. But if God is in it, and He chooses to providentially bless the work, He can insure an infallible translation as easy as He moved men to choose the correct Books of the Bible. God is able to translate correctly, even through imperfect men as His instruments. Enoch was *translated by* God:

Hebrews 11:5 By faith Enoch was **translated** that he should not see death; and was not found, because **God had translated him**: for before his translation he had this testimony, that he pleased God.

Was his nose or foot left behind? No! The same God who can translate people (Colossians 1:13), can certainly translate His words! He can insure that we have what we need in these last days. He has not left us to the subjective whims of present-day scribes. Was something lost in translation in Acts 2, when each man heard the preaching in his own language?

In the not-too-distant future, multitudes of people will be beheaded for their faith in the Word of God:

Revelation 20:4...and I saw the souls of them that were beheaded for the witness of Jesus, and **for the word of God**, and which had not worshipped the beast, neither his image, neither had received his mark upon their foreheads, or in their hands; and they lived and reigned with Christ a thousand years.

Obviously, these saints will *know* that they have a Bible that is inspired, true and authoritative. They will be willing to die for it!

It is a sword that can be held in their hands. An infallible, perfect, inspired, inerrant "Bible" that once existed, but can no longer be held in the hands of God's people today, is of no practical use. To resist the Devil, and fight the good fight of faith, the Christian must have a sword that he can hold!:

Psalms 149:6 Let the high praises of God be in their mouth, and a **twoedged sword in their hand;**

2 Samuel 23:10...and **his hand clave unto the sword**: and the LORD wrought a great victory...

Ephesians 6:17 And **take** the helmet of salvation, and **the sword of the Spirit, which is the word of God:**

CHAPTER 13

THE JERICHO SCHOLARS

2 Kings 2:1 And it came to pass, when the LORD would take up Elijah into heaven by a whirlwind, that Elijah went with Elisha from Gilgal.
11 And it came to pass, as they still went on, and talked, that, behold, there appeared a chariot of fire, and horses of fire, and parted them both asunder; and Elijah went up by a whirlwind into heaven.
15 And when **the sons of the prophets** which were to view at Jericho saw him, they said, The spirit of Elijah doth rest on Elisha. And they came to meet him, and bowed themselves to the ground before him.
16 And they said unto him, **Behold now, there be with thy servants fifty strong men; let them go, we pray thee, and seek thy master**: lest peradventure the Spirit of the LORD hath taken him up, and cast him upon some mountain, or into some valley. And he said, Ye shall not send.
17 And when they urged him till he was ashamed, he said, Send. They sent therefore fifty men; and they sought three days, but found him not.
18 And when they came again to him, (for he tarried at Jericho,) he said unto them, Did I not say unto you, Go not?

In 1919, Fundamental Baptist pastor, I.M. Haldeman, published a tract called *Jericho Theology, or The Modern Theological College A Menace and a Peril to the Church*. Notice some excerpts from this eye-opening tract:

THE WORD: GOD WILL KEEP IT!

"The day had now arrived when the Lord would take up Elijah by a whirlwind into heaven. Elijah and Elisha found themselves together at Gilgal...The two came to Jordan...Elisha desired that a double portion of the prophet's spirit might rest upon him. Elijah recognized that this was a hard thing. It afforded him, however, an opportunity to make a final test of his successor. He declared that if Elisha should see him when he was taken away the request would be granted, not otherwise...While they were going on together, suddenly Elijah was parted from his companion and swept by a whirlwind to heaven. Elisha cried out, 'My father, my father! the chariot of Israel, and the horsemen thereof'...He had met the test; he had had the heaven gaze - he saw the miracle...The theological students at Jericho who had stood afar off when the two men went down into Jordan came forward to meet him and testified that they were sure the spirit of Elijah was now in the world and that it was resting upon Elisha; but while they believed the spirit of Elijah was in the world they did not believe the body of Elijah was in heaven...the students urged and insisted to such a degree that the body of Elijah could be found on the earth; they were so anxious to demonstrate that the body of Elijah had not gone to heaven and that, in reality, Elijah himself was not there, that Elisha grew ashamed, yielded up his testimony and bade them go...The theological college at Jericho, president, faculty and students, accepted the presence of the spirit of Elijah in the world, but repudiated the presence of the living body of Elijah in heaven. In this the Jericho college gave a fore-view of the attitude of some theological colleges to-day, and sets forth the movement of the modern theological idea...The theological college at Jericho undertook to explain the miraculous disappearance of Elijah's body on rational and natural grounds...No matter where such a college may be, whether in New York, Chicago or New England, it is a Jericho college. The theology is Jericho theology and the professors are Jericho professors. They are influenced by the Jericho environment; by scientific thought, by modernism. It is an endeavor to bring the truth of God down to the level of the world's atmosphere...The next time you hear a preacher telling his audience that we must translate the theology of the New Testament into modern terminology; that we must accommodate our theology to the scientific spirit; that we must bring the exposition of the Bible into line with the twentieth century thought, you may know that you are listening to a Jericho preacher; no matter whether he is native born or imported, he is a Jericho preacher from a Jericho college, giving you Jericho theology...The Jericho theologians became so urgent and made such a clamor about going out to prove that Elijah's body did not ascend to heaven that Elisha became ashamed - and yielded his testimony to theirs. There were circumstances which combined to produce this surrender. The Jericho theologians had the prestige of professed scholarship and trained mentality. They had erected themselves into a final court of judgment. They looked with the same contempt upon a worker for God who had not passed through their doors as a West Point graduate does upon a volunteer. They fixed the interpretation and repudiated everything and everyone who did not go along with their decision. Elisha never had time to go to the Jericho college. The Lord called him from the field, the furrow and the plow, and bade him enter on his ministry at once. When therefore the men of the college insisted that he really did not know what he was talking about; that he was crassly ignorant in proclaiming such a thing as that the body of a man was living in heaven on the throne of God, he hesitated and surrendered...They talk continually of their own scholarship. They exploit it at every turn. They batter the ignorance of those who differ, with them. Their sacramental phrase is, 'Scholarship is agreed'...Men who really in their heart of hearts do not believe in the Bible as the living Word of God. These are the men the Jericho colleges of the twentieth century are turning out...The theological seminary at Jericho was an actual menace and peril to the ministry of Elisha...surrender to Jericho theology means the paralysis of the Jericho preacher himself. **He becomes filled with doubts** which find no limit, which extend over every range of professed truth. He becomes a peddler of other men's thoughts, of their doubts and guesses. He **speaks no longer with authority** as did his Master; he speaks as the scribes and the Pharisees. **There is nothing certain about him but his uncertainty** - and those who hear him become like him - totally paralyzed in relation to the supernatural and the divine...Let this surrender to Jericho theology continue for the next twenty-five years and the Bible will be practically repudiated from the pulpit, the church as a supernatural organization will cease to exist; it will become, on the one side, a club for rich men and women wherein they may gather to congratulate themselves on their moral tendencies...the church will drift into a social organization for the discussion of social inequalities and wrongs...Elisha's ministry became a ministry of power only when he repudiated the Jericho theology. Only when he repudiated the Jericho theology, turned his back on Jericho, and reaffirmed his testimony concerning the living body of Elijah in heaven, did his ministry become one of power and bear seal that it was heaven-sent..."

Preachers that believe in the resurrected Christ, who will soon return, are certainly needed today. But how will men believe these truths, with certainty, unless they believe in the preservation of the Scriptures which testify of these important doctrines?

Just as the scholars of Jericho, with their unbelief and natural minds, denied the *translation* of Elijah to heaven, so do modern Jericho scholars deny that the Holy Bible is really *translated miraculously by God* for us today in English. As the Jericho scholars in Elisha's day went *searching* for the missing Elijah, so do modern Jericho scholars search (and search and search!) for the lost words of the Bible (i.e. "modern" textual criticism). And if the Christian will listen to these Jericho scholars, he will find his time wasted, and his work, power and faith greatly hindered.

In Elijah, a type of the original languages of the Bible can be seen. When Elijah was translated, the Spirit fell upon Elisha (with a double portion of power). We can see in Elisha a picture of the Authorized Version. The Jericho scholars immediately praised Elisha, and acknowledged his spiritual power:

2 Kings 2:15 And when the sons of the prophets which were to view at Jericho saw him, they said, **The spirit of Elijah doth rest on Elisha. And they came to meet him, and bowed themselves to the ground before him.**

Nevertheless, they went seeking for the "lost" Elijah in the mountains and valleys!

In the same way, modern Jericho scholars refuse to believe that God has translated the Bible from a dead, ancient language into the international language of these last days. While they often praise the Authorized Version, and acknowledge much of its power and glory, they immediately set out to search for "the Greek." They continually send out their "strong men," over and over again. But regardless of how many times they search for Elijah, they never fully find him. They are like a greedy disease foundation that will never acknowledge a true cure, for it would then mean the end of their whole industry!

Good Christian leaders can be deceived. The disciples of Jesus after His resurrection were slow to believe that the Lord had been resurrected. In a similar manner, there are many modern disciples who are slow of heart to believe the promises of the preservation of the Scriptures. They will not acknowledge that the Bible has been given to us today in English. They are searching for the written Word among the dead languages:

Luke 24:4 And it came to pass, as they were much perplexed thereabout, behold, two men stood by them in shining garments:
5 And as they were afraid, and bowed down their faces to the

earth, they said unto them, **Why seek ye the living among the dead?**
10 It was Mary Magdalene, and Joanna, and Mary the mother of James, and other women that were with them, which told these things unto the apostles.
11 And **their words seemed to them as idle tales, and they believed them not.**

The prophets of Jericho never found Elijah on some mountain, or in some valley. And the disciples never found the body of Jesus in the tombs. In the same way, modern Christian scholars will never find a perfect, infallible Bible by searching the valleys, mountaintops, and tombs of ancient Greek. They have been looking for many years, and they are the first to confess that they will never find a perfect Bible.

Years ago, early psychologists, believing in determinism, promised that they would soon find the keys to perfectly predict behavior. They would thereby prove that psychology was a hard science. In denying free-will, they searched for decades. Soon, psychology was largely (and quietly) accepted as a "science," simply because psychologists were "investigating" human personality! Psychology never found (and never will find) the keys to perfectly predict human behavior. Likewise, the so-called "science" of textual criticism will never find an infallible Bible that anyone can hold in their hands and read. These so-called "sciences" are actually philosophies (vain philosophies); and they will spoil the faith and fruit of Christians:

Colossians 2:8 Beware lest any man **spoil you through philosophy** and vain deceit, after the tradition of men, after the rudiments of the world, and not after Christ.

Psychology harms Christians by shipwrecking their faith in the sufficiency of Scripture. Modern textual criticism shipwrecks the faith of Christians in the infallibility (and thus, the credibility) of the Bible. Textual critics speak highly of the lost Originals that they seek to piece back together, year after year, in a never-ending quest. But in doing so, they hinder assurance in a Bible that can be held in the hands, and studied, and believed. And ironically, they thereby shipwreck the faith of multitudes in the inspiration and infallibility of the Originals themselves! If God did not preserve His Scriptures, anywhere, to absolute perfection, how then can one believe that the original manuscripts were even written in perfection? Will one then quote a *Bible* verse to prove it?

For example, a scholar once argued that there is no perfect Bible because the perfect word is only "settled in Heaven" (Psalms 119:89). When asked how he knew for sure that the word is settled *in Heaven*, he then quoted Psalms 119, which is in the Bible that is *on earth!* When he was asked whether the Bible he was quoting was inspired and infallible, he said that it was not, since the only perfect and infallible Word was in Heaven:

2 Thessalonians 3:1 Finally, brethren, pray for us, that the word of the Lord may have free course, and be glorified, even as it is with you:
2 And that **we may be delivered from unreasonable** and wicked men: for all men have not faith.

How many millions of people have never believed, or have had their faith shipwrecked by these Jericho scholars?:

"The **authority of the translation was the first to be shaken**; then variation in the manuscript, **destroying confidence in the original texts.** If the original language was miraculously communicated, there was a natural presumption that it would be miraculously preserved. As it has not been, the inference of doubt extends backward on inspiration...How can the Protestant

Church establish its claim to any inspiration of the Bible itself when it is known that there are no autographs of the Bible writings extant..."
(James Anthony Froude; quoted in H.M. Tabor, *Faith Or Fact?,* 1897)

"The dogma of the one infallible book is now fast losing hold of thinking minds, even in the more conservative churches."
(George W. Buckley, *Politics and Morals*)

The God who inspired the *infallible* Word through *fallible* men, and recorded it through *fallible* writers (like Tertius), is well able to *preserve it perfectly* through fallible men. And there is not the slightest Bible verse that teaches that God will not preserve His Word through a perfect translation in English, in the international language of the end times:

Jeremiah 32:17 Ah Lord GOD! behold, thou hast made the heaven and the earth by thy great power and stretched out arm, and **there is nothing too hard for thee:**

Psalms 12:6 The words of the LORD are pure words: as silver tried in a furnace of earth, purified seven times.
7 **Thou shalt keep them**, O LORD, **thou shalt preserve them** from this generation for ever.

How do we know the perfect, inspired Bible is the King James Version? We know it the same way that we know that the Christian revelation itself is true, in comparison to the Koran, etc. The same objective standards that prove the Christian Bible over the Koran (or Vedas, etc.), can also be used to prove the KJV over any other copy, manuscript, version, etc. Many of these proofs are offered in this book.

When we examine the degree the KJV is hated, and by whom it is hated; and when we examine its fruit; and when we examine the testimonies of the multitudes of people that have clung to it as inspired and infallible, these things alone argue that there is no other Book around today that can give the same objective and subjective witness.

The Jericho scholars may mock our King James Bible. Like the Sadducees, they have their arrogant, hypothetical questions and objections (all of which originated from infidels and modernists). But who will not admit that our King James Bible is better than the "Bible" that they have not yet found? Let them continue to bring their spices to the tombs in their unbelief of our Lord's promises (Luke 24:1). Let them gather together and praise and mourn the lost manuscripts:

Luke 24:13 And, behold, two of them went that same day to a village called **Emmaus,** which was from Jerusalem about three-score furlongs.
17 And he said unto them, What manner of communications are these that ye have one to another, as ye walk, and are sad?
19 And he said unto them, What things? And they said unto him, Concerning Jesus of Nazareth, which was a prophet **mighty in deed and word** before God and all the people:
20 And how the chief priests and our rulers delivered him to be condemned to death, and have crucified him.

These Emmaus scholars (like the Jericho scholars) praised Jesus (e.g. like many praise the Originals). But they were discouraged that Jesus perished (as modern scholars teach that the Originals perished). But what did Jesus say to them?:

Luke 24:25 Then he said unto them, **O fools, and slow of heart to believe all that the prophets have spoken:**
26 Ought not Christ to have suffered these things, and to enter into his glory?
27 And beginning at Moses and all the prophets, he expounded

unto them in all the scriptures the things concerning himself.

The same Scriptures which speak of the preservation of Christ, also speak of the preservation of God's words!:

Isaiah 40:8 The grass withereth, the flower fadeth: but **the word of our God shall stand for ever.**

Will we heed the rebukes and warnings of Jesus?:

Mark 12:38 And he said unto them in his doctrine, **Beware of the scribes**, which love to go in long clothing, and love salutations in the marketplaces,

CHAPTER 14

THE MOST HATED BOOK

"No book has been so hated, opposed, analyzed, commented on, condemned, and cast out; and on the other hand, never any book so loved, defended, expounded, and illustrated by loyal hearts and holy lives. There must be something peculiar about a book which so excites the undying hatred of its enemies from age to age, and which so attracts the love and admiration of tens of millions..."
(*The Theological Monthly*, Volume 5, 1891)

John 16:7 Nevertheless I tell you the truth; It is expedient for you that I go away: for if I go not away, the Comforter will not come unto you; but if I depart, I will send him unto you.
8 And when he is come, **he will reprove the world of sin, and of righteousness, and of judgment**:

Jesus Christ, the Word, was hated by this world. Wherever the true, Written Word is found, it will be treated in the same manner. It is true that, at times, many false teachers lauded Jesus:

Matthew 22:16 And they sent out unto him their disciples with the Herodians, saying, **Master, we know that thou art true, and teachest the way of God in truth,** neither carest thou for any man: for thou regardest not the person of men.
18 But Jesus perceived their wickedness, and said, Why tempt ye me, ye hypocrites?

Even devils sometimes admitted His glorious identity (Acts 16:17):

Mark 1:23 And there was in their synagogue a man with an unclean spirit; and he cried out,
24 Saying, Let us alone; what have we to do with thee, thou Jesus of Nazareth? art thou come to destroy us? **I know thee who thou art, the Holy One of God.**

Wicked men sometimes hid their contempt for Jesus because they feared the people (Mark 12:12). Nevertheless, the world (especially these wicked leaders) certainly hated Jesus.

In the same manner, there is one Book that is hated above all others by false teachers and evil people. There is no other book that receives so much praise and so much hatred at the same time. This is another proof that the King James Bible is God's infallible Word in these last days.

A few quotes (out of thousands that could be provided) should reveal how the various adversaries of true, Biblical Christianity despise the King James Bible:

"This (King James) Bible was completed in 1611, and was bitterly opposed by Romanists, Hebraists, Armenians, Socinians, Arians, and others."
(Schaff; quoted in H.M. Tabor, *Faith Or Fact?,* 1897)

"When we find Unitarians, Modernists and Romanisers holding the RV in preference to the AV it should make us pause..."
(Charles Welch, *The Berean Expositor*, Vol. 29, 1939)

The Spiritualists and Occultists

In the 19th century, it became fashionable in some circles to investigate ghosts or spirits, through the aid of "mediums." The King James Bible condemns this attempt as divination and necromancy (Leviticus 19:31, Deuteronomy 18:10-11). Webster defines *necromancy* as:

"The art of revealing future events by means of a pretended communication with the dead. This imposture is prohibited. Deuteronomy 18. Enchantment; conjuration."
(*Webster's Dict.,* 1828)

John Worth Edmonds (1816-1874) was an influential early American spiritualist. He was the author of *Spiritualism* (1853). His daughter was a medium. In 1858, after resigning his position as a judge (based on public outcry against his necromancy), he authored, *Appeal to the Public on Spiritualism.* He became convinced that the so-called departed "spirits" were real:

"I have heard the mediums use Greek, Latin, Spanish, and French words when I knew they had no knowledge of any language but their own...facts were communicated which were unknown then..."

The Bible teaches that "seducing spirits" (i.e. devils, or fallen angels) are behind these manifestations. The Bible warns of such deceptions in the last days:

1 Timothy 4:1 Now the Spirit speaketh expressly, that in the latter times some shall depart from the faith, giving heed to **seducing spirits**, and **doctrines of devils**;

Notice that these seducing spirits will deceive people with certain "doctrines." A common doctrine that is found throughout these devilish writings is the lie that God has not perfectly preserved His Word in the King James Bible:

Genesis 3:1 Now the serpent was more subtil than any beast of the field which the LORD God had made. And he said unto the woman, **Yea, hath God said**...?

Observe the following words from *Sacred Circle* in 1855, which was a magazine edited by Judge Edmonds (mentioned previously):

"[Skeptic]: 'You are very severe upon the Sacred Word.'

[Spiritualist]: 'I **respect it** as much as you do, and believe that a thorough investigation can not harm it. **It is only when you claim too much for it; when you will have every translated word of King James' version *infallible*...'**

[Skeptic]: 'What would you have us do? **We have nothing but King James' version of the Bible, and wherever the English language is spoken, that is the authority**. Must I become an Oriental linguist - a perfect Hebraist...before I read my Bible?'

[Spiritualist]: 'No; but **those who have studied those languages, and thrown light upon the dark mysteries of the ancient record, should be listened to**...'"

(Judge Edmonds, Dr. Dexter, O.G. Warren, *The Sacred Circle*, Volume 1, 1855, Vol. 1, 1855)

It can be clearly seen that the old Serpent seeks to seduce people away from the clarity and certainty of the King James Bible. His "light" is the same lie that he offered to Eve, *after* he tempted her to doubt the certainty of God's words.

Wherever we find spiritualism (i.e. spiritism), occultism and Satanism, we find the infallibility of the King James Bible decried, and the RV exalted:

"I am proud to have been one of the pioneer workers in the Spiritualistic field, and have suffered much for the cause of Spiritualism, in upholding its purity and promulgating its truth. I am

writing this in defense of the glorious truth I love so well...The King James Bible is admittedly one of the most incorrect versions..."
(Franklin Alonzo Thomas, *Philosophy and Phenomena of Spiritualism*, 1922)

Another example is Helena Petrovna Blavatsky (1831-1891). She was an early leader of the occult Theosophy movement. Her devilish philosophies are spread around the world today in the *Harry Potter* books, etc. She founded the Theosophical Society in 1875. Blavatsky was a Satanist, who claimed to be a medium (i.e. possessed!). She wrote:

"In general, the so-called *orthodox* Christian conceptions about the 'fallen' angels or Satan, are as remarkable as they are absurd ...the author of 'Earth's Earliest Ages'...Pember, M.A., devotes a thick volume to proving Theosophists, Spiritualists, Metaphysicians, Agnostics, Mystics, poets, and every contemporary author on oriental speculations, to be the devoted servants of the 'Prince of the Air,' and irretrievably damned... It is 'Satan who is the god of our planet and the only god'...When the Church, therefore, curses Satan, it curses the cosmic reflection of God; it anathematizes God made manifest in matter..."
(H.P. Blavatsky, *The Secret Doctrine*, 1888)

What do these Satanically-inspired writers think about the King James Bible and the new versions? Blavatsky's words on the subject are frighteningly close to those of many modern, conservative scholars. She calls Westcott, "a learned scholar" (i.e. *Isis Unveiled*), and quotes him often. Statements from Blavatsky could be multiplied, such as, "...the Revised Version does not repeat the mistake of the Authorized Version..." For example, she writes:

"In King James's version, as it stands translated, it has no resemblance to the original."
(Blavatsky, *Isis Unveiled*)

"Add to this the fact that out of the forty-seven translators of King James' Bible 'only three understood Hebrew'...and one may easily understand what reliance can be placed on the English version of the Bible...Now that the **revised version** of the gospels has been published and the most glaring mistranslations of the old versions are **corrected**, one will understand better the words in St. John [chapter 5:6-7]..."
(Blavatsky, *The Secret Doctrine*, 1888)

Some of the followers of Blavatsky also claimed to be under the control of spirits through automatic writing, etc. In 1891, Annie Besant (1847-1933) succeeded Blavatsky as head of the Theosophical Society. From 1889, until Blavatsky's death in 1891, Besant was a co-editor of the Theosophical Society's *Lucifer* magazine. Besant, and her associates, hated the King James Bible:

"The English translation (Authorised Version) is **wretchedly imperfect. Errors abound in it,** and some of them are of a **most laughable** description. On this account great calls have been made for the **new translation**..."
(Charles Bradlaugh, Annie Wood Besant, Charles Watts, *The Freethinker's Text-book*, 1876)

Later Theosophical writings continued to attack the King James Bible:

"...the English translation called the Authorized Version...while it is dear to English people...yet lacks entirely the proper spirit of the mystical Hebrew original; and the very fact that Englishmen love their King James's version so much distracts their attention away from the original mystical sense of the Hebrew scripture. Go then to the original tongue..."
(*Lucifer Magazine*, January to December, 1930)

Another influential occult writer is Manly Palmer Hall. Notice the following short biography of this Satanic writer:

"Manly Palmer Hall [1901-1990] was a Canadian-born author and mystic. He is perhaps most famous for his work *The Secret Teachings of All Ages: An Encyclopedic Outline of Masonic, Hermetic, Qabbalistic and Rosicrucian Symbolical Philosophy,* which is widely regarded as his magnum opus, and which he published at the age of 25 (or 27, 1928)...In 1973 (47 years after writing *The Secret Teachings of All Ages*), Hall was recognized as a 33° Mason (the highest honor conferred by the Supreme Council of the Scottish Rite), at a ceremony held at PRS on December 8th, despite never being initiated into the physical craft."
(www.manlyphall.org)

Manly P. Hall (as documented elsewhere in this book) often wrote against the King James Bible. He sometimes slandered it with historical lies; but his main goal (like the earlier necromancers) was to oppose the popular view of its infallibility!:

"The King James version is especially rich in errors..."
(Manly P. Hall, *Reincarnation: The Cycle of Necessity*, 1956)

"We know that the Authorized Version by no means satisfies the requirements of advanced Biblical scholarship..."
(Manly P. Hall, *Horizon,* Issue 9. Vol. 1, 1949)

"...we will **have to undo** much that is cherished error. The **problem** of revising the Bible shows how difficult it is to do this. For the last hundred years, **we have been trying** to get out an edition of the Bible that is reasonably correct; **but** nobody wants it. What's wanted is the good old King James version, every jot and tittle of it, because **most people are convinced that God dictated the Bible to King James in English**."
(Manly P. Hall, *Horizon*, Philosophical Research Society, 1944)

The occult plan is plainly confessed above. What book did Hall (who boasted of having the keys to channeling the power of Lucifer) call one of the great books of the world? It was one of the principle manuscripts that is used by all modern versions, and many modern scholars to supposedly "correct" the King James Bible!:

"The **Codex Sinaiticus** is a manuscript of the 4th Century...This manuscript is **one of the great books of the world**, and although it was discovered long after the publication of the **now universally accepted King James version** of the Bible, it is sufficiently important to justify considerable revision of our popular conception of the Scriptural writings."
(Manly P. Hall, *Horizon the Magazine of Useful and Intelligent Living,* 1946)

Another Masonic writer views discarding the King James Bible as a key to advancing Masonry in the world:

"I remember distinctly the shock which I experienced the first time **the revised version** published in common English as it is spoken today was shown to me. It seemed positively sacrilegious. To me the wording and peculiar language of **the old King James** version seemed essentially a part of the Bible itself and I was sure that I could never part with those old associations. That feeling has long since changed, however, and I have come to know that **the newer translations** are the best and most accurate. I survived the **transition from my old ideas** and am better for it today. So it is ever in the history of **progress** and so it will be with us as **we advance in the work of pushing Masonry ahead** in the van of human progress."
(Carl W. Mason, *Nature and Powers of a General Grand Lodge*, September 5, 1910)

How long will the eyes of so many Christians remain closed? These men praised the very manuscripts that Westcott and Hort used to construct the Greek text that is behind the English RV, and other new versions. The principle leaders who worked on the Revised Version, etc., practiced necromancy (communicating with the "dead"). The early "research" of Westcott and Hort not only helped spawn a new age of textual criticism - these men helped launch the so-called New Age movement itself! (See chapter 16).

Freemasons regularly advised students to study the newer versions:

"The Scripture readings should be from **the American Revision** ...The great Light of Masonry can only be understood through the illumination of the Spirit..."
(Robert D. Graham, *The Foundation Stones of Masonic Study*, Grand Lodge Bulletin, Volumes 21-25, 1920)

"...some of the newer translations, by virtue of more recent researches, are often more accurate..."
(Joseph Fort Newton, *Great Light in Masonry*, 1940)

Elizabeth Clare Prophet (a New Age astrologist) even justifies her astrology by attacking the KJV:

"*Observe times* does not appear in modern translations, which are considered to be more accurate and literal than the King James Version."
(Elizabeth Clare Prophet, *The Astrology of the Four Horsemen*, 1991)

Homosexuals

Homosexuals also hate the King James Bible (or at least they abhor the idea that it is infallible). Notice the following words of a homosexual theologian:

"The term 'sodomite' in the King James Version of Deuteronomy 23:17 and I Kings 14:24 is an incorrect translation of the Hebrew word for 'temple prostitute.'"
(Dr. Rembert S. Truluck)

Homosexuals adore the new versions. They participated in producing the NIV in various ways. Both Marten Woudstra (chairman of the NIV's Old Testament Committee) and Virginia Mollenkott (stylistic editor of the NIV) were homosexuals!

It is therefore not surprising that Jim Swilley, the homosexual bishop of the Church in the Now (Conyers, Georgia), rejects the infallibility of the King James Bible, and praises the NIV as one of the most accurate versions. On his blog, he writes:

"...I **wholeheartedly reject the notion of an official 'authorized version'**...When I was young, Kenneth Taylor's beautifully accessible *Living Bible* changed my life and set the course for my whole ministry. Many years later, Eugene Peterson's daring paraphrase called *The Message* affected me nearly as dramatically. In recent years I have grown to respect the *Today's New International Version* for its modernity and clarity and lack of religious sexism. In my opinion, it is probably the most accurate mainstream translation of them all...You may ask then, 'If you love all these translations so much, why write a new one?' My only answer is that this writing is my way to pay homage to those who have already blazed this trail of translation before me."

Roman Catholics

In the 1800's, Roman Catholics publicly burned the King James Bible (see John Dowling, *The Burning of the Bibles: Defense of the Protestant Version of the Scriptures, Against the Attacks of Popish Apologists,* 1843).

In support of this atrocity, a Catholic priest in Rhode Island was not shy in revealing how he really felt about the King James Bible:

"If, then, such a version of the Bible should not be tolerated, the question then is, which is the best and most respectful manner to make away with it...As for myself I would not hesitate to say, that the most respectful would be **to burn it**, rather than give it to grocers and dealers to wrap their wares in, **or consign it to more dishonourable purposes**..."
(John Corry, a Catholic priest, *Providence Journal*, January 9, 1843)

Catholics believed the King James Bible competed with the authority of their church, in the eyes of men:

"Pope Pius VII. denounced...[the] Authorised Version in no measured terms; as, 'Not the Gospel of man, but the Gospel of the Devil.'"
(Franz Anton Knittel, "*New Criticisms on the Celebrated Text: 1 John V,*" 1829)

"Can you consistently reject the authority of the great universal Church [Roman Catholicism], and yet build upon that of *some obscure translator* in the reign of James I.?"
(John Milner, *The End of Religious Controversy*)

Roman Catholics were largely responsible for outlawing the King James Bible from public schools in various states.

Is Modern Conservatism the Old Liberalism?

Sadly, many so-called conservative scholars are joining with the enemies of Christ and His Gospel in their scornful contempt for the King James Version. They sometimes praise it when they must; but they also take every opportunity to deride it so that its authority will be lessened in the eyes of the people. In other words, many envy it! The proud prediction of a 19th century Liberal has largely come to pass:

"The Liberalism of today will be the Conservatism of tomorrow, and as for the Conservatism of today, it will be utterly forgotten and ignored in the future, which is near..."
(Frederic Edwards, *The Revised Old Testament*, 1885)

Grave errors in history, after some time, gain the appearance of orthodoxy through tradition. Thankfully, a growing remnant is still holding "fast the form of sound words" (2 Timothy 1:13), during this "falling away" (2 Thessalonians 2:3).

Notice the following arguments from the so-called "freethinkers" (i.e. blatant infidels) of the 19th century. These same arguments are found in many conservative circles today (2 Timothy 3:5):

"Accordingly, in November, 1852, a Bible Convention was held at Salem, Mr. Barker being appointed President. We extract the following from his speech, as illustrating the **uncertainty of the Bible translations**...: 'We say, that the Bible bears on its very face the marks of human imperfection and error. This is true of every Bible **in existence.** We will begin with the Bible in common use, and what do we find? The title-page tells us it is a *translation* from the original tongues, by the special command of one of the kings of England. **Does any one pretend that the translators were infallible** - men above the possibility of error? Nothing of the kind...The sects and priesthoods themselves show that they regard the common translation as imperfect. They all take the liberty to alter it. They alter it in thousands and tens of thousands of places. Nothing is more common than for theological disputants to appeal from the common translation of the Bible to what they call the original Greek and Hebrew. Every commentator takes the same liberty. The leaders of the sects and

priesthoods of the day have testified their belief that **the Bibles in common use are imperfect** and erroneous by making *new* translations...English Unitarians, published a new translation of the New Testament...Mr. Taylor published a new translation of the New Testament from Griesbach's Greek New Testament...We are not alone, therefore, in believing that **the Bibles in common use bear marks of human imperfection and error**...We add, if the translators of the Bible had been the best and wisest men that ever lived, **their work would not have been perfect**. **A translation from Greek and Hebrew cannot be perfect.** But the translators employed by King James were not the best or wisest men that ever lived. They were, in some respects, exceedingly ignorant, prejudiced, and immoral. They were liars and false-swearers...To make the Bible agree with their creed, they, put into their translation things which were not in the Greek or Hebrew Bibles, and mistranslated vast multitudes of things which were in the Greek and Hebrew Bibles. I will give you an instance or two. Their creed taught that God once died, or laid down his life. There was nothing in the Greek or Hebrew Bibles to uphold this doctrine, so in translating the Bible they so altered a passage as to make it to teach the doctrine...The Greek and Hebrew languages, from which the Bible has to be translated, are dead languages - languages which are no longer spoken or written by any people - languages which exist only in ancient writings. The meaning of many of the words of those languages is, in consequence, lost."
(*Half-hours With the Freethinkers*, 1857)

In this extensive quote, we find that the "textual criticism" of many professing conservative scholars today, is really the old, so-called "higher criticism" of a century ago. It was born in the unbelief of these infidels, and they received it from the original "free thinker" of the Garden of Eden (i.e. the king of pride and father of lies):

Genesis 3:1 Now the serpent was more subtil than any beast of the field which the LORD God had made. And he said unto the woman, Yea**, hath God said**, Ye shall not eat of every tree of the garden?

Humanist Scholars

Charles Francis Potter (1885-1962) is another example of how infidels hate the King James Version. Potter was greatly used by Satan to attack the KJV. He began as a Baptist preacher; but he soon became a Unitarian minister, denying almost everything in the Bible. He gained national attention when he participated in a series of radio debates with the fundamental Baptist pastor, John Roach Straton in 1923-24. During the Scopes evolution trial in Dayton, Tennessee, Potter wrote out what he perceived to be contradictions in the Bible for the defense. He founded the First Humanist Society of New York in 1929. In 1930, he authored, *Humanism: A New Religion*. In this book, Potter boasts that public education in America is controlled by Humanists, and is really a state-funded Humanist "church" that is far more powerful than a once-a-week Sunday School. He was a signer of the *Humanist Manifesto* with John Dewey, and became an honorary president of the National Education Association (NEA). In his autobiography, Potter writes:

"What gave me a jolt was the discovery that the **King James version** of the Old Testament might be beautiful poetry and prose, but **it was as inaccurate a translation as was ever sold** to a trusting public."
(Charles F. Potter, *The Preacher and I*, 1951)

In, *The Faiths Men Live By,* Potter explains how revised versions (which lack 1 John 5:7, etc.), promote the Unitarian viewpoint, which finally led him to Humanism.

In his autobiography, Potter also speaks of his contact with a medium (a person claiming to be in contact with the spirit world), and his growing interest in occult phenomena:

"...my contact with a medium who tried to get me to incorporate Spiritualism into Humanism led me to think that his whole performance was a staged fake, but that then his undoubted telepathic ability, and the other experiences...gave me the somewhat disturbing impression of having come momentarily into contact with some field or sphere - or perhaps even some world or dimension - *beyond the senses*...I am no Spiritualist, but I do believe that the future of religion...will be intimately concerned with these natural forces, faculties, and phenomena...Telepathy... is an unexplored ability of human beings..."
(Charles F. Potter, *The Preacher and I*, 1951)

"Research" is usually the justification for exploring evil. Eve "investigated" the forbidden fruit. She wanted her eyes to be opened, so she could be "as gods" (Genesis 3:5). Again, contact with spirits (regardless of how such divination is justified) is a recurring theme in those who hate the King James Bible, and deny the perfect preservation of God's Word. Casting doubt upon God's Word is the first step of Satan. This prepares his victims to doubt God's warnings. Finally, with these two foundations shaken, he then tempts his victims to eat the forbidden fruit in an attempt to gain godhood (usually by the aid of "spirits"), in defiance of the true God.

In all of this, we see that the King James Bible is hated by foolish rebels because of its power. Yet, often this hatred and envy is hidden behind words of doubt. Satan tried to tempt Jesus with the same insinuating questions:

Matthew 4:6 And saith unto him, **If** thou be the Son of God...

THE WORD: GOD WILL KEEP IT!

We can be sure that wherever the true, preserved Word of God is found today, it will have this same, Satanic doubt heaped upon it by all who envy its authority:

Mark 15:10 For he knew that the chief priests had delivered him **for envy.**
11 But the chief priests moved the people...

Many flatterers will arise with a feigned praise for the Word of God. But their true motive is its destruction:

Matthew 22:16 And they sent out unto him their disciples with the Herodians, saying, **Master, we know that thou art true**, and **teachest the way of God in truth**...
18 But Jesus perceived their wickedness, and said, Why tempt ye me, ye hypocrites?

Psalms 12:2 They speak vanity every one with his neighbour: **with flattering lips and with a double heart do they speak.**
3 The LORD shall cut off all flattering lips, and the tongue that speaketh proud things:
6 The **words of the LORD** are pure words: as silver tried in a furnace of earth, purified seven times.
7 **Thou shalt keep them, O LORD, thou shalt preserve them from this generation for ever.**

There is no other book that is hated, scorned, resented, envied, despised and criticized like the Authorized Version of the Holy Scriptures! It is the Word of God in these last days:

John 7:7 The world cannot hate you; but **me it hateth**, **because I testify of it, that the works thereof are evil.**

John 17:17 Sanctify them through thy truth: **thy word is truth.**

CHAPTER 15

THE MOST FRUITFUL BOOK

Matthew 7:20 Wherefore by their fruits ye shall know them.

2 Timothy 2:9 Wherein I suffer trouble, as an evil doer, even unto bonds; but **the word of God is not bound.**

Isaiah 55:11 So shall **my word** be that goeth forth out of my mouth: it shall not return unto me void, but it shall accomplish that which I please, and **it shall prosper** in the thing whereto I sent it.

"Will a new and modern version make more Christians or bring more solace in the next 349 years than the King James version has in the last 349 years?"
(*Raleigh Register*, October 10, 1960)

Ecclesiastes 8:4 Where the word of a king is, there is power...

Many so-called "Bible versions" have arisen to challenge the spiritual influence of the Authorized Version:

"American Bible Society spokesmen predict that within a generation the new bible [i.e. the RSV] will have supplanted the King James version as the standard source of Biblical quotations, sermons and study...the RSV will replace the King James...300 years is too long for one [Version] to reign supreme..."
(*The Stars and Stripes,* November 11, 1958)

Yet, before long, these new versions fade into the background, as the Authorized Version remains victorious in its majestic power. Indeed, the Authorized Version is the only Book that has brought forth the amazing, *enduring* fruit that we would expect from the true, preserved Word of God in these last days. People from all philosophical or theological viewpoints are forced to admit that there is something different about this Book:

"...the English Bible, and specifically the King James version...was couched in a prose so rich with the genius of a great language, and so invariably read with reverence, love, or fear, that **there is perhaps no equivalent instance of the style as well as the substance of a single book influencing and sometimes dominating the mold of thought and form of expression of a whole people**...The most sophisticated megalopolitan can not read Isaiah today, or Paul, without yielding to the spell ...Enter to scoff and you remain to be stirred and exalted...***Ye shall know them by their fruits*** **applies to books as well as to men**..."
(Henry Seidel Canby, *Saturday Review*, 1928)

Jesus Christ (the Word) was hated by the world. At the same time, He went about doing good, with so much power and light, that His enemies were compelled to complain that the whole world had gone after Him!:

John 12:19 The Pharisees therefore said among themselves, Perceive ye how ye prevail nothing? behold, the world is gone after him.

God has magnified His Word above His very name (Psalms 138:2). It is therefore reasonable to expect that we will find, in the Written Word, the same paradox as we find in Jesus Himself. The Written Word (wherever it may be found, as God preserves it), will be hated and scorned (especially by those who crave the praise and respect of men); yet it will also have a miraculous, fruitful, enduring influence above and beyond any and every merely human book. The Authorized Version has these qualities. There is no other book that can be found today that can merit the following high praises:

"The book [the KJV] that has influenced more human lives than any other printed document observes its 350th anniversary this year."
(*The Newark Advocate*, September 27, 1961)

"It's barely possible to overstate the significance of this Bible. Hundreds of millions have been sold...By the end of the 17th century it was, simply, the Bible."
(*The New York Times*, "The King James Bible at 400," January 8, 2011)

"It [the AV] is rightly regarded as the most influential book in the history of English civilization."
(*Compton's Encyclopedia,* www.Britannica.com)

"It is impossible to overestimate the influence of the King James version of the Bible on English life and thought..."
(Charles Austin Beard, William Chandler Bagley, *Our Old World Background*, 1922)

"The King James Bible is the cornerstone of Anglo-Saxon civilization...Our economic systems, our literary and cultural pursuits are rooted in this single fructifying source."
(*The Dallas Morning News*, 1941)

"...that chief legacy of our language, bought with the tears, and prayers, and blood of millions, the King James Bible, our supreme literary masterpiece of translation, which more than all other spiritual forces has molded the lives and characters of the English-speaking peoples."
(*Bulletin*, Issues 26-30, North Carolina State Dept. of Archives and History, 1919)

"Bishop Anderson, who spoke on 'The Bible of the People,' said 'that the people of the present day scarcely realize their debt to the **authorized version of the Bible**. It has become an unconscious part of their thoughts and language. Our most laconic expressions, our pointed paragraphs, our tersest sayings are borrowed from the Scriptures. The Bible has consecrated monogamy and liberty and freedom. It has consecrated such words as home and wife and child and brother. It has laid the corner stones of our highest civilizations. It has been the preacher of fraternity and equality. I hope that this Tercentenary [of the AV] will have the effect of sending men back to their Bibles for fresh inspiration for life and service. I hope that it may have the effect of sending a lot of careless, slovenly people back to the Bible and of leading American mothers to teach the Bible to their children. Go back to the custom of your grandmothers who used to teach their children that the Bible is the true and living word of God. No nation or people having this priceless possession can afford to undervalue it, to misuse it or to neglect it."
(*The Advance*, Volume 61, 1911)

"Lord Macaulay [said] that 'if everything else in our language should perish, this book alone would suffice to show the whole extent of its beauty and power'...J. R. Green that it is 'the noblest example of the English tongue'...Time would fail us to tell of Carlyle and Coleridge and Walter Scott and Ruskin...nor is it necessary. Perhaps Professor Saintsbury of Oxford, great among living authorities, may speak for them all when he says, 'It is unnecessary to praise the Authorized Version of the English Bible - because of the mastery which its language has attained over the whole course of English literature.' Professor Phelps of Yale, charmed and amused us all in New York at the Tercentenary Celebration by adopting the phrase of the moment, - 'The English Bible,' he said, 'is simply the whole thing'...It may be truly said of them that they translated in the selfsame spirit which moved the original writers of Holy Scripture...Not only the great

masters of literature admit their debt to our Version, but English speech everywhere is permeated with it in incalculable ways. It is the gold basis for our major coinage; but it also supplies the smaller coin of popular phrase. Everybody talks about 'highways and hedges,' the 'still small voice' and 'the thorn in the flesh' and the 'root of all evil' and 'the sweat of the brow' and 'coals of fire' and 'pearls before swine' - the list can be drawn out *ad infinitum*...The literary reputation of the English Bible is the consequence and not the cause of its power. The true cause of its whole influence is the conviction, bred into the bone of English Christendom, that **it is the very Word of God** - the ultimatum of Deity...When men cease to believe in its full divine authority, they will presently find plausible reasons for denying its supreme value as literature...Is it not wonderful that though only a translation and not indigenous to our soil, it should yet dominate our literature? How fair it seems, our much loved English Bible, like a stately vessel coming from some distant ocean laden with rare spices and costly treasures to visit our shores!"
(Charles R. Erdman, *The Influence of the English Bible on English Literature*, 1911)

"Such was the origin of this venerable and truly national work: which immediately became the standard English Bible, and superseded all the other versions. Confined at first to the limited territory of the British Islands, and intended only for a population of a few millions, it had the effect at once to develop and fix the structure and character of the English language; and with that language it has since been borne abroad even to the ends of the earth. And now, during the lapse of almost two and a half centuries, it has gladdened the hearts, and still gladdens the hearts, of millions upon millions, not only in Great Britain, but throughout North America and India, in portions of Africa, and in Australia. At the present day, the English is probably the vernacular tongue of more millions than any other one language under heaven; and the English Bible has brought and still brings home the know-

ledge of God's revealed truth to myriads more of minds, than ever received it through the original tongues. The translators little foresaw the vast results and immeasurable influence of what they had thus done, both for time and for eternity. Venerated men! their very names are now hardly known to more than a few persons; yet, in the providence of God, the fruits of their labours have spread to far distant climes; have laid broad and deep the foundations of mighty empires; have afforded to multitudes strength to endure adversity, and grace to resist the temptations of prosperity; and only the revelations of the judgment day can disclose, how many millions and millions, through the instrumentality of their labours, have been made wise unto salvation."
(Isaac Ferris, *Jubilee Memorial of the American Bible Society,* 1867)

"It became at once the Bible of our American forefathers. Its classic English has given shape to American literature. Its spirit has influenced American ideals in life and laws and government."
(President William H. Taft, *New York Times*, April 26, 1911)

"In all study of English literature, if there be any one axiom which may be accepted without question, it is that the ultimate standard of English prose style is set by the King James version of the Bible...here, at any rate, is one question of literature settled for good: the standard of English prose style is the standard of the Authorized Version of the Bible; that style is so clear and so noble that there is nothing more to be accounted for...There is something in the genius of the people which brings the language to its noblest heights when it carries a message that is to arouse the people above themselves; and something in the genius of the language which makes it inevitable that when the language reaches these high points it shall show most strongly these two qualities of simplicity and earnestness...With this simplicity of language goes always an immense earnestness and dignity of style: the translation as we have it seems fused and transfigured

by the glow of an inward fervor...These translators could find nothing trivial in the word of God, and their reverence lifted everything to the same plane of earnest and inspired dignity."
(*The Atlantic Monthly*, Volume 85, 1900)

"...the Authorized Version of the English Bible is the best example of English literature that the world has ever seen. It combines the noblest elevations of thought, aspiration, imagination, passion and religion with simplicity of diction. Everyone who has a thorough knowledge of the Bible may truly be called educated; and no other learning or culture, no matter how extensive or elegant, can, among Europeans and Americans, form a proper substitute. Western civilization is founded upon the Bible; our ideas, our wisdom, our philosophy, our literature, our art, our ideals come more from the Bible than from all other books put together. It is a revelation of divinity and of humanity; it contains the loftiest religious aspiration along with a candid representation of all that is earthly, sensual and devilish. I thoroughly believe in a university education for both men and women; but I believe a knowledge of the Bible without a college course is more valuable than a college course without the Bible...Now as the English-speaking people have the best Bible in the world, and as it is the most beautiful monument ever erected with the English alphabet, we ought to make the most of it, for it is an incomparably rich inheritance, free to all who can read. This means that we ought invariably in the church and on public occasions to use the Authorized Version; all others are inferior."
(*The Biblical Review*, Volume 7, Biblical Seminary in New York, 1922)

John 7:31 And **many of the people believed on him**, and said, When Christ cometh, **will he do more miracles than these** which this man hath done?
32 The Pharisees heard that **the people** murmured such things concerning him; and the Pharisees and the chief priests sent officers to take him.

46 The officers answered, **Never man spake like this man.**
47 Then answered them the Pharisees, Are ye also deceived?
48 Have any of **the rulers or of the Pharisees** believed on him?
49 But **this people** who knoweth not the law are cursed.

CHAPTER 16

THE NECROMANCY OF WESTCOTT AND HORT

1 Timothy 4:1 Now the Spirit speaketh expressly, that in the latter times some shall depart from the faith, **giving heed to seducing spirits, and doctrines of devils;**
2 Speaking lies in hypocrisy...

2 Timothy 3:13 But evil men and seducers shall wax worse and worse, deceiving, and being deceived.
14 But continue thou in the things which thou hast learned and hast been assured of, **knowing of whom thou hast learned them;**
15 And that from a child thou hast known **the holy scriptures**, which are able to make thee wise unto salvation through faith which is in Christ Jesus.

These Bible verses teach that in the last days many will be deceived by seducing spirits and doctrines of devils. It is therefore crucial that Christians know the true history behind the various doctrines that they have been taught. Where did they originate? Do they have their source in the Holy Scriptures? Any doctrine that has arisen from satanically inspired men, or from men who have practiced necromancy and divination, cannot be of God's Spirit. After reading the views of occultists, Humanists and infidels concerning textual criticism, the King James Bible, and their applause for men like Westcott and Hort (the primary fathers of the modern versions), it should not be a surprise to find that Westcott and Hort practiced necromancy (i.e. the attempt to communicate with the dead through divination, mediums, etc.).

Brooke Foss Westcott (1825-1901) and Fenton John Anthony Hort (1828-1892) were Anglican scholars. In 1881, they published a Greek New Testament based upon their theories. The Westcott and Hort Greek text was used as the primary basis for the Revised Version (and it is also the general foundation for other modern versions).

In 1853, Westcott and Hort formulated their plan to revise the text of the Greek New Testament (see *The New Schaff-Herzog Encyclopedia of Religious Knowledge*, Vol. 5, 1908, p. 368). Before, during, and after this date, these men used mediums and divination to attempt to contact the dead. They were necromancers, which God calls an abomination (Deuteronomy 18:11-12).

Occultists commonly use so-called "scientific investigation" as an excuse to practice magic and divination. The infamous Satanist, Aleister Crowley, defined his *magic* as, "the **science** and art of causing change to occur in conformity with will." Occultists often claim to be merely using the "scientific method." But God forbids the practice of necromancy, and condemns people who regard familiar spirits, etc. "Scientific investigation" is no justification before God for practicing magic, divination, etc. These things expose the seekers to dangerous, satanic deceptions.

The following documentation proves that Westcott and Hort practiced necromancy:

"He [Westcott] devoted himself with ardour, during his last year at Cambridge, to two new societies. One of these was **the 'Ghostlie Guild'**...The 'Ghostlie Guild,' which numbered amongst its members A. Barry, E. W. Benson, H. Bradshaw, the Hon. A. Gordon, **F. J. A. Hort**, H. Luard, and C. B. Scott, was

established for the investigation of all supernatural appearances and effects. **Westcott took a leading part in their proceedings, and their inquiry circular was originally drawn up by him**...Outsiders, failing to appreciate the fact that these investigators **were in earnest** and only seeking the truth, called them the 'Cock and Bull Club.' One of my father's earliest letters to Mr. Hort concerns this Guild. Writing from Bristol in January **1852**, he says: 'I am sorry I have delayed so long to write to you about our 'ghostlie circular'...'"
(Arthur Westcott, *Life and Letters of Brooke Foss Westcott*, 1903)

"In the early fifties of the last century there was formed in Trinity College, Cambridge, a 'Ghost Society.' The founder was Brooke Foss Westcott..."
(*University of Ceylon Review,* Volumes 12-14, 1954)

"Besides Benson, **the chief instigator seems to have been B. F. Westcott**, the theologian and Biblical scholar, later Bishop of Durham. **Westcott apparently wrote the society's circular and served as its Secretary**..."
(*The Journal of the American Society for Psychical Research*, Volume 29, 1935)

"Westcott had drawn up a schedule of questions for the ethereal beings supposed to be disembodied to answer..."
(*Country Life*, Volume 10, 1901)

Likewise, Hort's son writes:

"The 'Bogie Club,' as scoffers called it, aroused a certain amount of derision, and even some alarm; it was apparently born too soon."
(Arthur Fenton Hort, *Life and Letters of Fenton John Anthony Hort*, 1896)

He provides the following letter written by his father concerning this club:

"**Westcott**, Gorham, C. B. Scott, Benson, Bradshaw, Luard, etc., and I have started a society for the **investigation of ghosts** and all supernatural appearances and effects, **being all disposed to believe that such things really exist**, and ought to be discriminated from hoaxes and mere subjective delusions...Westcott is drawing up a schedule of questions. Cope calls us the 'Cock and Bull Club'; our own temporary name is the 'Ghostly Guild.'"
(Arthur Fenton Hort, *Life and Letters of Fenton John Anthony Hort*, 1896)

Westcott and Hort were fathers (or at least popularizers) of modern textual criticism (of which new Bible versions are derived). New versions are largely based upon the work and theories of Westcott and Hort:

"It is scarcely possible to overstate the significance of this new [Westcott and Hort] text...Their achievement was revolutionary...the Westcott-Hort text represented...an acknowledged dependence on Sinaitic and Vatican manuscripts...There have been, of course, other editions of the Greek text since Westcott-Hort; however, time has but confirmed their immense contribution to the status of our New Testament text."
(Neil R. Lightfoot, *How We Got Our Bible*, Baker Books, 2010)

Quotes such as these could be multiplied. But it is important to realize that Westcott and Hort were also fathers in another manner. Through their experiments in necromancy, they became progenitors of modern *spiritualism* (or more properly *spiritism*), which is the foundation of the New Age movement. This necromancy, at the time, was commonly viewed as wild fanaticism or superstition. Westcott, Hort, and other members of their club, such as Edward White Benson (later archbishop of Canterbury), J.B. Lightfoot, etc., added a cloak of academic respectability to the dangerous movement. Subsequent occult and New Age organizations appealed to Westcott's ghost society as their principle root!:

"Spiritualism has progressed so rapidly, has grown to such stature in so short a time...In the year 1851, the Cambridge Ghost Club published a circular, to which the **distinguished** name of **Brooke Foss Westcott** is appended...It was the earliest venture we know of..."
(*Light*, Volume 1, Issue 1, London Spiritualist Alliance, 1881)

When Satan's first words in Genesis are considered (i.e. "Yea, hath God said...?"), it is not surprising that the men behind the new Bible version movement (bringing confusion and doubt), also helped launch the New Age movement itself:

"The **original** Ghost Club had been **founded** by a group of students and fellows at Trinity College [Cambridge]...and was **continued** more formally in London from 1862 when Charles Dickens had joined...it was reestablished in 1882...the Ghost Club remained a highly selective, but informal, private dining club whose members were convinced believers in psychic phenomena and the occult...it was a specific rule that nothing would be published...all deceased members were still considered to be present...The membership was an eclectic mixture of spiritualists, Theosophists and occultists..."
(William Hodson Brock, *William Crookes...*, 2008)

"The Cambridge Ghost Club, founded in 1851, was followed by the London-based Ghost Club in 1862. These and other organizations **investigated** mediums as well as reported apparitions, hauntings, and poltergeists."
(James Houran, *From Shaman to Scientist*, 2004)

"A striking characteristic, especially of Hort's earlier manhood, is his hospitality to new views and practices. He...believes in a kind of communism; thinks well of universal suffrage, women included...As early as 1851, with a knot of inquisitive souls, he started a society known as the **'Ghostly Guild,'** for the purpose

of collecting and classifying authenticated instances of exceptional mental phenomena, - **a kind of forerunner, possibly a progenitor, of the modern societies for 'Psychical Research'**... The truth in Darwinism he was prompt to recognize...On one occasion he even went so far as to broach the notion that Protestantism itself might be but a 'parenthetical and temporary' stage of ecclesiastical progress."
(*The New World*, Volume 6, 1897)

"Dr. **Westcott**, afterwards Bishop of Durham, while in residence at Cambridge, had apparently acted as secretary; and in **1860**, when he had left for Harrow, we find him **sending Sidgwick a story**, 'produced by the old 'ghostly' circular,' and adding, 'I trust I am right in believing you are still engaged in the pursuit of the question.' **This investigation of ghost stories was the beginning, so far as Sidgwick was concerned, of 'Psychical Research,'** in which, as will be seen in the following pages, he was engaged, with brief intervals, during the rest of his life."
(Arthur Sidgwick, Eleanor Mildred Sidgwick, *Henry Sidgwick*, Volume 3, 1906)

Benson, one of the member's of Westcott's ghost club, married Sidgwick's sister. Henry Sidgwick (1838-1900) became a more open, popular leader in psychical research. When the Society for Psychical Research (SPR) was founded in 1882, he served as its president for eight of its first eleven years. Sidgwick was also a member of the Eranus society in 1872, which included Westcott and Hort. A letter of Sidgwick to his sister in 1858 is revealing:

"...my ghostological investigations are flourishing; I have taken unto myself associates here, and am prosecuting my researches with vigour; meeting with failures and vexatious exaggerations **but still getting a good deal of real matter**."

Sidgwick renounced orthodox Christianity. When Sidgwick died,

Westcott wrote that some of the happiest memories of his life were spent with him, and that he believed the blessings of God were upon him. Sidgwick also believed that the whole psychical research movement started with this ghost club, and these "investigations" at Cambridge! Many others in the 19th century agreed:

"Parenthetically one may observe that some **movements** which the present day thinks especially characteristic of itself **were then already in full swing**, among others a 'society for the investigation of ghosts,' **exactly similar to the S.P.R.** [Society for Psychical Research], having been started by **Hort, Westcott, Benson**, and some others in **1851**..."
(*The Academy and Literature*, Volume 50, 1896)

"Among my father's [Benson] diversions at Cambridge was the foundation of a 'Ghost' Society, **the forerunner of the Psychical Society**, for the investigation of the supernatural [called S.P.R.]. **Lightfoot, Westcott and Hort were among the members.** He was then, as always, more interested in psychical phenomena **than he cared to admit**."
(A.C. Benson, *The Life of Edward White Benson,* 1899)

It was often necessary for members of such clubs to publicly distance themselves from spiritism.

Notice that Joseph Barber Lightfoot (1828-1889) was another member of this ghost club. He also served on the Revision Committee (1871-1885) of the Revised Version! Westcott was Benson's tutor.

Other sources reveal that Westcott and Hort's original ghost club was a forerunner and root of the New Age movement:

"More or less connected with these interests was an inquiry into

supernatural or, as people now prefer to call them, psychical phenomena, which was made about the year 1851. A paper, inviting the communication of any experiences of this nature, was drawn up by a sort of committee, including among its members **a good many friends of Bradshaw's, now well known in the university** and in the world at large....**This curious anticipation of the 'Psychical Society' of our own day called itself the 'Ghostly Guild'**...Sir Arthur Gordon informs me that they came to a conclusion very similar to that which the modern Psychical Society has arrived at - namely, that, while for the ordinary run of ghost-stories there is nothing in the nature of trustworthy evidence, **an exception must be made in favour of phantasms of the living, or appearances of persons at the point of death**."
(George Walter Prothero, *A Memoir of Henry Bradshaw,* 1888)

In 1860, Robert Dale Owen wrote a book seeking to defend the new spiritualism (necromancy). He praised Westcott and Hort's ghostly society as proof that spiritualism was gaining ground:

"The majority of educated men set aside, with little thought or scruple, all stories of haunted houses, all narratives of apparitions...as the ignoble offshoots of vulgar superstition. **Yet there has been of late a reaction in this matter.** Here and there we come upon indications of this. It is within my knowledge, that a few years since, at one of the chief English universities, **a society was formed out of some of its most distinguished members**, for the purpose of instituting, as their printed circular expresses it, 'serious and earnest inquiry into the nature of the phenomena which are vaguely called supernatural'...**The society referred to was formed in the latter part of the year 1851**, at Cambridge, by certain members of the University, some of them now at the head of well-known institutions...The names of the more active among them were kindly furnished to me...by one of the leading members. To him, also, I am indebted for a copy of the printed circular of the society...The same gentleman informed me that

the researches of the society had resulted in a conviction, **shared, he believed, by all its members**, that there *is* sufficient testimony for the appearance, about the time of death or after it, of the apparitions of deceased persons...To a gentleman who had been one of the more active members of the society, **the Rev. Mr. W.**, I wrote, giving him the title of the present work, and stating in general terms the spirit and manner in which I proposed to write it. In his reply he says, 'I wish that I were able to make any contribution to your proposed work at all commensurate with **the interest which I feel** in the subject of it'...'I **rejoice extremely** to learn that the subject is likely to receive a calm and philosophic treatment. This, at least, it demands; and, for my own part, I feel little doubt that **great good will result from the publication of the work which you are preparing**. **My own experience has led me to form a conclusion similar to that which you express**, - that the possibility of supramundane interference is a question which is gradually attracting more and more attention, especially with men of education. This circumstance makes me the more anxious that a selection of facts should be fairly laid before them.' The society, popularly known as **'The Ghost Club,'** attracted a good deal of attention...."
(Robert Dale Owen, *Footfalls on the Boundary of Another World*, 1860)

Owen's book was reproved by discerning Christians, who also rebuked the necromancy of Westcott and Hort. One publication reviewed Owen's book under the heading "Modern Necromancy":

"The work of Mr. Owen is a collection of ghost stories, intended to have a scientific application...Now, these professedly **scientific spiritualists** acknowledge that many phenomena, hitherto termed spiritual, are due to morbid functional activity of the nervous system; but there are others which are inexplicable by any current physical or physiological theory, and *therefore* (they say) belong to the spiritual or ultra-mundane...**We learn from**

Mr. Owen that a society was formed in 1851, at the University of Cambridge, for the purpose of instituting, as their printed circular expresses it, 'a serious and earnest inquiry into the nature of the phenomena which are vaguely termed supernatural.' It was popularly known as the 'Ghost Club.' Most of the members, we are told, were clergymen, and Fellows of Trinity College. The Bishop...was one of the most active, and brought it under the notice of Mr. Owen...this **spiritualistic necromancy**...[is] found to be only dust and ashes, - a delusion and a snare."
(*The North British Review*, 1861)

"...the **Cambridge Spiritual Association**, called in jest the **Cambridge Ghost Club**, and including many of the most distinguished members of that university, clergymen and professors of high note, and one or more bishops, has been established to enquire into the existence of spiritual phenomena, and has already decided on the reality of apparitions...The **Cambridge Association for Spiritual Enquiry**, familiarly called **the Ghost Club**, consisting of eminent members of the university, have stated that their carefully-conducted researches on the subject of apparitions have led them to regard such appearances as a settled fact. **A member of this association informed Mr. Dale Owen that he had collected 2,000 cases** of apparitions..."
(William Howitt, *The History of the Supernatural*, 1863)

New version advocates must do their best to downplay this dark history:

"The club was formed to *investigate* strange occurrences, not engage in devilish activity."
(James R. White, *The King James Only Controversy*, 2009, p. 245)

Notice White's careful wording. He uses the words "strange occurrences" to try to sugarcoat the investigation of ghosts, spirit communications, etc. White appears to be unaware that "investigating" the occult by participating in séances, etc., is divination and necromancy! Many in the Bible "sought after" (i.e. investigated) such things, and were condemned by God:

Leviticus 19:31 Regard not them that have familiar spirits, **neither seek after** wizards, to be defiled by them: I am the LORD your God.

Isaiah 8:19 And when they shall say unto you, **Seek unto them** that have familiar spirits, and unto wizards that peep, and that mutter: should not a people seek unto their God? for the living to the dead?
20 To the law and to the testimony: if they speak not according to this word, it is because there is no light in them.

The whole spiritualist movement was made up of people who were "investigating" the spirit world. But in their investigations, they were practicing necromancy, etc.:

"In their quest for scientific proof of life after death the psychical researchers have from time to time made discoveries...At only one place - the University of Cambridge - was sustained effort made to get at the 'bottom facts.' There, in 1850, under the leadership of **Edward White Benson**, afterwards Archbishop of Canterbury, a number of serious-minded undergraduates organized **a 'Ghost Society,' for the investigation, not only of 'mediumistic,'** but also of all phenomena of a seemingly supernatural character - apparitions, hauntings, and the like. **The members industriously attended spiritistic séances...In this way the Ghost Society...really did much to lay the foundations of the English Society for Psychical Research**...Indeed, there is a direct connection between the Ghost Society and the Society for Psychical Research in the fact that the famous English philosopher **Henry Sidgwick**, who was the first President of the Society for Psychical Research...was also the most prominent and

active member of the Ghost Society during its later years. 'Spiritualism,' he wrote to his friend H. G. Dakyns, 'progresses but slowly...I can only assure you that **an evening with 'spirits'** is as fascinating to me as any novel. **I talk with Arabs, Hindus, Spaniards, Counts Cavour, etc.** I yield to the belief at the time, and recover my philosophical skepticism next morning.'"
(Henry Addington Bruce, *The Outlook*, Volume 94, "The Ghost Society And What Came of It," 1910)

According to the research of Bruce above, Westcott and Hort's ghost club members "industriously attended" séances, etc. Details of similar meetings are described by Robert Chambers (1802-1871). Chambers (born with six fingers and six toes) was an early (though sometimes secret) advocate of evolution and spiritism. He writes:

"My happiest evenings - with the most miserable nights to follow - are spent, weekly, at a Society for the Investigation of Spiritual Phenomena, or, as some of the unbelieving have disrespectfully termed it, **the Cock-and-Bull Club.** We assemble every Friday, at seven o'clock. If the police were suddenly to break in upon our speculations, **as we sit, thirteen in number, looking at one another, around a table with lighted candles**, they would, I believe, proceed to collar and shake us..."
(William and Robert Chambers, *Chamber's Journal*, 1858)

In his final years, Westcott became known as the Bishop of Durham (1890-1901). On one occasion, in 1893, he distanced himself from spiritism:

"Many years ago I had occasion to investigate 'spiritualistic' phenomena with some care, and I came to a clear conclusion, which I feel bound to express in answer to your circular. It appears to me that in this, as in all spiritual questions, Holy Scripture is our supreme guide. I observe, then, that while spiritual

ministries are constantly recorded in the Bible, there is not the faintest encouragement to seek them. The case, indeed, is far otherwise. I cannot, therefore, but regard every voluntary approach to beings such as those who are supposed to hold communication with men through mediums as unlawful and perilous."
(*Borderland,* Vol. I, No. 1, July 1893)

There are two problems with this confession (assuming it is sincere). First, the damage had already been done. Westcott did not fully realize the Satanic delusions he had fallen under by opening himself up to evil spirits though his "investigations." Secondly, Westcott and Hort also practiced "communion with the saints," which is another form of spiritism with a "Christian" dressing. Westcott never repented of this practice. These men believed that the spirits of those who had died could appear and fellowship with the living.

It is a common practice of deceived, professing Christians to advocate good and bad magic. For example, new versions call the "wise men" who visited Jesus as a child, "magi," implying a good brand of magic or witchcraft (see Matthew 2 in the NIV, NAS, etc., and the footnote and chapter heading of the ASV). Actually, these men were *wise* for searching the Scriptures and understanding the prophecies of Daniel concerning the time of the Saviour's first coming. They were not magicians. Nevertheless, occultists commonly excuse their necromancy by claiming that there is a good form of magic; they also argue that they are merely *scientists* investigating the strange phenomena:

"We all have heard the sneer 'modern necromancy!'...the travelers from the East [Matthew 2] made **good use** of their occult powers, while Simon and Bar-Jesus prostituted theirs...If occult powers had once such possibilities as in this instance came to fruition they may have now. How can any fair-minded person

who accepts as history the incident of the **Magi**...rebuke men who are **scientifically testing** occult phenomena in our days to ascertain their real nature, sources and capacities?"
(Walter F. Prince, *Journal of the American Society for Psychical Research*, Volume 6, 1912)

Notice the following words of a modern advocate of "communion of saints" as he attempts to distinguish this practice from ordinary necromancy or spiritism:

"This **communion of saints** involves remembrance, **mutual intercession and conversation**. This **communication** must be sharply distinguished from 'spirit communication' or necromancy...The communion of saints concerns **real interaction** between the faithful in heaven and the faithful on earth."
(Donald G. Bloesch, *The Last Things: Resurrection, Judgment, Glory*, 2006)

"Communing" with supposed departed spirits is necromancy, regardless of whether it is practiced by Roman Catholics, deceived Anglicans, or occult mediums in séances. The attempt to communicate with "holy," departed saints through prayer, "meditation," etc., is just as evil as sitting around a candlelit table in an attempt to communicate with one's dead aunt!

In 1880, Westcott gave an address on the subject of the communion of saints:

"The Communion is a Communion of Saints as Saints, and not as men under the present conditions of humanity. It is independent of limitations of time and space, both in its range and in its fulfilment...We are learning, by the help of many teachers, the extent and the authority of the dominion which the dead exercise over us, and which we ourselves are shaping for our descendants. We feel, as perhaps it was impossible to feel before, how at every moment **influences from the past enter our souls**...It is be-

coming clear to us, that we **are literally parts of others, and they of us**...Men must be dependent on one another. For saints this dependence is transfigured into **fellowship**...We are constrained, in our attempts to give distinctness to it, to use the language of earth, but in itself the spiritual life, of which the Communion of Saints is the foretaste, belongs to another order...The Communion of Saints in the largest sense, the communion of angels and men, of men already perfected...The Communion of Saints must, therefore, be realised socially and personally - socially, to speak briefly, by commemoration; personally, by meditation...to our great loss, the faculty and the habit of meditation have not as yet been cultivated among us...**This fellowship of spirit with spirit is closer**, and may be more powerful, than the precious fellowship which we can hold with books...Meditation on the saintliness of saintly men must be **supplemented by meditation on angels** as the representatives of the unseen world, if we are to feel the full extent of the Communion of Saints... the Communion of Saints, with its manifold supplies of strength, with its boundless wealth of promise, becomes a **fact of immediate experience**."
(*The Official Report of the Church Congress Held at Leicester, 1880*; 1881)

Westcott (at this late date) was advocating mysticism and necromancy dressed up in Christian language. Westcott's son writes:

"The subject [Communion of the Saints], too, is one so very dear to himself. **He had an extraordinary power of realising this Communion**. It was his delight to be alone at night in the great Cathedral, for there he could meditate and pray in full sympathy with all that was good and great in the past. I have been with him there on a moonlight evening when the vast building was haunted with strange lights and shades, and the ticking of the great clock sounded like some giant's footsteps in the deep silence. **Then he had always abundant company.** Once a daughter in later years met him returning from one of his customary

meditations in the solitary darkness of the chapel at Auckland Castle, and she said to him, 'I expect you do not feel alone?' 'Oh no,' he said, 'it is full'; and as he spoke his face shone with one of his beautiful smiles."
(Arthur Westcott, *Life and Letters of Brooke Foss Westcott*, 1903)

Westcott also addressed this doctrine in his commentary on the Epistle to the Hebrews:

"Christian believers in Christ, alike living and dead, are united in the Body of Christ. In that Body **we have fellowship** with a society of 'eldest sons' of God...Thus the idea of the Communion of Saints gains distinctness."
(Brooke Foss Westcott, *The Epistle to the Hebrews*, 1892)

In 1868, Westcott called for a return to Roman Catholic *asceticism,* which preserved the pagan practice of necromancy with Christian terminology (Oscar Hardman, *The Ideals of Asceticism*, 1921).

F.J.A Hort also embraced the doctrine of the Communion of Saints in a heretical fashion. In 1851, he wrote:

"Have you heard of a new book, [Henry Bristow] Wilson's *Bampton Lectures,* which are making a great stir at Oxford? I have read part of them...and they seem to me **perfectly horrible**...It is on **the Communion of Saints**, and the object is to show that **there is no communion** between **the living and the dead**..."
(Arthur Fenton Hort, *Life and Letters of Fenton John Anthony Hort*, Vol. 1, 1896)

Actually, a pattern is developing. Westcott, Hort and Lightfoot were not the only men behind the new versions who practiced necromancy. John Bertram Phillips (1906-1982) was the author of the *New Testament in Modern English* (1958), which claims to be a paraphrase of the New Testament. He believed that the spirit of C.S. Lewis appeared to him, more than once, after his death!:

"A few days after his death, while I was watching television, he 'appeared' sitting in a chair within a few feet of me, and spoke a few words..."
(J.B. Phillips, *The Newborn Christian*, 1984)

All of these revelations are frightening when one considers that Westcott and Hort's plan to "revise" the Bible was conceived in this environment. This is very troubling when coupled with the fact that these evil spirits (disguised as departed saints, etc.) often gave their "investigators" advice and even work to do:

"The establishment of the University of California, I am credibly informed, was through suggestions made from the spirit world."
(*Galveston Daily News*, July 30, 1893)

The text that they produced certainly reveals signs of satanic deception. As these men were searching for psychic signs, the Devil was busy deluding their minds, and using them to hinder the faith of millions in Biblical Christianity.

The delusions these evil spirits seek to generate and encourage can be plainly seen in the revealed words of Satan and his spirits in the Bible. In Genesis 3, Satan casts doubt on the certainty of God's Word, diminishes the fear of God, and entices Eve to godhood through forbidden knowledge or practices. Spiritualists (spiritists) who have spent their lives following the messages of these evil spirits have summed up the content of their teaching. Notice the doctrines of these spirits:

"...spiritualists as a rule do not believe that Jesus Christ was the

son of God in any higher sense than that taught by Christ himself when he said, 'So, are we all sons of God.' They believe that he was higher or more advanced...We do not believe in the doctrine of the atonement as it is ordinarily taught in the churches...Spiritualists believe that all who practice the teachings of Jesus Christ and seek entrance into heaven by the modes and methods in which he instructed his disciples, living a Christ-like life, that they will attain the highest degrees of happiness in the spiritual world. They believe that every man must suffer for the sins that he commits, that there is no escape from the penalty of sin."
(*Galveston Daily News*, July 30, 1893)

People who participate in séances, practice the communion of saints, and such like, will usually end up believing that everyone on earth is a spiritual child of God; that Jesus Christ was only a more advanced mystic than others (i.e. denying His Divine distinctions); that the doctrine of the Atonement is false (i.e. denying eternal salvation through the shed Blood of Christ); and that eternal salvation is through following Christ as a good example (i.e. instead of through faith alone in the Gospel); etc.

It is not surprising that these doctrines of devils are found in the views of Westcott and Hort. They are also found in the new versions that are derived from their work and theories. Observe the following letters from Hort:

"My dear **Westcott**...I entirely agree - correcting one word - with what you there say on the **Atonement**, having for many years believed that 'the absolute union of the Christian (or rather, of man) with Christ Himself' is the spiritual truth of which **the popular doctrine of substitution is an immoral and material counterfeit**. But I doubt whether that answers the question as to the nature of the satisfaction. Certainly nothing can be more unscriptural than the modern limiting of Christ's bearing our sins

and sufferings to His death; but indeed that is only one aspect of an almost universal heresy."
(Arthur Fenton Hort, *Life and Letters of Fenton John Anthony Hort*, Vol. 1, 1896)

"...not only are the Epistles almost free (as far as I can recollect) from allusions to everlasting torments, but their whole tone is such that the introduction of such a notion would seem to render it discordant and jarring. And little as I like to rest on isolated texts, I cannot get over the words, 'As in Adam all die, even so in Christ shall all be made alive'...finite sins cannot deserve an infinite punishment...here is the question of Substituted Punishment, which, as it seems to me, is quite distinct from the Atonement and reconciliation of the person of sinning man and God...the corresponding heresy (as it appears to me) of a fictitious substituted *penalty*...I *do not see how* God's justice can be satisfied without *every man's* suffering in his own person the full penalty for his sins."
(Arthur Fenton Hort, *Life and Letters of Fenton John Anthony Hort*, Vol. 1, 1896)

When Westcott and Hort's Revised Version (RV) was published, many Christians upbraided it for despising the Deity of Christ in many places, and removing the Blood of Christ, etc.:

"in whom we have our redemption, the forgiveness of our sins:"
(RV)

Colossians 1:14 In whom we have redemption **through his blood**, even the forgiveness of sins:
(KJV)

Spiritualists (i.e. occultists) longed for a new Bible version in the 1850's. This desire began to be realized in the new text and version that was later published by Westcott and Hort. These men opened the door; and subsequent versions have continued the satanic seduction, step by step:

2 Timothy 3:13 But evil men and seducers shall wax worse and worse, deceiving, and being deceived.

The Spiritism of Johannes Greber

One final spiritist should be mentioned. Johannes Greber (1876-1944) was a Roman Catholic priest who became a spiritist. In 1932, he authored, *Communication with the Spirit World: Its Laws and Its Purpose*. And in 1937 he produced, *The New Testament: A New Translation Based on the Oldest Manuscripts*. Greber claimed that his translation was authored by spirits.

He adopted the view that the Bible only condemns communication with *evil* spirits:

"If, therefore, we, as faithful servants of God, or at any rate, as honest seekers after the truth, try to get into touch with the world of good spirits we are committing no sin...There is no other way."
(*Communication with the Spirit World: Its Laws and Its Purpose*, 1932)

The seducing spirits taught Greber that Jesus Christ was not God, and many other heresies, such as eternal salvation through works:

"Whoever believes in God and relies upon Him, **whoever obeys God's will according to the best of his knowledge**, will arrive at God."
(Ibid.)

These devils taught Greber that verses such as Philippians 2:5, etc. had been wrongly translated in the King James Bible. For many years, the so-called Jehovah's Witnesses quoted Greber's translation in support of their own heretical doctrines (e.g. *The Watchtower*, Sept. 15, 1962; Oct. 15, 1975; April 15, 1976, etc.). Again, it is seen that evil spirits seek to deny the doctrine of the Deity of Christ, etc. The Watchtower Society not only embraced Gerber's translation by spirits, it regularly claims to be led by angels!:

"Certain duties and kingdom interests have been committed by the Lord to his angels, which include the transmission of information to God's anointed people on earth for their aid and comfort...at the convention in 1922, the angel of the Lord 'spoke' to the 'young man' class...and brought information to them..."
(J.F. Rutherford, *Preparation,* 1933)

The Watchtower's *New World Translation* is therefore inspired by evil spirits - the same class of spirits that "inspired" Westcott and Hort and the new versions that are based upon their work. A careful comparison of the *New World Translation* with the *NIV, NASB*, etc., reveals that these versions share many of the same heretical readings (e.g. compare Matthew 17:21, 18:11, 23:14; Mark 9:44,46, 11:26, 15:28; Luke 2:33, 17:36; John 1:18, 5:4; Acts 8:37, 15:34, 17:29, 24:7, 28:29; Romans 16:24; Philippians 2:6; 1 Timothy 3:16; 1 John 5:7; Revelation 1:11; etc.).

CHAPTER 17

HERETICS BEHIND THE ASV

"The old gross charges against the Bible are, for the most part, abandoned. The weapons now are more keen-edged and the tactics more subtle...not a few, who had sworn to maintain and defend it, have, betraying their trust, co-operated with the enemy in their assaults; while others, who love it and desire to maintain and defend it, in ignorance and fear have surrendered the outposts...Higher Criticism…it boasteth great things. It is fitted to awe and overcome, and **does awe and overcome many weak minds...Many young divines...are hypnotized by the eye of a German critic**..."
(*The Theological Monthly*, Volume 5, 1891)

Matthew 7:18 A good tree cannot bring forth evil fruit, neither can a corrupt tree bring forth good fruit.

1 Samuel 21:15 Have I need of mad men, that ye have brought this fellow to play the mad man in my presence? **shall this fellow come into my house?**

The above words of Achish, a Philistine king, are a strong rebuke to many Christians today. Even he had enough common sense to avoid madmen, and to keep them from *his* house. But many Christians bring worse men and women into their living rooms everyday through their modern amusements, etc. The Bible teaches that evil communications corrupt good manners (1 Corinthians 15:33). *Evil communications* speaks of more than just corrupt entertainment. Satan has deceived many men, and he has used them to corrupt the Word of God and produce counterfeit *Bibles*:

2 Corinthians 2:17 For we are not as many, which corrupt the word of God…

This is why believers are commanded to prove all things (1 Thessalonians 5:21):

2 Timothy 3:13 But evil men and seducers shall wax worse and worse, deceiving, and being deceived.
14 But continue thou in the things which thou hast learned and hast been assured of, **knowing of whom thou hast learned them**;
15 And that from a child thou hast known the holy scriptures…

Modern "Bible" versions like the NIV and the NASB are rooted in the RV and, more specifically, the ASV (American Standard Version) of 1901. The Preface to the NASB states:

"The American counterpart of this last work was published in 1901 as the American Standard Version. Recognizing the values of the American Standard Version, the Lockman Foundation felt an urgency to update it…Therefore, in 1959 a new translation project was launched, based on the ASV. The result is the New American Standard Bible…The American Standard Version (1901)…has frequently been used as a standard for other translations…"
(*Preface to the New American Standard Bible*, *The New Open Bible, Study Edition,* Thomas Nelson, 1990)

The ASV was first revised in 1952 and published as the RSV (Revised Standard Version). Due to its openly liberal connections and biases, it was largely rejected by fundamentalists and evangelicals. But what many do not realize is that this whole line of so-called Bibles is corrupt! The root (i.e. ASV/RV) itself is sick. The men behind these new versions (even in America) are tainted with freemasonry, occult societies, and modernism/liberalism.

The principle men behind the RV have already been examined (e.g. Westcott, Hort, Lightfoot, etc.). It should not be surprising to find that the American revision committee was also filled with heretical men. These men professed to be opposed to the openly hostile, destructive criticism of blatant infidels. This makes their particular brand of heresy all the more dangerous, since it is dressed in Biblical language:

Romans 16:18...by good words and fair speeches deceive the hearts of the simple.

For example, the heretics behind the ASV argued that Christians wrongly replaced the infallible pope with the infallible Bible. The men behind the ASV viewed themselves as new reformers, called to replace the doctrine of an infallible Bible with the doctrine of the infallible Christ! They scorned the advocates of an infallible Bible as dogmatists, etc. They apparently overlooked the fact that our knowledge of the infallibility of Christ is grounded in the trustworthiness of the Bible! Notice the following arguments of Charles Marsh Mead, one of the men who worked on the ASV:

"Christ, it is said, is the ultimate authority for all Christians, so that we need not anxiously attempt to defend the exact accuracy of every part of the Bible. If we believe in him and follow him, we can safely let criticism have free range, and not be troubled at any discoveries it may make of defects and mistakes in the Biblical writers. **As Christians we put our supreme faith in Christ, not in the utterances of any of his followers**. Inasmuch as the ultimate ground of our faith in the authority of the Bible is our faith in the authority of Christ, nothing is gained, while much may be lost, by attempting to defend, as absolutely infallible, everything found in the books of the Bible…Both the Protestant and the Roman Catholic doctrine ultimately rest on the assumption of the supreme, infallible authority of Christ. The Bible on the one hand and the Pope on the other are admitted to be infallible only because Christ is first accepted as the supreme authority. **Why, then, rest our faith on the secondary, derivative ground** rather than on the primary one?...Here, then, we seem to have an impregnable position, and one which enables us calmly to await and accept whatever scientific investigation may bring to light…"

(Charles Marsh Mead, *Christ and Criticism*, 1892)

Many were deceived by such subtle, pious-sounding wordplay. It permitted destructive criticism of the Bible by professing to hold to the infallibility of Christ! Some Christian leaders reproved this game:

"The gravest defection from the faith is the denial of the authority of the Word of God…The people generally believe that the Word is authoritative…it became fashionable to class the idea of an infallible Book with the Romanist figment of an infallible Pope or Church…Many [therefore] think that the authority of Christ is all that we ought to regard; but the whole point lies just here, What is the expression of the authority of Christ? It is the written Word."

(Dr. McCaig, "The New Theology," quoted in *Sword & Trowel*, Feb., 1907)

Men like McCaig argued that there was no antagonism between the authority of the Bible and the authority of Christ. Yet, the rotten seeds of the "New Theology" were sown by the principle men behind the ASV. These men viewed the Bible as *secondary* to what they called the person of Christ. These seeds have come to fruition in this present age. For example, a former pastor of Broadway Baptist (a church in Fort Worth, Texas that is pro-homosexual) justifies his acceptance of homosexuality by arguing that the true Word is in Heaven (and therefore the Bible is secondary and largely irrelevant).

Down Grade Bible Versions

Charles Spurgeon, before his death, became aware of the fact that many grievous wolves had entered in with their "new theology," and he began to reprove them in a series of articles (i.e. the *Down-Grade* controversy). The "broad school" views that Spurgeon exposed are the exact views advocated by the men on the ASV translation committee! Notice some of Spurgeon's reproofs:

"Read those newspapers which represent the Broad School of Dissent, and ask yourself, How much farther could they go?...A new religion has been initiated...the inspiration of Scripture is derided...and yet these enemies of our faith expect us to call them brethren...At the back of doctrinal falsehood comes a natural decline of spiritual life, evidenced by a taste for questionable amusements...no man can possess the confidence of even of the most worldly, who is known to be a haunter of theaters..."
(*The Sword and the Trowel*, August, 1887)

"Germany was made unbelieving by her preachers..."
(*The Sword and the Trowel*, August, 1887)

"A little plain-speaking would do a world of good just now. These gentlemen desire to be let alone. **They want no noise raised**. Of course thieves hate watch-dogs, and **love darkness**."
(*The Sword and the Trowel*, August, 1887)

"...no one has set himself to disprove our allegations...no one has denied that certain ministers frequent theaters; no one has claimed that the Broad School newspapers have respected a sin-

gle truth...Now we submit that these are the main points at issue...the new theology is introducing, not only a new code of morals, but a new tone and spirit...We are grateful to the editor of Word and Work for speaking out so plainly. He says: - 'In *The Sword and Trowel* for the present month Mr. Spurgeon gives no uncertain sound...he will be called a 'troubler of Israel'...The preachers of false doctrine dislike nothing more than the premature detection of their doings...'...That ugly word 'pessimist' has been hurled at our devoted head...Are all of the orthodox afraid of the ridicule of the 'cultured'?...**We cannot hold the inspiration of the Word, and yet reject it**..."
(*The Sword and the Trowel*, September, 1887)

"...Jesuitical craft may be at the bottom of this 'modern thought'..."
(*The Sword and the Trowel*, April, 1888)

"The error in the Baptist denomination is ten times more widely spread than we knew of when we wrote the 'Down-Grade' papers...the controversy has revealed what we little dreamt of..."
(*The Sword and the Trowel*, May 1888)

"The inspiration of Holy Scripture in the sense of its being the infallible Word of God, is not held sincerely by all those who wish to appear evangelical."
(*The Sword and the Trowel*, October, 1888)

Spurgeon, before his death, was "at the door" of discovering the devilish agenda behind the new versions. All that he rebuked as part of the "down grade" was found in the men who translated and promoted the new versions. And these men planned to use their new versions in order to replace, not only the old Bible, but the fundamental truths so plainly taught in the old Bible.

With these things in mind, notice the dangerous views of some of the main leaders behind the ASV of 1901.

Philip Schaff

A history of the men behind the ASV must begin with Philip Schaff (1819-1893). He was a well-known textual critic and historian, and he served as the chairman of the American Standard Version translation committee:

"It is possible that his connection with the Revised Version is the feature which will preserve his name longest in remembrance. This was the judgment of the secular press at his decease..."
(David Schley Schaff, *The Life of Philip Schaff*, 1897)

Schaff worked for a one-world religion, and he used his new version to lay the groundwork for accomplishing this goal:

"...he was convinced that such an ecumenical revision would foster the bond of interdenominational and international union."
(George Shriver, *Philip Schaff, Christian Scholar and Ecumenical Prophet*)

His final, literary work was a paper read at the Parliament of World Religions (1893) in Chicago. Schaff attended but did not speak at this event. The Theosophical Society (i.e. followers of Lucifer) and many other occult and blasphemous religious organizations were represented at this meeting. The Theosophists considered the Parliament of World Religions to be a wonderful "breakthrough" for them, as thousands gathered to hear their teachers for the first time. Annie Besant (the editor of *Lucifer* magazine) was one of the speakers. As she praised evolution, karma, Buddha, and reincarnation, she exclaimed:

"Unity is the foundation of our brotherhood..."

No rebuke was issued by Philip Schaff. His own paper, *The Reunion of Christendom,* was read at this meeting, and it also exalted the Roman Catholic Church:

"...union must include the Greek and Roman churches...if any one church is to be the center of unification, that honor must be conceded to the Greek or the Roman communion...[For they] trace their origin back to the apostolic age..."

Schaff's paper also called for a religious, ecumenical council in Jerusalem led by the Pope! He ridiculed the Biblical proof-texts that Christians have used against Popery; he justified evolution; and he felt that the new English translation he was helping to produce would aid in breaking down the walls of separation.

Schaff continued:

"There is room for all these [Unitarians and Universalists] and many other churches and societies in the kingdom of God..."
(Quoted in, John Henry Barrows, *The World's Parliament of Religions*, 1893)

Not long after these words were uttered, Schaff "gave up the ghost." It is not difficult to see why his death was greatly eulogized by Catholics at the time.

This evil ecumenism was nothing new for Schaff:

"His first major work in America was *The Principle of Protestantism* (1845)...This work...brought upon Schaff charges of heresy and Romanism..."
(*Dictionary of Christianity in America*, InterVarsity Press, 1990)

Schaff also associated with openly heretical men like Charles Briggs (his former student), and other higher critics, in the Society of Biblical Literature and Exegesis, which he helped to organize:

"Throughout the 1880s Briggs published works which championed the higher-critical method...Briggs denied the verbal inspi-

ration, inerrancy and authenticity of Scripture…"
(*Dictionary of Christianity in America*, InterVarsity Press, 1990)

Schaff was praised by the University of Berlin for his work of mediation in bringing German criticism into American churches:

Jude 1:4 For there are certain men **crept** in unawares…

Acts 20:30 Also of your own selves shall men arise, speaking perverse things, to draw away disciples after them.

In his writings, Schaff derided the literal inspiration and inerrancy of the Scriptures, and he often refused to reprove even the most destructive criticisms of the Bible:

"As for the Old Testament, Dr. Schaff was cautious about expressing his judgment, holding that research and scholarship must be allowed to do their work before a categorical sentence is passed."
(David Schley Schaff, *The Life of Philip Schaff*, 1897)

Most of the other men behind the ASV were as corrupt as Schaff in their doctrinal views. Several of the main leaders will be examined in this chapter. They knew how to cloak their higher criticism in orthodox-sounding language, thereby serving as a bridge for destructive criticism to enter into the theological schools and churches.

John De Witt

John De Witt (1821-1906) was a member of the Old Testament revision committee for the ASV. His heretical views of inspiration were summed up in his book, *What Is Inspiration?* (1893). Notice some reviews of his book:

"*What Is Inspiration?* In a neat little book of less than 200 pages Prof. John De Witt, D.D., discusses this burning question…Here

is a man seventy-two years old who has been all his mature life a student of the Bible in the original tongues. As a faithful pastor who wrote, nearly fifty years ago, *The Sure Foundation: How to Build on It*, he taught according to that mass of Latin theology and reformed symbolism with which his denomination, the Reformed Church in America, is loaded...Now, after thirty years' professional labors in Hebrew and Greek and experience as a member of the company of Old Testament revisers, he realizes the problem...The old notions about the Bible, the hard and fast ideas of inspiration, are as chaff before the whirlwind... What shall the people have in place of their old faith?...His candid discussion results in this judgment: 'Whatever in the Old Testament revelation, or in any professed revelation from God, is not in accord with the righteousness, or love, or purity, or truth, in the words and life of Christ has been annulled and superseded and is practically no revelation for us.' **The errancy of Scripture, therefore, does not disturb Dr. De Witt.** Elsewhere this axiom is expanded into ample proportions. On the final pages are noble words for all young men, inquirers who are forming their judgments, and preachers who would be honest but who have not the fame and honor and the weight of years which in the author's case shield him from the dangers of a possible heresy trial."
(*The Literary World*, Volume 24, 1893)

"*What Is Inspiration?* By John De Witt, D.D...He treats the question in a scholarly way, **admits the errors of the Bible**, is **in sympathy with the 'Higher Criticism,' evolution, progressive revelation.** His definition of inspiration is in accord with these views..."
(Albert Shaw, William Thomas Stead, *The Review of Reviews*, Volume 8, 1893)

Biblical Christians rejected and reproved the views of John De Witt. They argued that progress in revelation does not imply error to be corrected, or a higher inspiration. Yet, such higher critical views (i.e. modernism) were found in these men who produced the ASV!:

"Dr. De Witt was invited to become a member of the American Old Testament Revision Company, at its formation in 1872. When the Anglo-American edition was published, in 1885, he was requested by the American committee to prepare the Old Testament for a future American edition, by incorporating the Appendix in the text...With the surviving members of the company, Dr. De Witt labored upon this edition up to its very issue..."
(Charles Edward Corwin, *A Manual of the Reformed Church in America*, 1922)

The *New Schaff-Herzog Encyclopedia* (1909) obscures the identity of John De Witt by assigning the authorship of the book, *What Is Inspiration?* to another John De Witt who was not a member of the Old Testament revision committee! Other resources simply ignore the controversy surrounding his liberal, heretical views, altogether. However, there is no doubt that the John De Witt who wrote *What Is Inspiration?* is the John De Witt who was a member of the Old Testament revision committee. The opening page of the heretical *What is Inspiration*? (1892), reads:

"John De Witt...A Member of the American Old Testament Revision Company...Author of 'The Psalms'..."

New Brunswick Theological Seminary is proud of John De Witt. In a publication in 1984, John W. Beardslee writes:

"John De Witt...A member of the class of 1842, Dr. De Witt taught in the seminary from 1863 to 1892. He was prominent in the preparation and publication of the American Standard Version of the Bible (1901). His *What is Inspiration?* (1893) is perhaps, given its time, the most significant piece of theological

writing produced by New Brunswick Theological Seminary, combining a firm evangelical faith with the **insights of historical criticism and evolutionary** thought."
(John W. Beardslee, *Vision From the Hill: Selections From Works of Faculty & Alumni*, New Brunswick Theological Seminary, 1984)

By "historical" criticism, they mean the German, higher criticism, which is really infidelity disguised as intelligence. Men like John De Witt served as bridges so the enemy could break down walls and shake the foundations of the faith. At times, many of these men had to hide their corrupt views. For example, F.J.A. Hort, in a letter to Westcott (April 12, 1861), wrote:

"Also - but this may be cowardice - I have a sort of craving that our text should be cast upon the world before we deal with matters likely to brand us with suspicion. I mean, a text, issued by men already known for what will undoubtedly be treated as dangerous heresy, will have great difficulties in finding its way to regions which it might otherwise hope to reach, and whence it would not easily be banished by subsequent alarms."
(Arthur Fenton Hort, *Life and letters of Fenton John Anthony Hort*, Volume 1, 1896)

Charles A. Aiken

Charles Augustus Aiken (1827-1892) was also a member of the Old Testament Revision company. He likewise praised the higher criticism of Germany:

"It is worthy of remark, that the development of Biblical science has been for the last hundred years much more rapid in Germany than in England...It should further be observed, that Biblical criticism has been prosecuted most scientifically in Germany. True science loves order and method. Nowhere have the various departments of sacred science been so sharply defined, nowhere the prerogatives of each guarded with such jealous care as in

Germany."
(Charles A. Aiken, *Bibliotheca Sacra*, "The Comparative Value of English and German Biblical Science," Volume 11, 1854)

Edward A. Washburn

Edward A. Washburn (Calvary Church, New York) was a member of the New Testament committee of the ASV:

"Edward A. Washburn, D.D. (1819-1881)...was, I think, the best representative of **the 'Broad Church'** school in the American Episcopal Church...He was a member of the American company of New Testament revisers of the Authorized Version of the Bible, and read papers before the Evangelical Alliance (1873-79) on 'Reason and Faith' and on 'Socialism.'"
(Jesse Ames Spencer, *Memorabilia of Sixty-Five Years, 1820-1886*, 1890)

Again, men like Washburn served as bridges to allow the criticism of what was known as modernism to enter into American schools and churches. Washburn admits as much:

"I speak as one of those who earnestly hope for such **mediation** between the Church and the criticism of the time."
(Rev. E. A. Washburn, "Reason and Faith," quoted in *History, Essays, Orations, and Other Documents of the Sixth General Conference of the Evangelical Alliance: Held in New York, October 2-12, 1873*, 1874)

These men behind the ASV rejected rationalism, on one side, while also opposing what they called *dogmatism* on the other. By dogmatism, they meant orthodox, fundamental Christianity! Washburn writes:

"...I can answer as truly the same spirit when it comes in the shape of a **dogmatism** that fears the advance of modern critical thought...If we have grasped the one spiritual law of revelation, we shall be in no danger of clinging to some **mechanical theory** of Scripture for fear of losing its substance. **The Book of God**

will be for us no record of astronomy or geology, no chronicle which a verbal criticism can overthrow...Rationalism builds its fabric of theoretical notions, **dogmatism does the same**: rationalism robs Christianity of all that can touch conscience or affection, **dogmatism does the same**."
(Edward Abiel Washburn, *The Social Law of God: Sermons on the Ten Commandments*, 1881)

Washburn condemned the doctrine of the verbal infallibility of the Scriptures. Shall Christians allow such madmen in their houses?

Tayler Lewis

Tayler Lewis (1802-1877) was also a member of the Old Testament translating committee of the ASV. He died before the project was finished. He is known for inventing the wicked doctrine of evolution, and reading it into the Scriptures, before Darwin!

"...Lewis, who in 1855, several years before Darwin proclaimed evolution as a theory in harmony with the teachings of science, suggested the same theory of creation by development, as in harmony with the teachings of Scripture, for which he was sneered at and denounced..."
(*The Treasury; A Magazine of Religious and Current Thought*, Volume 2, 1885)

"Before Darwin was heard of, our own able biblical scholar, Professor Tayler Lewis, taught it, by biblical exegesis, as implied in the Mosaic Cosmology. He was a Darwinist before Darwin..."
(Daniel Dorchester, *Christianity in the United States*, 1888)

Joseph Henry Thayer

J. Henry Thayer (1828-1901) was the author of *Thayer's Lexicon*. He worked on the RV and the ASV (i.e. New Testament committee). He was a Unitarian (he denied the Divinity of Jesus)! He (like so many others who worked on the ASV) did not believe in the infallibility of the Bible. He also used the infallibility of "Christ" to excuse his disbelief in the infallibility of the Scriptures. He writes:

"...when we set the book up as the infallible and final appeal in all matters of religious belief and life, we are doing something for which we are destitute of historic warrant; we are assigning it a place and a function which it neither held nor exercised at the outset...We may find another reason for questioning the theory of the coequal and infallible authority of all parts of the New Testament in the fact that that theory sets at defiance the law of historic sequence and proportion...But Christianity is Christ...The mistaken views we are considering involve a misuse of the Biblical term 'Word of God'...No descriptive appellation of the Bible is oftener on the lips of certain persons than this...the persons referred to hold that it warrants them in quoting every phrase in the book with a 'Thus saith the Lord.' The man who questions any statement in it is [seen as] impeaching the divine veracity...It is the spoken word...And when we hear well-meaning but over-zealous believers reiterating 'The Bible is the Word of God'...it will often have a salutary effect to ask them whether they think God's word was written in English?...anything, to set them a-thinking...Who now would declare that the Bible...restricts the work of creation to six days of twenty-four hours each; compels us to believe in witchcraft, and make it a capital offense..."
(J. Henry Thayer, *The Change of Attitude Toward the Bible, A Lecture Given Under the Auspices of the American Institute of Sacred Literature, February 17, 1891*)

"Said Dr. Channing, 'The Bible is a book written by men, for men, in the language of men, and its meaning is to be sought in the same manner as that of other books.' This is precisely the ground to-day taken by Dr. A. Briggs, who has been in danger of

excommunication from the Presbyterian body on account of his heresies. The old-fashioned Presbyterian believes that his faith stands or falls with the verbal accuracy of the Scriptures. Dr. Briggs denounces this as a superstition. It is the blind worship of a book. It is Bibliolatry…**Prof. J. Henry Thayer, addressing an evangelical audience in Boston, made to them this startling statement: 'The critics are agreed that the view of Scripture in which you and I were educated, which has been prevalent in New England for generations, is untenable.'** Such announcements are received by most persons in the orthodox world as novel and startling declarations; but to us they are no novelty, for upon this very belief we have always proceeded in examining the contents of the Bible, pointing out its errors and inconsistencies and setting aside the crude and immoral teachings which belong to a past age…"
(*The Unitarian*, Volume 7, 1892)

Charles Marsh Mead

Charles M. Mead (1836-1911) was a member of the Old Testament committee of the ASV. His views were quoted at the beginning of this chapter, as he sought to justify higher criticism on the basis of Christ being infallible (as if this somehow excuses disbelief in an infallible Bible):

"...let me at the outset emphatically say that I regard the higher criticism as not only entirely legitimate, but as very useful... According to [the Protestant doctrine]…the Bible is to be regarded as of divine and infallible authority. But here too it is no easy task to justify to doubters, or even to ourselves, the validity of **this assumption**…For we are now dealing with the problem of certitude: how can men be assured that the Bible gives them an infallible body of religious history and doctrine? In general, all histories are assumed to be more or less imperfect. It is not claimed for them that they are inerrant. The presumption always

is that errors creep into the most conscientiously prepared works ...This brings us then to the last of the principal methods by which religious assurance is sought. **Christ, it is said, is the ultimate authority for all Christians, so that we need not anxiously attempt to defend the exact accuracy of every part of the Bible.** If we believe in him and follow him, we can safely let criticism have free range, and not be troubled at any discoveries it may make of defects and mistakes in the Biblical writers. As Christians we put our supreme faith in Christ, not in the utterances of any of his followers. Inasmuch as the ultimate ground of our faith in the authority of the Bible is our faith in the authority of Christ, nothing is gained, while much may be lost, by attempting to defend, as absolutely infallible, everything found in the books of the Bible...This seems, therefore, to be the only defensible ground on which one can rest when assurance of Christian faith is sought...Christ is the object of a Christian's faith; and however much he may find that is questionable in the Christian Scriptures, this faith can remain undisturbed...Both the Protestant and the Roman Catholic doctrine ultimately rest on the assumption of the supreme, infallible authority of Christ. The Bible on the one hand and the Pope on the other are admitted to be infallible only because Christ is first accepted as the supreme authority. **Why, then, rest our faith on the secondary, derivative ground rather than on the primary one?**...Here, then, we seem to have an impregnable position, and one which enables us calmly to await and **accept** whatever scientific investigation may bring to light as regards the history or the character of the Bible."
(Charles Marsh Mead, *Christ and Criticism*, 1892)

"In so far as the Biblical writers told the truth, it is quite immaterial whether in telling it they were worked on by an extraordinary divine influence or not...So those who made the written record which has come down to us may possibly have made it with the exercise of only ordinary powers of observation and acquisition...The foregoing considerations, while they may seem to de-

grade the importance of the doctrine of inspiration, or even to make the fact of it questionable, serve to guard what is more important than this doctrine from resting on an insecure foundation...It certainly does follow from what we have here conceded concerning inspiration, **that it is not of the central importance** which it has often been made to assume. One may hold to all the essential doctrines of revealed religion; one may exercise the most perfect faith in Jesus Christ; one may insist on the unique value of the Bible, and yet see no sufficient reason to believe that any exceptional supernatural influence was exerted on its authors when they were writing it...not the Scriptures, but only the Scriptural writers, can be said to be inspired...**A book, as a mere book, can no more be inspired than a rock**...The question, then, is: Was the inspiration of the Biblical writers specifically different from that which all members of the believing community enjoy? The answer to the question is encumbered with grave difficulties…"
(Charles Marsh Mead, *Supernatural Revelation*, 1889)

"Trying to prove its absolute inerrancy is nearly as harmful as trying to prove its general fallibility."
(Charles M. Mead, *The Biblical World*, Volume 25, "The Ground of the Authority of the Bible," 1905)

Timothy Dwight

Timothy Dwight (1828-1916) served on the New Testament committee of the *ASV*, and was the president of Yale (1886-1898). Dwight was a member of the occult, secret society called *Skull and Bones*:

"Among the long list of distinguished 'Bones' men are numbered…**President Timothy Dwight**, '49, of Yale…"
(Frank Leslie, *Frank Leslie's Popular Monthly*, Volume 42, 1896)

"The following are the names of some of the better known Yale graduates who are 'Bones' men: **President Dwight**..."
(Albert Clark Stevens, *The Cyclopædia of Fraternities*, 1899)

"Out of every class Skull and Bones takes its men. They have gone out into the world and have become, in many instances, leaders in society. They have obtained control of Yale."
(*The Iconoclast*, Vol. 1, No. 1, October, 1873)

"This association was organized in 1832 by fifteen members of the class of 1833, one of whom is now Ex-Attorney General Taft."
(William Emery Decrow, *Yale and The City of Elms*, 1882)

This occult society was sometimes in the news (though almost always in a trivial manner) during the Bush presidencies:

"In his junior year, George W. was 'tapped' (invited by existing membership) for Skull and Bones, the well-known Yale senior-year secret society that was founded in 1832...Bonesman have risen to be United States cabinet secretaries, Supreme Court justices, and even on three occasions, presidents of the United States - most recently, Bush Senior and George W...Bush Senior's father, Prescott Bush, later himself a U.S. Senator, were all Bonesmen..."
(David Aikman, *A Man of Faith: The Spiritual Journey of George W. Bush*, Thomas Nelson, Inc., 2005)

Men such as William F. Buckley (author), Henry Luce (*Time-Life*), Pierre Jay (first chairman of the Federal Reserve Bank of New York), and many other powerful leaders in government, the media, etc., have been "Bonesmen." It is often seen as an international mafia organized for the purpose of bringing about a "new world order" controlled by themselves.

At least one other member of the ASV translating committee had connections to Skull and Bones. Theodore Dwight Woolsey (also Yale College president and cousin of Timothy Dwight) was the chairman of the New Testament committee of the ASV. His son (Theodore S. Woolsey, Professor of International Law at Yale University) and his grandson (Heathcote Muirson Woolsey) were members of Skull and Bones.

"For decades, mystery has surrounded an elite secret society at Yale University called the Order of Skull and Bones…" (National Public Radio, March 11, 2009, NPR.org)

A fascination with ghosts and skulls, and such like, is a sign of devil possession and influence:

Luke 8:27 And when he went forth to land, there met him out of the city a certain man, which had devils long time, and ware no clothes, neither abode in any house, **but in the tombs**.

Masonry and the *NASB*

The New American Standard Bible is published by the Lockman Foundation. Dewey Lockman (1898-1974) was a Mason. The website for the Lockman Foundation (www.Lockman.org) contains the following information:

"[Dewey Lockman] was active in the Gideon Society for 31 years, and a **member of the Masonic Order**…A little more than three years before he left us…on January 11, 1974, Lockman lived to see the ultimate completion of his dream: the dedication of the *NASB* to God…"

Conclusion

God will keep His Word. He will preserve it from men who seek to hide in their dark, secret societies and corrupt His Word to accomplish their goals (Psalms 12:6-8):

Isaiah 29:15 Woe unto them that **seek deep to hide** their counsel from the LORD, and their works are **in the dark**, and they say, Who seeth us? and who knoweth us?

Ezekiel 8:12 Then said he unto me, Son of man, hast thou seen what the ancients of the house of Israel **do in the dark**, every man in the chambers of his imagery?...

Jeremiah 23:24 Can any hide himself in **secret places** that I shall not see him? saith the LORD…
30 Therefore, behold, I am against the prophets, saith the LORD, that **steal my words every one from his neighbour.**

The words of God are found today in the Authorized Version. This Holy Bible teaches that every person has sinned against God and His moral law (Romans 3:23). The punishment for sin is eternal damnation in the Lake of Fire (Revelation 20:15). But it also teaches some very good news:

John 3:16 For God so loved the world, that he gave his only begotten Son, that whosoever **believeth** in him should not perish, but have everlasting life.

Jesus Christ, the Divine, sinless Son of God, died on the cross, and shed His Blood for our sins, and resurrected the third day. Do not trust in anything else (or anyone else) for forgiveness of sins and eternal salvation:

John 3:36 He that **believeth** on the Son hath everlasting life: and he that believeth not the Son shall not see life; but the wrath of God abideth on him.

Sadly, this precious, good news of eternal salvation by God's grace, through faith alone, is obscured by the *ASV, NASB*, etc. The *ASV* in John 3:36 (the context of the Gospel!), reads:

"...but he that **obeyeth not** the Son shall not see life, but the wrath of God abideth on him."

The final, world religion (with its new "Bible") must teach salvation through works in order to unite deceived Christians, Catholics, and all the other religions and sects of the world that teach this false gospel of works:

Galatians 1:9 As we said before, so say I now again, If any man preach any other gospel unto you than that ye have received, let him be accursed.

Romans 3:28 Therefore we conclude that a man is justified by faith **without the deeds of the law.**

Romans 4:5 But to him that **worketh not, but believeth** on him that justifieth the ungodly, his faith is counted for righteousness.

Obedience to God's commandments is how we show our love and gratitude to Jesus, and obtain rewards, after we are saved:

Acts 8:36 And as they went on their way, they came unto a certain water: and the eunuch said, See, here is water; what doth hinder me to be baptized?
37 And Philip said, **If thou believest** with all thine heart, thou mayest. And he answered and said, I believe that Jesus Christ is the Son of God.

Notice, good works, such as submitting to baptism, should come after we believe the Gospel. But again, the *ASV* (*NASB*, etc.), deletes verse 37, allowing for infant baptism, and baptismal regeneration. This change, along with many others, promotes the final, compromised unity that the Bible calls the "falling away" (2 Thessalonians 2:3).

This "falling away" will result in the worst time of deception the word has ever known, called the Great Tribulation period. Even in the midst of this coming age, the true Bible will still be found, and many will be slain for it:

Revelation 20:4 And I saw thrones, and they sat upon them, and judgment was given unto them: and I saw the souls of them that were beheaded for the witness of Jesus, and **for the word of God**, and which had not worshipped the beast, neither his image, neither had received his mark upon their foreheads, or in their hands; and they lived and reigned with Christ a thousand years.

There are some serious consequences for rejecting this truth about the infallibility of the King James Bible. Christians that do not believe every word of the Bible is given by God will be hindered in their growth:

1 Thessalonians 2:13 For this cause also thank we God without ceasing, because, when ye received the word of God which ye heard of us, ye received it **not as the word of men**, but as it is in truth, **the word of God**, which effectually worketh also in you that believe.

And by promoting false translations, etc., one runs the risk of receiving great punishments from the Lord:

Revelation 22:18 For I testify unto every man that heareth the **words** of the prophecy of this book, If any man shall **add unto** these things, God shall add unto him the plagues that are written in this book:
19 And if any man shall **take away** from the **words** of the book of this prophecy, God shall take away his part out of the book of

life, and out of the holy city, and from the things which are written in this book.

2 Corinthians 5:9 Wherefore we labour, that, whether present or absent, we may be accepted of him.
10 For we must all appear before the judgment seat of Christ; that every one may receive the things done in his body, according to that he hath done, whether it be good or bad.
11 Knowing therefore the terror of the Lord, we persuade men…

Let's fear the Lord in these perilous times, and believe that He has not allowed His wonderful words to perish. God will keep His Word:

Psalms 12:6 The words of the LORD are pure words: as silver tried in a furnace of earth, purified seven times.
7 Thou **shalt keep them**, O LORD, thou shalt preserve them from this generation for ever.

Numbers 23:19 God is not a man, that he should lie…